D0988688

Dominic Carman

Dominic Carman was educated at Manchester Grammar School and Durham University. He worked in banking before beginning a publishing career at News International, and later joined Euromoney Publications in London and in Hong Kong. He then worked for the world's largest conference company before setting up his own business in 2000, publishing a quarterly magazine, *London Business Review*. He is married, has four children and lives in London.

No Ordinary Man

A Life of George Carman, QC

Dominic Carman

CORONET BOOKS
Hodder & Stoughton

For Rachel

First published in Great Britain in 2002 by Hodder and Stoughton

First published in paperback in 2002
by Hodder and Stoughton
A division of Hodder Headline

A Coronet paperback

2 4 6 8 10 9 7 5 3 1

Copyright © 2002 by Dominic Carman

The right of Dominic Carman to be identified as the Author of
the Work has been asserted by him in accordance with the
Copyright, Designs and Patents Act 1988.

All rights reserved. No part of this publication may be
reproduced, stored in a retrieval system, or transmitted,
in any form or by any means without the prior written
permission of the publisher, nor be otherwise circulated
in any form of binding or cover other than that in which
it is published and without a similar condition being
imposed on the subsequent purchaser.

A CIP catalogue record for this title is available from the British Library

ISBN 0 340 82099 3

Printed and bound in Great Britain by
Clays Ltd, St Ives plc

Hodder and Stoughton
A division of Hodder Headline
338 Euston Road
London NW1 3BH

Contents

List of Illustrations

Section 1

Page 1
George, aged eight, altar boy at St Kentigern's Catholic Church

Page 2
George with unknown dog near Dungarvon, Ireland, 1934
George with elder sister Joyce in a Blackpool street, 1932
School holiday overlooking Rome, Easter 1938

Page 3
Carman family group, 1948
St Joseph's College Rugby 1st XV, 1947

Page 4
George standing in front of Riber Castle, Derbyshire, August
   1945
Balliol Younger Society, Oxford, 1951

Page 5
Ursula Groves, George's first wife from 1955 to 1960
Celia Sparrow, George's second wife from 1960 to 1976
George Best with Eva Haraldsted, August 1969

Page 6
George fulfils ambition of becoming a QC in 1971
George relaxing with cigarette outside Knightsbridge
   Crown Court

List of Illustrations

List of Illustrations

Preface

It isn't enough to tell us what a man did, you've got to tell us who he was.

Citizen Kane

Ten days before he died, my father handed me a watch. 'I want you to have it. Take it,' he said. Inscribed on the round white face were the words 'Sword of Truth' and the date, 20 June 1997. This had been a present from the *Guardian* newspaper to celebrate the libel victory over Jonathan Aitken. Since his death, the watch has assumed greater significance. For with the gift came a simple request: 'I'm not going to be able to do it. You'd better have a go.' He was acknowledging that an autobiography was now beyond him and asking me to write his life story in its place. This book is the result.

Filial biographies are often inadequate. In suffering from a variety of sins, they can be too subjective, too apologetic, too critical or too selective. I have tried to bear these potential deficiencies in mind when deciding exactly what to examine. The easy book would have chronicled the life of the public man – his childhood and education, his legal skills, his dazzling array of clients and his celebrated victories. It would have glossed over the details of private torment and trouble. That is what some have suggested and many may have expected me to produce. I have instead chosen the more difficult option.

After listening to plenty of advice on what to put in and what to leave out, I have stuck firmly to the belief that the duty of a responsible biographer is to be as objective, balanced and comprehensive as he can be. In telling the story of someone else's life, you have to make judgments. It has been my judgment that I must tell the full story. The only issue has been where to draw the line. Some things are not included because of the sensitivities of others. A few matters have been excluded because the available information is incomplete or inconclusive. Notwithstanding these omissions, the story of George Carman is told without being sanitised or partial. Events have been chosen that best illustrate the man and his contribution to the courtroom while explaining some of the problems which plagued him and the dramatic effect on those around him. It is a sad story. It is a difficult story to tell. It is the truth.

Many children see their father as superman. They grow up to realise that he is just a man. I grew up with a father who was hailed by the press as a superman of the courts. Recognition of that talent went well beyond the newspapers. For his clients, for the solicitors who instructed him and for many who came into contact with him, here was a barrister with special gifts who could sometimes achieve the impossible with a jury. Respect, admiration and praise were almost universally delivered from all sides. If success carried a Faustian price, it came at the expense of personal happiness. That deal demands examination.

The reader is presented with George at work and at play. As in Cromwell's request to the painter Sir Peter Lely, it is a 'warts and all' portrait. Some of those who do not wish to countenance the complete picture may criticise me for being too intimate, for laying bare his failures as a person alongside his triumphs as an advocate. My view is that they are inseparable in understanding the man. The scale of his achievements and the validity of the results he obtained are in no way devalued or diminished. If anything, their magnitude is amplified given the enormous self-harm that he inflicted.

Writing has not been easy. The Odyssey of reliving the past has produced a few surprises and brought back painful memories. Inevitably, it has been a cathartic process. Consolation has come with a deeper understanding of my father and some better explanation of events in my childhood. For the reader, all of this may prove interesting and informative, but no more than that. In the future, when this book lies forgotten on library shelves, it will remain as a permanent record for my four children of the grandfather whose famous name they share. It will form part of my legacy to them.

Research has been essential. Of more than a hundred interviews undertaken by me, half were conducted face to face in London, Manchester, Brighton, Oxford and Scotland. Most of the remainder were done by telephone. With the exception of two sets of written answers and a few informal conversations, all were tape-recorded. From these, quotations and anecdotes have been incorporated which add appropriate substance to the story. Given the sensitive nature of some material, confidentiality and anonymity have occasionally been necessary. I am very grateful that so many people have taken their time to co-operate. Especial thanks should be given to the following for their contribution: Jonathan Aitken, Lord Archer, Max Armstrong, Michael Beloff QC, Marcel Berlins, Tony Blair MP, Christopher Blane, Nicholas Blane, Judge Graham Boal, Cherie Booth QC, Stanley Brodie QC, Michael Brompton, Desmond Browne QC, Ian Burton, Andrew Caldecott QC, Paul Callan, Nick Carter, James Clements, Bill Conner, Dr Annie Coxon, Edwina Currie, Jonathan Dark, Sir Maurice Drake, Clare Dyer, John Edwards, Paul Foot, Edward Gee, Frances Gibb, Elizabeth Gloster QC, Christina Gorna, Muriel Gorna, Sir Charles Gray, David Green, Rosemary Green, Stephen Grosz, Richard Hartley QC, Charles Howard QC, Benet Hytner QC, Richard Ingrams, Barbara Jones, John Jones, Sir Anthony Kenny, Roger Lane-Smith, Samuel Lee, Alan Montefiore, Sir Michael Morland, Dr Peter Mueller, Christopher Murray, Leah, Lady Napley, Pat Nolan, John Obertelli, Phyllis Pacey, Adrienne Page QC, George Papageorgis, Sir Oliver Popplewell, Judith Preston-Rouse, James Price QC, Vivian Price QC, Gerald Quinlan, Maggie Rae, Lord Rees-Mogg, Frederic Reynold QC, James Robertson, Joshua Rozenberg, Sir Patrick Russell, Lionel Scott, Father Michael Seed,

Victoria Sharp QC, Monsignor Frank Slattery, Father Vincent Smith, David Speker, Basil Stein, Professor George Steiner, Lord Taverne, Jeremy Thorpe, Marion Thorpe, Hugh Tomlinson, John Townend, David Waller, John Walton, Sir Ronald Waterhouse, Tony Whalley, Lord Williams, Mary Williamson.

Separate interviews with Max Clifford and David Mellor were conducted in the autumn of 2000, before this biography was planned. Their relevant comments have been included.

This is my first book. Without the advantage or experience of being a professional author, I have tried to produce a succinct and digestible account. For simplicity, my father is referred to throughout as George. Since he would usually introduce himself with the informal line 'Call me George', that is how the reader should think of him. The structure may be summarised as follows: Chapters 1 to 6 follow a mostly chronological path while Chapters 7 to 12 are thematic. Chapter 13, 'The Three Graces', covers George's three marriages over thirty years. This space has been devoted to the thoughts and recollections of his wives – Ursula, Celia and Frances. Each has been formally interviewed at length. The addition of brief comment at the end is not intended to colour the narrative of their experience.

The text has been written without assistance in a little under four months. Writing quickly develops a natural rhythm as words start to sing off the page, albeit sometimes out of key. It also increases the chance of error. Although I have checked and rechecked information wherever possible, I am sure that something may have slipped the net. Readers will, I hope, accept my apologies for any deficiencies, errors or omissions. Throughout, I have been very fortunate to be advised by excellent publishing professionals. The combination of great experience and good instinct has made my agent, Gillon Aitken, a source of wise counsel. I am grateful too for the sound judgment of Roland Philipps at Hodder Headline, who has given me just what was needed – straightforward comment and clear instructions. My thanks also go to Peter James for tightening and reshaping my prose, to Juliet Brightmore for her efforts on picture research and to the rest of the team at Hodder and Stoughton.

A word or two about the law. Without legal training, it would have been inappropriate for me to write about cases with any pretence of expert knowledge. Technical issues are not therefore addressed in these pages. This biography is designed for people with an interest in the life of a lawyer who made the practice of law an artform through advocacy. There is, I am sure, room for another, more specialist book that analyses George's courtroom technique. My thanks go to James Price QC for providing me with an excellent note on this. Regrettably, it has not been possible to incorporate his observations. I am indebted also to David Hooper, whose excellent book, *Reputations Under Fire*, was a very useful source. Again, if there are mistakes of interpretation or analysis that are obvious to trained legal eyes, I trust that they will be forgiven.

It should not be forgotten that this book deals with the life of a very complex man. In trying to examine the various facets of his personality, I have recalled on many occasions Churchill's description of Soviet foreign policy: a riddle wrapped in a mystery inside an enigma. That was the way George played it and I do not pretend to provide all of the answers. The objective has been to deliver a more complete understanding of George Carman beyond a mere catalogue of his cases. It is for each reader to judge for themselves the adequacy of that endeavour. The hardest task – line by line, page by page – has been reconciling the love which I felt and still feel for my father with the uncomfortable reality that many aspects of his behaviour were very difficult to live with and to understand. This account is not so much a voyage round my father as describing my voyage with him. Writing about that journey has caused a degree of anguish. To those who will argue that many things would have been better left unsaid, I can only comment that after a lifetime of enforced silence, there is no choice other than to tell the truth.

So concluded the original preface to the hardback edition.

From widespread comment that followed publication, the view of some senior barristers was best summarised by Jonathan Sumption QC: 'George Carman was not important enough for his personal problems to become public property. There is no need to lie about them, when it is possible to say nothing about them at all.' *Guardian* editor Alan Rusbridger echoed this message, cautioning me to remember that 'keeping silent is not a bad tactic'. Elsewhere, critics savaged his three wives, questioning their right to speak about married life with George: 'Why, faced with such supposed cruelty, were the wives all so supine? Why, physically or verbally battered, didn't they threaten a career more vulnerable than most?' It is quite remarkable that Peter Preston, a former *Guardian* editor, posed such questions, given the outstanding coverage of domestic-violence issues in his newspaper.

Of course, George's private life has absolutely no bearing, in the strictest sense, on his public achievements. But for closing establishment ranks of the London Bar, former Fleet Street friends (a.k.a. grateful clients) and even Mohamed Al-Fayed (who banned this book from being sole at Harrods) to suggest that this biography should have stopped short at the courtroom door and say nothing of the private man, is plainly absurd. Their argument for Stalinist self-censorship seems to be that detailing a man's personal life tells readers nothing useful. As George was fond of saying, *Cui bono?*

Reaction elsewhere has been more illuminating. 'Everyone here knew about his wild behaviour,' concluded Peter Birkett QC, Northern Circuit leader of the Bar, when describing George's drunken escapades in Manchester. He recalled his failure to turn up at court in the morning (not unusual in the 1970s) and one particular occasion when Frances, his third wife, confirmed that he'd not come home. A city-wide search was undertaken. Eventually, he was found in a hotel suite alongside two teenage prostitutes angrily demanding money for their time. His clerk duly paid up. Carman QC was then shaved and dressed, before being pushed into (a specially adjourned) court to settle a multi-million pound insurance claim for Norwich Union. Somehow, George managed to get the best figure on offer. 'By midday, he was back celebrating in Goblets wine bar!' beamed Birkett in admiration.

One of many letters came from Elizabeth Llewellyn-Smith CB, former Prinipal of St Hilda's College, Oxford and biographer of George's undergraduate fiancée, Dame Anne Mueller, who died in July 2000. Llewellyn-Smith wrote of 'George's brutal behaviour towards Anne' and went on to put me in touch with her brother, Dr Peter Mueller, and her former husband, James Robertson. They recounted what Anne had told them about her two-year engagement – a familiar pattern of violence and sustained abuse, culminating in 'a serious attempt by George to strangle her'. In Peter Mueller's words, 'She had a very lucky escape.' These traumatic events were further described to me by George's Balliol contemporary Professor George Steiner as 'a very ugly business, widely known by his circle at Oxford'. Luckily for George, everyone stayed silent.

Should there be a posthumous right of silence that excludes from his biography the debauchery and domestic violence that permeated George's daily life for more than four decades? Are the private transgressions of a distinguished public figure eternally to be swept under the carpet, simply because he was famous and had a first-class mind? Many argue the case. Former *Express* and *Independent* editor Rosie Boycott commented in the BBC2 drama-documentary *Get Carman*: 'George was safe. George was golden. Nobody in Fleet Street would criticise George because they never knew when they would need him.' To how many other public figures does that special treatment apply?

I confess that the conspiracy of silence running through George's life extends even to these pages. Some deeply unpleasant memories have been kept out. But enough is probably included to give a reasonably complete picture. It must be right to acknowlege properly as the centrepiece of this volume the brilliance of a truly great advocate, universally admired and championed for his skill and dedication. But it must also be right that there is nothing ordinary in a man who, for example, repeatedly kicked his third wife when she lay in spasms on the ground, suffering an epileptic fit. Now, the child who watched in terror as his father assaulted the supine figure of his stepmother has at last broken years of silence. I would respectfully ask those who have argued to the contrary, please think again.

Summer 2002

I

Father and Son

Children begin by loving their parents; after a time they judge them; rarely, if ever, do they forgive them.

Oscar Wilde

George made his way through the middle of 1960s Manchester where buildings were blackened by generations of grime. I felt important sitting next to him as he steered the Ford Zephyr towards our destination. Dusty Peter Street chambers greeted us with a stale cigarette smell and leftover mints. These Saturday-morning visits had only one purpose: money. Desperate to see what had arrived, he went straight in to the clerk's room to open his mail, leaving me to play on a swivel chair behind his cracked leather desk. A large solicitor's cheque brought sighs of relief. Usually, there was nothing except frustration.

A short Sunday drive took us from Park Road, Hale to the Bull's Head pub less than a mile away. In blazer and cravat, George lingered with the lunchtime whisky crowd that cheerfully chatted until closing time. I sat by the bowling green, drinking Coca-Cola and waiting. Other Sundays stayed silent. I watched as the unshaven figure in pyjamas puffed away thoughtfully at his cigarette, removing the pink ribbon from each set of papers.

These are early memories of my father, George Carman, an unconventional man, who made few concessions in life to other people's expectations. His approach to fatherhood was no different. Without doubt, he loved me very much on his own terms and talked of me with pride. Introductions came with a theatrical delivery: 'This is my son, Dominic.' The words suggested that I would be guaranteed to impress but in truth, I felt very small and insignificant.

My parents had been married for a little over a year when their only child was born in August 1961. George was thirty-one, and my mother, Celia, twenty-three. I was immersed in an adult world from which there was no turning back. Their constant arguments were bitter and unrelenting. Keeping out of the way as much as possible, I developed a separate relationship with each of them since we did very little *en famille*. In the full swing of the 1960s, they made few friends together. Whilst other family members were unwelcome, Celia became isolated at home as her husband spent his time working and socialising.

Daytime drinkers were invited impromptu. George was a generous host who enjoyed entertaining pals from the pub or Hale Conservative Club. But formal dinner parties or family social occasions were generally avoided. The arrival of new dining-room furniture for the sparsely furnished house did not bring many couples over to eat. Nor did I have friends to play when he was around: noise was an irritant for the man who mostly preferred to maintain privacy at home.

As is often true for the early reader, nothing proved more enjoyable than shutting myself away with books. I was encouraged to recite poems and read stories aloud. Through a suspension of smoke, George read legal papers in return. Dictating on to tapes for transcription by a typist, the cadence of his language was compelling. Each personal injury opinion opened with the same mantra: 'Under the Factories Act 1961 . . . at all material times the plaintiff was employed as a . . .' It did not matter if meanings were lost. The gravelly voice was hypnotic. Smiles of appreciation appeared when I mimicked the words. Yet his strong personality did not distract from my infant awareness that here was a very different person.

For a man who lived his life to win, fatherhood and family were unfulfilling. Neither held out the prospect of tangible victory. In a role that did not come naturally, he tried to be a good father, even if the ground rules were unclear. He focused on what he knew best by teaching me in intricate detail the one skill he had mastered to perfection: arguing a case in court. If his love came cloaked in legal conversation, I tried my best to comprehend. There was little advice or guidance. On most things, I was left to my own devices. Living with the eternal hope that we would one day have a normal father-son relationship, I wanted so much for him just to say well done for something, anything. Every phrase and every look held out the prospect of better times ahead. By not articulating his parental feelings, he was no more than a creature of his generation. But nothing could destroy the love which I felt. Through everything, the bond between us remained very strong.

Part of my childhood was spent in the witness box. 'Speak up.' 'Tell the truth.' 'Take your time.' 'I'll ask you once again.' His blue eyes narrowed. The advocate's considerate manner could turn sour, as he delivered his words through gritted teeth. For, in bringing home with him an outstanding ability to cross-examine and humiliate, he sometimes left courtesy and the safeguard of a judge and jury in the courtroom. It paid to be careful what you said and when you spoke. One out-of-place response could cause problems. Given his mercurial nature, silence presented the safest option. As a model of studied quietness, I was too quiet even for George. Refusal to answer questions infuriated my interrogator. He made me stand in the corner for 'dumb insolence'. Any contradiction could make him fly into a rage. There was no way out at the receiving end of this sustained verbal punishment. His capacity to inspire feelings of guilt for whatever you had done or said, and the consequent dissection of your personality, was far worse than any smacking. To escape the miasma of stinging words, I took refuge in defiance.

He once took me to Old Trafford. It was amazing to meet Bobby Charlton, George Best and others of the European Cup winning team. Sir Matt Busby, Louis Edwards and Manchester United players were by now his clients. They all called him 'Mr Carman'. Charlton told me: 'Your father is a great man.' I was thrilled and proud to think that these men, my heroes, held him in such high regard. It made me realise that he was someone very special to other people. I idolised him too.

Games of football or cricket in the garden did not happen with George. He was not that sort of father. We were close in a more adult way. Endless talk of his working life stretched the limits of my understanding. But I never tired of listening. I enjoyed it. Whatever the subject mater, he invested it with a natural gravitas and authority. Every word seemed important. I learned about 'taking silk' (becoming a Queen's Counsel), 'going on the bench' (appointment as a High Court judge) and 'members of the jury' speeches. He appeared to be in complete control of this magical, complicated world.

On the journey home one January morning in 1968, his car smashed at high speed into Brooklands Roundabout, near Altrincham. Well over the limit, he was miraculously thrown clear as the steering wheel punctured the driver's seat. Wearing a safety belt would have meant instant death. He escaped with a few stitches and a bruised leg. George was a lucky man. Smiling at me from a hospital bed, he said: 'It's all right, I'm okay.' I was very relieved. Police photographs from the traffic accident shook him. They showed his new blue Ford Corsair crumpled to half its original size. 'Skidded on black ice' became the party line. The decision was reached not to push his luck any further. He did not venture behind the wheel again for nearly ten years. It was taxis only from now on.

Alcohol, gambling and talking to people remained the pastimes of choice outside work. Even now, the exploits of George Carman are legendary among those of a certain generation in Manchester. Older black-cab drivers in the city still recall the six- and seven-hour fares that took him from bar to club to casino, and the waiting between stops before the trip home. If he came home. It was convenient to keep a driver on tap with the meter ticking all the while, and the familiar sound of a cab's diesel engine outside our house would herald his return.

4

Weekday evenings followed a pattern. Drunk more often than sober, he called me out of bed to introduce fellow drinkers who had made the journey with him. I welcomed the attention since we rarely ate together at night, and mornings were filled with panic, as he shouted at Celia to find his wallet and cufflinks. His companions – sometimes two or more – varied depending on where he had been. Solicitors, bar clerks, policemen, journalists and barmaids would arrive slightly bemused or embarrassed, apologising for their intrusion. He insisted that they stay. Celia was sometimes asked to cook as they drank the small hours away.

Many late-night visitors seemed to have been specially chosen because they were malleable. Most were deferential. Controlling the conversation was not hard. It was never serious stuff. George did most of the talking, or singing if he felt frivolous. Sinatra was a hero. He identified with this small tough guy and particularly liked the line on the live album, *Sinatra at the Sands*: 'I feel sorry for the guy who doesn't drink. When he wakes up in the morning, that's the best he's gonna feel all day.' Piaf's 'La Vie en Rose' was another favourite. At the piano, he played 'Lily Marlene' and 'Smoke Gets in Your Eyes' – cabaret style. I was asked to perform, by reciting a poem or recalling the names and dates of each reigning monarch since 1066.

More often George would return by himself, and then he could be unpredictable and volatile. Much depended on the day in court, the night at the casino, what he had drunk or just how he felt at that moment. Being sick on arrival would make him subdued, but not for long. You would never know what to expect from the hunched figure across the table, his spirit restless and ill at ease, his mind in turmoil. Tie, stiff collar and studs would be removed – with help. Wincing occasionally, he breathed heavily through pointed nostrils before his slurred speech settled on some highlight of the day. His slowly burning cigarette angled downwards, accumulating a curved column of ash. It was fixed into small manicured fingers that gradually turned brown from the smoke creeping up between them. If I had stayed asleep, he moved me in the middle of the night to share his bed where the smell of whisky hovered in the darkness.

On a good evening, there might be jokes he had heard, tales of courtroom battles – obtuse or difficult judges attracting the full range of expletives – or stories of an unusual bar encounter. When in the mood and not too much the worse for wear, tomorrow's case monopolised the conversation. Talking about work was therapeutic. Launching into a lengthy analysis, he would spread out papers relating to personal injury cases on the table, turning over photographs, if there were any, of the victim who was claiming compensation and of the relevant equipment, machinery or vehicle. Although gruesome, the effects of industrial or traffic accidents were of great interest. In explaining the nature of the injury and the various heads of damages – amounts claimed for loss of earnings, pain and suffering and so on – he would draw you into a better understanding and sympathy with the victim. This gave him great satisfaction. A good settlement or award, particularly if the amount made a new record at the time, would mean coverage by local and occasionally national press. Public recognition for doing the job well thrilled him. Winning mattered. He would wave the newspaper proudly as confirmation of victory.

Bundles of one-, five- and ten-pound notes were put on the table for me to sort and count on the rare occasions when George won at blackjack. For a brief moment he seemed rich. The reality was rather different. Heavy gambling had disastrous consequences, as one of his colleagues recalls: 'He would often cash fees from a big case and go straight to Salford casino, where he lost the lot.' Day to day, things became desperate. Cheques bounced. Celia did not have enough to pay the milkman – we hid in silence when he called. There were no luxuries at home. Many promises remained unfulfilled: a safari holiday, tennis lessons and a racing bike. Others did not involve money. The days out to the park that never happened or the sports days he never attended. His work was important. He was busy. I knew that.

Our first holiday came with a week in Scarborough. I was seven. The following year, he complained about noise from the Dublin hotel generator. George was good at complaining. He got results. We were moved to a better room. By August 1971, the Côte d'Azur was a smarter destination for the new forty-one-year-old silk. Celia and I waited outside as the holiday spending money went at the Monte Carlo casino. The exchange control regulations still in force caused several days' wait before more funds could be transferred.

Gambling had seen greater consequences. Our Hale home was quickly sold to pay mounting debts in 1968. For nearly nine years, we lived in a rented house in Didsbury, a suburb of Manchester. At £8 a week, it was a bargain. The rent never increased. Situated directly opposite my new prep school, Moor Allerton, 112 Barlow Moor Road had entertained Dickens in the 1850s and, after we left, became home to the daughter of Ruth Ellis in the late 1980s. George's wild behaviour added to its history. As the new local talking point, he heard nothing about himself.

Every week brought a fresh crisis. Neighbours, reluctantly dragged in, kept a respectful distance. Following bad parental arguments, I was frequently sent to stay with different people in Manchester – sometimes for a week or more. On occasion, I was taken to London to stay with friends. The police would become involved. Policemen were handled with consummate skill. Quickly adopting a cool and menacing tone, George took charge of the situation by putting them in a metaphorical witness box, immediately letting it be known exactly who he was and whom he knew. Portraying himself as the innocent victim of a 'neurotic wife', his control of events was imperious. There was an immediate metamorphosis. Language and attitude were transformed. A fuming body of rage became the epitome of reasoned calm. This was Carman chameleon in action. Not wishing to get further involved in a 'domestic' with an awkward barrister, the enforcers of law made a strategic withdrawal.

My parents' marriage broke down in 1972. Adamant that I should stay with him, George repeatedly delivered a forceful message in arguments with Celia: 'Dominic stays with me. I will fight for custody in every court in the land.' He got his way. Given the constant conflict, their split came as a relief. For a while, Celia moved to an hotel nearby. In the autumn of 1973, she went to live permanently near her parents in London. I was to see her only once a year from then on until my mid-twenties. George disliked me visiting her or even talking to her on the phone when she called. Celia was regarded as non-existent. He expected me to think the same, but I did not. As usual, I kept my feelings hidden.

By now, George had become a Queen's Counsel, involved in both heavy civil and criminal work. I had moved on to a more demanding school, Manchester Grammar. We lived alone together. It was an abnormal arrangement that made me grow up fast. Trying to keep him on the rails was a challenge. To some degree, he depended on me. In more depressed states, I was 'all he had' as he talked of dying or killing himself. Changing the subject to work made him forget and invariably lifted his mood.

For several months, we moved out of the Didsbury house to stay in service flats. When he was away doing a case in London or elsewhere, I would stay at Holly House Hotel owned by George's friend, Phyllis Pacey, or with other friends. After school, we met at his chambers, at the Doubles Bar of the Café Royal next door, the Midland Hotel, the Grapes or the Fifth Inn. Typically, we would then go on to Indian or Chinese restaurants. He ate very little, talking animatedly of the day's events in court.

My attempts to moderate his alcohol intake had little effect. George would never be told to do anything. On some evenings, he got into such a bad state that, after crashing out, he needed help to get dressed the following morning before we went off in a taxi together. He acquired a reputation for turning up at court sometimes late and often inebriated. But he never went completely over the edge, knowing somehow just when to stop. An inner steel kept him going. Despite self-inflicted problems, the work went on.

After a heavy session and only an hour or two of sleep, he could, if necessary, get up at 4 or 5 a.m. and read papers for court: a method of working that was common throughout much of his career. There were times when he did not go to bed at all and did no preparation. He simply came home, had a bath, changed his clothes and went straight to court. Such stamina was phenomenal. His practice remained healthy. As one Manchester solicitor, who instructed him regularly, told me: 'Many thought George actually performed better in court when he was drunk!'

Several women were pursued in quick succession, each provoking rhapsodies from George. The thrill of the chase was another form of winning – hopeful travel being better than arrival. Yet his vulnerability was obvious. Clearly desperate to have a new partner, George poured out his heart, describing in intimate detail his feelings for the latest object of his desire. There was not much practical advice available from me. As a twelve-year-old schoolboy, I felt responsible, yet totally useless.

The most passionate words were for Janet Smith, a young female barrister in his chambers, who later became Dame Janet Smith, a High Court judge and chair of the 2001 enquiry into the mass murderer Dr Harold Shipman. Things did not work out. Disappointed, he punched a clenched fist so hard against the brickwork of our house that his knuckles bled. In the summer of 1973, we went to Igls in Austria. He developed an instant crush on a local woman. On our return, he rushed out to buy new bedroom furniture in the hope that she would come and stay in Manchester. She developed gallstones and failed to turn up. That Christmas, we stayed in Dalhousie Castle, north of

Edinburgh, and there he met Frances, the talented chef in residence.

Within a few months, she moved down to live with us. George negotiated an early contract release with her employers. She was kind. I hoped that the relationship might provide a new beginning. It did not. Problems that existed between my parents soon resurfaced with Frances. Her crusade to create a reformed George never had a chance. As he drank and gambled with the same gusto as before, she soon stopped preparing gourmet food for dinner because he was never there to eat it. When he did return home, a number of creations ended up on the wall or ceiling thanks to his outbursts of temper.

Holly House Hotel, just around the corner, was established as the regular local haunt – open all hours for George. For several years, I spent more time with him there than at home. Absence of natural light made the basement bar feel much the same at 4 a.m. or 4 p.m. A varied cast of characters made for a lively atmosphere. They included James Clements, a Territorial Army major, who had introduced George to his first wife Ursula; Patrick Collard, a bacteriologist from Manchester University, who resembled the Barry Humphries character Sir Les Patterson; and Alex Higgins, the hell-raising snooker player, who stayed at the hotel to do exhibition matches in Manchester until Phyllis asked him to leave. The drinkers blended with hotel residents – homeless families and travelling salespeople – to create an exotic cocktail.

Phyllis always gave a warm welcome. She was George's oldest friend and describes herself as 'like a big sister to him'. Trained as a hairdresser before she became an hotelier, she first met him in 1958 when her brief marriage to a Greek club owner broke down. A close and loyal confidante, she looked after him in Manchester's nightclubs and casinos and in the illegal drinking bars that were quite common in the days of stricter licensing laws. She recalls that 'He enjoyed himself as a complete party animal at night with the same energy that he had in court.'

When there was conflict between my parents or between George and Frances, she tried to humour him – with occasional success.

When the mood took him, George talked to anyone, entertaining fellow drinkers with natural eloquence and jovial banter. His engaging charm could be considerable. It was the same charisma he used to such good effect with juries. Not a natural joke-teller or raconteur, the best stories came from his own professional life and the lives of his clients. They offered a vicarious fund of experience on which to draw and helped avoid too much discussion of himself. 'More than once after a good night, George would help me cook breakfast for thirty or forty people. He was quite good at doing sausages, eggs and bacon,' remembers Phyllis.

George decided that, in contrast to his own strict Catholic childhood, I would not have any religious upbringing. Baptism remained my only formal church visit. A good education was the paramount concern. Judging performance and potential, he thought my school 'academically sound, but socially inferior'. That was the reason I 'lacked polish and finesse'. Speech attracted special criticism. Anything that smacked of a Manchester accent would be jumped on immediately as 'completely unacceptable'. Because I followed his example, my voice has no discernible origin.

I had sat the St Paul's entrance exam in London when he thought of moving there and been taken for interviews at Winchester and Rugby. Westminster was considered. The headmaster of Eton was consulted about a transfer. Public school would knock me into shape. Despite endless discussion of moving me 'somewhere better', higher fees were unaffordable. Not academic enough to win Eton or Winchester scholarships, I stayed on at Manchester Grammar. Among clever boys at a high-powered school, I was bright – passing my O Levels at fourteen – but by no means outstanding and certainly not in George's league. There were frequent reminders of his own academic prowess: the scholarships and the unvivaed first from Balliol. Dominic, however, was not first-class material.

Another obsession was manners. From early childhood, the supreme importance of behaving at the table and being polite were drummed into me. You did not forget. Public school mores were encouraged by example. Evolving as a typically awkward teenager with an edge, I felt out of place. George's furious response to his teenage son's untidy bedroom on a Saturday morning was to throw books, records and clothes over the banisters into the hall. 'Now tidy it up,' was the parting shot. This trick, learned from his officer training, seemed to provide great satisfaction.

Given his concern for me to do well, the same dogmatic point – 'work hard, go to Balliol' – was delivered with measured persistence. Yet he showed very little interest in my homework or other school activities. When at home, he continued to be either working or drinking. My request for help with an essay prompted him to rewrite the whole thing. It was a much better effort. The tactic backfired when Chris Johnson, my English master, gave the following mark and incisive comment: '19/20–6=13/20. Far too good to be all your own work.' I learned to write my own essays.

Lacking the motivation to push myself hard, I worked well within my limits. Fear was not a great incentive to change. Damning school reports arrived. Although many of the results were good, they contained occasional withering comments such as 'A boy of his ability should be ashamed.' The predictable outrage would be drawn out over many tortuous days. It was apparent that failure to realise my full potential caused much grief, which would be manifested as pure anger.

Instead of studying textbooks, I pretentiously devoured a wealth of literature that mirrored my angst and introspection or created a world that was not mine: Sartre, Kafka, Camus, Gogol, Dostoevsky and Tolstoy. These, together with punk rock singers of the period, became my new heroes. George was anxious that his moody, awkward son did not go off the rails. But I did not dabble in drugs and drank no more than friends of my age. By sixteen, I had developed a good relationship with my girlfriend.

In March 1976, George married Frances. By then, following our move to Altrincham, George played no conventional part in suburban life. He stood out as the father who liked girls clubs and gambling. My introduction to Manchester nightlife came early. 'He was not a conventional father. Unlike other parents, he treated his son as an adult and a friend. The effect that this had on Dominic was profound. We all recognised it,' comments the writer and journalist David Waller, who knew me well. Some of my friends felt intimidated and uncomfortable in George's presence. Others laughed when he repeatedly banged his Mercedes at the exit of the Griffin pub car park in Bowdon, the new local.

Laissez-faire did not feature in his personal vocabulary. Reasoned discussions never happened. A difficult teenager did not suit his style. As with many fathers in that situation, he hoped that I would 'snap out of it', whatever 'it' was. Determined for me to follow in his footsteps and read law at Balliol, we went to Oxford three times in as many years. He assumed that I would fall in love with the place by osmosis. If he wanted something, George usually got it. Any challenge to his authority was unwelcome. But his desire to control my life created strong resentment. A quiet rebellion followed as I resolved not to go under any circumstances and never to study law. Deliberately doing the opposite of what he wanted had become a mission in life. It made no difference if I repeatedly lost out in the process.

Jeremy Thorpe's trial was the major watershed in George's professional career, propelling him to national prominence and creating for the first time his wider public reputation as a great advocate. It also represented a personal rite of passage for me. The trial took place during my A Level exams in May and June 1979, a few months before my eighteenth birthday, and conversations with George matured in the months leading up to the case. Other matters were forgotten. Our relationship improved as one subject reigned supreme.

The hundreds of hours spent discussing the issues set a pattern for the future. George liked to let cases simmer in his mind like a casserole, testing the ingredients on quite a wide range of people in order to refine the recipe. Apart from junior barristers and solicitors, he would happily discuss ideas with journalists watching a case, or with drinking companions, to whom he would relay the facts. Always keen to sound out views, he was sensibly pragmatic, often taking on board the appropriate suggestions of others. Bouncing ideas around helped to identify the most emotional issues very early on. In his view, emotion rather than logic more often swayed a jury. Unable to quiz jurors directly, asking those closely involved or with an intelligent view was the next best alternative.

During Thorpe, my role developed as a sounding board and one-man audience. This became the basis of our adult relationship, the focal point between father and son. I felt important when asked to comment. He seemed to listen. By acknowledging that my opinions had some merit, he was taking me seriously. I was flattered as, over the years, he incorporated some of my ideas or phrases in different cases – it gave me some value in his life. Evidence, draft speeches and areas for cross-examination would be explored. Books of quotations were plundered. I learned by watching and listening. Carefully formulating different themes in outline, he pursued them to their full extent in discussion. By evaluating the options, George reviewed the key evidence in great detail. Long passages were read out. 'What do you think?' he asked intermittently. You had to make sure that you were concentrating at all times. If not, he would respond impatiently: 'Do listen.' This would happen in case after case. If I was not with him, the phone would do just as well. Calls would start with 'Let me try this one on you' and 'Is that any better?' or 'Have you got a minute?' An hour or two later, his opening or closing speech to the jury would be refined. Sometimes, there would be five or six different calls spread out over a day or an evening.

When involved in a big trial, which was most of the time, everything else in George's world ceased to exist. Entirely consumed by the process, he made no distinction between work and the rest of his life. Work was his life. He expected you to undergo the same total immersion. As he talked over the issues, their various nuances and subtleties, his energy and enthusiasm for the task were limitless. He paced up and down with little, quick steps, smoking incessantly. Peripatetic speech aided his concentration – in direct contrast to the stillness he maintained in court. There was no deviation from the subject, no loss of focus on what he was trying to achieve. Sifting through a mass of evidence enabled him to filter the important detail in his mind. Key points were then distilled. Listening to your responses and reactions assisted in deciding what might work with the jury.

Under duress, I agreed to go to Durham University. After one year I left. George's eighteen-year-old son had been a huge disappointment. He told me often. Initially, I worked seven days a week in a Mayfair restaurant, living with George and Frances in their rented Lincoln's Inn flat after their move to London in 1980. At the time, this was their only residence. I wanted desperately to escape and find a normal, stable life, for which I was very much ill equipped. At George's instigation, I moved into banking and stayed in the job for six years. At just twenty, I married and three years later, in December 1984, had a son, Matthew.

George's marriage to Frances had ended in the summer of 1983. At his request, I spent virtually every night in Lincoln's Inn for many months afterwards. His drinking and despair followed a similar pattern to the aftermath of the split with Celia. My own marriage ended in early 1985. Now available to spend time with him each week, I hoped to understand the man who kept himself hidden under a blanket of protective language. He arrived late for sessions after court. It created tension. You always heard George before you saw him. His approach would be heralded by distinct coughing, audible from some distance, as he cleared his throat forcefully. On entering the several different worlds which he inhabited, it was essential for me to stay sober. For some hours, he could be very good company, but invariably he needed looking after by the end of proceedings.

A common rendezvous was the famed Fleet Street haunt of the claret-drinking classes, El Vino's. George stood at the bar gossiping or sat huddled in conversation with small groups of barristers. Among his frequent companions were Mungo Fitzpatrick, a bespectacled P. G. Wodehouse figure, and James Crespi QC, reputed to have inspired Sir John Mortimer in conceiving the Rumpole character. Crespi was an eccentric, highly intelligent and humorous man of traditional outlook whose bulky frame and gout-inspired lifestyle (copious nightly port at the Garrick dinner table) made him the embodiment of a Rowlandson caricature. George admired his intellect. Sadly, he had married a young nightclub hostess who left him after three weeks.

Daly's Wine Bar, opposite the Royal Courts of Justice, became the other watering hole of choice. From the mid-1980s onwards, this was a regular starting point for evenings out. Holding court at the bar with a small crowd in attendance, listening to the form on his latest client and anecdotes from the courtroom, George insisted on buying the champagne. Keen to encourage and motivate, he adopted an avuncular approach towards young barristers, often going out of his way to give them a friendly word or two. Occasionally, he came unstuck in chatting to female pupils not so appreciative of his charms. But he was generally lucky to attract people who were in awe of his talent, understood his weaknesses, indulged him with their time and forgave him almost anything. Of the band of admirers around him, most were genuine.

Barristers like gossip. George liked it more than most, revelling in detail and minutiae. When we talked alone together, he loved to fill me in on the latest from solicitors, chambers or clients. He thrived on the many stories that came his way. Given the highly sensitive information at his disposal, confidentiality caused problems. As some journalists and lawyers know, he was a notoriously bad keeper of secrets. Notes of caution included 'strictly *entre nous*' or 'keep it under your hat'. Yet he could be wildly indiscreet, telling the same 'you mustn't tell anyone' story to four or five people in quick succession. As Bill Conner, his clerk in the 1980s and 1990s, recalls: 'Your father once flew back with another silk from Singapore and came in the following day to tell me, "You'll never guess what Mr X has just told me in confidence."' Scandalous tales that circulated the Bar about his own antics were disregarded as irrelevant.

Elsewhere, he got into arguments. In the days when Fleet Street watering holes were packed with lawyers and journalists rather than accountants and bankers, the Wine Press became a secondary staging post. Here one evening, without provocation, he launched a sustained verbal assault on Kelvin MacKenzie and his newspaper. The thick-skinned *Sun* editor laughed it off, subsequently employing his attacker for personal legal advice. George later found himself banned from the same hostelry. Not long afterwards, having spent the evening drinking at El Vino's, he took the arm of cultivated eccentric Paul Callan, a bowtie-and-pinstripe-wearing feature writer for the *Mirror* and *Express*, and crossed Fleet Street with him to enter the Wine Press. There George requested another bottle. The South African barman told him to leave immediately and never to return. When he was asked the reason, the response was an enigmatic 'Mr Carman knows why.' As they left, George quipped: 'If you tell me why you are banning me, I will sue you for slander.' The story soon did the rounds.

George had little appetite when in drinking mood. If I said I was hungry, he insisted on taking me to the Savoy or Ritz dining rooms, or to the Garrick Club, where leading actors mix with others who emulate their theatrical achievements – politicians, newspaper editors, lawyers and High Court judges. On Centre

Table – a long dining table seating maybe forty people – he would make polite conversation with the assorted company, but he preferred more intimate chatter. One Oxford contemporary, Sir Robin Day, was always pleased to oblige. They had been young barristers together in the early 1950s. Robin felt that his television success left him somehow second best to the star advocate of the courts. For George, whose constant insecurity required the acknowledgment of others, such recognition was very important.

On a March evening in 1986, we dined with Robin some weeks before George was due to cross-examine Arthur Scargill, who was suing Peter Wright, chief constable of South Yorkshire, claiming damages for false imprisonment four years before. His NUM driver had been caught speeding on the M1 motorway at between 110 and 120 m.p.h. in the union Jaguar. A faulty cruise control was blamed. Scargill stated that at journey's end he was detained at length by the police on the pavement outside his home – this was the basis of his claim. After discussing the case over dinner, Day decided on a mock cross-examination in which he would play Scargill, whom he had questioned many times during the 1984–5 miners' strike. This would give George an idea of what to expect. When Day proceeded to rebuff questions with evasions and long-winded speeches that answered a totally different question, it was at once evident that his acute observation of Scargill's phrases and mannerisms was spot on. Beyond wonderful entertainment lay a serious message. And when the case came to court in Manchester, George did not forget his Garrick dinner warm-up. He told the NUM president: 'On television, they run out of time, but in court we have the time to wait for your answers and not let you steamroller your way through.' He got under Scargill's skin. The closing speech produced one of his best *bons mots*: 'To entrust Arthur Scargill with the task of upholding your civil liberties might be regarded as dangerous as entrusting Satan with the task of abolishing Sin.' The jury found in favour of the police.

Enjoyable evenings with Robin apart, the rich food, cerebral company and faded elegance of the Garrick were not always to George's liking. He found a number of members 'too stuffy'. Inherited privilege, understated charm and old money – part of the club's fabric – made him feel ill at ease. Yet most Garrick Club members are meritocratic in outlook. It was a little different from dining on the bench at Lincoln's Inn, where tales from the courtroom were the accepted norm. The reality was that broader conversation could discomfit George. He had no real interest in, or knowledge of, the arts or politics beyond superficial chitchat. On a 1988 weekend trip with him to Amsterdam, I had wanted to visit the Van Gogh museum. He was more minded to tour the sex clubs. We compromised and did both.

The act that he put on was an obvious strain. Yearning to be part of the establishment, or at least to be accepted by it for his achievements, he knew that some regarded him with suspicion. Naturally diffident and unsure of what was expected, he never quite knew how to fit in or what to say. Background was not the problem. It was more the person he was and the lifestyle he pursued. Some club members recognised that the contrived quips, quiet modesty and self-deprecating manner were, to a degree, affected. George craved respectability. He thought it very important to create the right impression with people who mattered. But it was a thin veneer. In several interviews, he called himself a keen and regular theatregoer. Yet West End visits seemed to make little impact. His cultural tastes were more tabloid. He preferred the prosaic. Apart from the news, *Blind Date* and prize money quiz shows were among the television favourites. Infrequent concerts were usually at the pop end of the classical repertoire. Ill at ease with those whose knowledge exceeded his own, he read few books and was uninterested in art. At a David Tang reception, Prince Charles asked him: 'Do you like Bach?' George replied: 'No, not really.' It was something of a conversation stopper. There were similarly sticky moments at the Garrick. Visits became infrequent. Largely discarding his distinctive green and salmon-pink members' tie, the 'best club in London' entered George's list of boring places. The legal journalist Joshua Rozenberg, a club regular in the 1990s, was surprised to learn that he had ever been a member at all.

A preferred late-night venue was Jimmy'z Bar in Sloane Avenue. As George arrived, a bottle of Bailey's would appear. He would then chat with the former insurance whiz-kid and playboy property tycoon Christopher Moran. The restorer of Crosby Hall, an eighteen-bedroom Tudor mansion in Chelsea, and purchaser of Glenfiddich, a 47,000-acre estate near Balmoral, Moran was entirely self-made. Often dressed in new green country tweeds, he had a similarly colourful background. Successful business people fascinated George. He admired their money. Another respected talent was the immaculate Aidan Barclay, chairman of Press Holdings, proprietor of the Ritz and a client (George won the hotel's casino licence application). He became a lunch companion in later years amid the restored gilt splendour and overstated opulence of the Ritz dining room. It was new money at its brightest. These were George's kind of people.

Blondes was even more fun. This Dover Street club, owned by two former Manchester clients for whom he had done licensing work, became a place to let his hair down. It attracted an extraordinary variety of punters, including some of London's best-known underworld characters and their brightly attired partners. In this environment, George was much more at home, totally relaxed, buying Dom Pérignon for the crowd around him. No pretence here. George Best became front man at the bar, shortly after his release from prison for assaulting a policeman. The two Georges chatted about their old times drinking together in Manchester. Best had also been a client. George mixed effortlessly in this *demi-monde*, enjoying the frisson of talking to men like Frankie Fraser, a gangland peer of the Krays and the Richardsons.

It was only a short walk from Blondes to Le Rififi in Hay

Hill, Mayfair. George liked to take me here and to other 'gentlemen's' clubs such as the Bruton Suite, Toppers, Chaplin's and L'Hirondelle. These were filled with ageing businessmen and champagne-guzzling hostesses in low-cut dresses. At L'Hirondelle in Swallow Street, there were topless cabaret girls with high heels and sequined cutaway leotards. Hostesses would sit at the table. Champagne was bought, £150 a bottle. The girls killed the fizz with swizzle sticks – they could drink more that way. He chatted to his bought companions with silly questions. I would be introduced: 'This is my friend Dominic.' The girls ordered more champagne. Being seen with young women like this in public gave him a thrill. Even more embarrassing was finding him at his Chelsea flat in 1991 with teenage escorts – tall, blonde and on good money. He was unashamed. Again, I was introduced as a friend. George, it seemed, could resist everything except temptation. His private world was hard to fathom. Like so much in my father's life, I tried to put it out of my mind.

Visits to different clubs were an integral part of his routine. The owners, such as Oscar at the Stork Club or John Obertelli at Le Rififi, enjoyed his patronage and conversation. For many years, he talked idly about opening his own nightclub. It remained a pipe dream. Watching him hard at work burnishing his reputation as a womaniser, I was never sure what message he was trying to convey. It made me feel uncomfortable. Just as he relished the service and attention he got in five-star hotels, he enjoyed being pandered to by obsequious flunkies and head waiters. He liked being recognised. 'Ah hello, Mr Carman,' they would say reverentially. The young, glamorous girls whose time he bought were told of his VIP status. Their conversation was unchallenging and undemanding. Their attention made him feel important. He gave generous tips. In wanting to be king pin, he did not care how insincere the company was.

The casino also beckoned. Aspinalls in Curzon Street had the highest rollers in Europe. Although George was a small-time player in their terms, his drop at the blackjack table was remarkable by any normal standard. His passion for gambling had been only too apparent on my first visit with him to the Playboy Club when I was sixteen, and it had never diminished. To watch him lose was not for the faint-hearted. He often encouraged me to gamble, which I could ill afford to do. At the table, his manner was similar to that of the courtroom – quiet, calm and patient, smiling in victory or defeat. As £500 or £1,000 went at the turn of a card, he was unmoved. On a bad evening, losses ran to tens of thousands – more than I earned in a year. 'Gorgeous George' – the journalists' favoured tag – was now known as a high-risk player. As Henry Porter observed in 1993 after interviewing him for the *Sunday Telegraph* magazine: 'He is dedicated to the avoidance of personal revelation . . . During lunch I struggled to think what this very careful man reminded me of. Certainly it was neither an actor nor a politician. As I left him in the Strand, chain-smoking and watchful as ever, it came to me: he is exactly like every professional gambler I have ever met. He's a loner hooked on the terrible fear of losing.' A very astute observation.

After a good evening at the tables, he would be visibly energised. It was the same adrenalin rush that he experienced in court. Demanding that the cashier return his original cheque or cheques used in exchange for gambling chips – typically for £10,000 or £15,000 – he would tear them into small pieces in an instant. Winnings had to be cash only. That way his bank would never know. The scale of his overdraft caused considerable pressure from Barclays to curb his gambling. George continued to walk a dangerous tightrope. The bundles of £50 notes in plastic wallets, each containing £2,500, made him feel good. He would walk down Curzon Street towards Park Lane with £50,000 or £60,000 stuffed into his pockets, showing no concern for safety. In the 'cash for questions' *Hamilton* v *Al-Fayed* case, he referred knowingly to 'how surprisingly slim these bundles are'. No one took much notice. But winning at the casino came less often than in court. The piles of cash, kept in an unlocked sideboard drawer at Evelyn Gardens in Chelsea – his home from 1987 to 1993 – would usually make a return journey to Curzon Street within days. In fighting a number of big licensing cases for casinos – the best-paid briefs of all – it pleased George to get some of his money back. As Tim Blackstone commented in the City Diary of the *Standard* in 1992: 'I can think of few better qualified to represent London Clubs International in its fight for new casino licences. Carman has the advantage of close experience with the green baize, being much given to trying his luck at the tables.'

George could be generous and gave me money on a number of occasions to clear an overdraft or credit card bills when my income was low. Generosity came at a price. There would be sharp rebukes and frequent reminders of how much he had given. In 1991, he gave me a small deposit on a house and later helped with a large sum to reduce my mortgage. I did not ask him for either. My income had increased significantly. These gifts were then used as a device to chastise and criticise when I did not do as he asked. His desire to help and his desire to control were in conflict.

My priorities changed when I married Rachel in October 1992. During our wedding reception at the Royal Crescent Hotel in Bath, George went into a sulk after lunch. He disappeared to a private suite with Phyllis and his companion Karen, the only two people whom he had himself invited. I was summoned. He was deeply offended because I had not thanked him 'properly' in my speech nor had I asked him to speak. His thin skin was showing. I was made to grovel and apologise. It was a familiar control mechanism. His mood then changed. Sweeping downstairs to announce the purchase of copious champagne for the wedding guests, he beamed at us all – restored as the centre of popular attention.

Now that I was a married man again, striking the right balance between family life and work was important for me. Raising children with Rachel combined with a demanding job and frequent international business travel put an end to my late nights out with George. He did not like this. He wanted me by myself. But looking after him as he degenerated during the evening was never easy and was not particularly enjoyable. Bundling him into taxis caused problems. Many black cabs refuse to take people who are obviously well oiled. Just as he had wanted me to go to Oxford and read law, he hoped that I would replicate his night-time activities. The way in which he conducted himself held little attraction, however. That side of George was not very gorgeous. Never a big drinker, I eventually became teetotal.

My employment caused him problems. He enthused to others about how well I was doing in every job I did. Privately, there was a constant flow of sustained criticism for lack of achievement. He was right. I did fall short of my potential. That was entirely my fault. I resigned from several jobs and did myself no favours. I was letting him down again. He was probably correct that I could do much better. Yet the encouragement I craved was never forthcoming. He told me that I was an embarrassment, a comment designed to kick-start me into action. Praise was something he could not give, yet he constantly demanded it for himself: a common paradox of the high achiever. George's son was seen as subordinate to his will, a satellite to his achievement.

Until the 1990s, my earnings were modest. When I did achieve some success at the international publishers Euromoney, he was unimpressed that I should be managing a magazine business. I owe a great debt to my boss Chris Brown, who became a role model. He restored my self-esteem and helped me to believe in myself. When I thanked him for this, he did not understand what I meant. The acknowledgment and praise he had given me over seven years were very important. But George continued to criticise – with subtlety. He dismissed the fact that I now had a six-figure income, telling me that it wasn't enough. Without warning, he bought £50,000 worth of Euromoney shares. He carped about the men running the company, Richard Ensor and Padraic Fallon, who earned more than he did. 'You should aim for their job,' he told me. This was ridiculous. His intention may have been to inspire, but I knew that the top jobs were well outside my reach. I lacked the experience and, more importantly, the self-confidence.

Our encounters were now limited to sharing a cup of tea and a sandwich in his chambers and to chats in courtroom corridors. He was encouraged to have dinner at our home and to see his three younger grandchildren, Charlie, Tristan and Isobel, born in 1994, 1996 and 1999. Occasionally, he did come. But he was easily irritated by the noise and exuberance of very young children. With my eldest son Matthew, who had never lived with me, George was able to achieve a more adult relationship, having got to know him gradually over sixteen years. He made a real effort with him and enjoyed talking about his achievements to colleagues such as Elizabeth Appleby QC.

'Highly improbable,' was George's response to being asked by Ginny Dougary of *The Times* if he would remarry and have any more children at the age of seventy, 'but I do like other people's babies.' In talking to other people's children, he could be quite charming. As Dougary wrote in a lengthy profile in July 2000: 'He and a lady friend spend Christmas Day together at the Ritz Hotel, which he finds jolly, surrounded by children queuing up to see Father Christmas.' Regrettably, these were never his own grandchildren. Dougary's interview continued: 'I get the impression that Carman is not exactly over-zealous about performing his grandfatherly duties.' He took Charlie and Tristan out once – to a children's party at the Islington house of Hugh Tomlinson, a barrister in his chambers. It was an experience that he chose not to repeat. The death of my father-in-law Philip in 1995 meant that George was their only living grandpa. His infrequent visits excited them. He was the grandpa who appeared on television. Sometimes, he played a game of chess with Charlie. But mostly the two boys watched in fascination as he smoked and talked to me about his latest case before they disappeared to play elsewhere.

While his drinking inevitably moderated with age, the impact of alcohol remained as great. Lengthy late-night telephone calls, sometimes at 1 or 2 a.m., followed these heavy sessions. Once a week was the norm, but two or three weeks might go by without him bingeing. Because of an eight-hour time difference, contact became more prevalent in the form of morning phone calls (local time) when we moved to Hong Kong. I lived there with my family from mid-1995 to January 1998 after agreeing to run a Euromoney subsidiary business in the region. During our stay, he went through some bad patches, often calling on my direct line when I had a meeting in my office. It was quite embarrassing. He would not understand that I was busy and could not talk freely with colleagues sitting around my desk. But it was no good my putting the phone down politely. He would just call back. I listened, hoping that he would soon stop. Sometimes, he would ring three or four times in the space of a few hours. I didn't have the time to chat. It set a bad example. Eventually, my secretary Nancy Tan had to screen all calls, but he soon worked his way round her.

He enjoyed having me to himself when I stayed with him on the seven or eight business trips to London which I made at that time. He managed one week-long visit to us in Hong Kong. Agitated and awkward, he preferred to go off in mid-afternoon 'to have a break'. On the fifth day, he didn't show up at all. Family life remained something of an alien concept to him. In his will, he settled money on each grandchild. The real sadness is that he could not give of his time or attention with the same generosity.

'Trust no one' was one of his favourite phrases in private. He remained deeply suspicious. Puffing away anxiously over a drink in a bar, his eyes would resemble those of a hunted animal, darting around to see who was watching him. It was the reverse in court, where he was the hunter, the bird of prey quietly tearing apart some rodent in the witness box. Even when laughing and joking with colleagues, he was still uneasily alert. Despite an ability to drop into apparently comfortable chat and talk to anyone when it suited, he was afraid to reveal much of himself, except to a trusted few. And even then, there were strict limits. For the most part, he did not disclose vulnerable areas of his personality, instead wearing different masks according to the situation. In this way he projected an image of what he thought other people expected him to be. Meanwhile, the real George stayed out of sight. The barriers stayed up. Questions were deflected. He did not want to let the mask slip. Even when expected to, as in his 1990 appearance on *Desert Island Discs*, he showed little of the person underneath. This clearly frustrated the presenter, Sue Lawley. Making a choice of music was problematic. He agonised over the selections. Pieces of music were tossed around like ideas for a speech. Safe and uncontroversial was the impression he wished to give of the private man.

We spoke very regularly in his final years. When something preoccupied him, he might ring several times a day. Generally, our conversations focused, as ever, on his work. If I tried to move on to other things, he was not really interested. I avoided talking about my life as he sometimes reverted to quiet cross-examination mode. Probing into my thoughts, actions or plans could be a precursor to criticism. Evasion was the best tactic. I remained a hostile witness, adept at changing the subject or turning the question back on him. My best defence was always to get George talking about himself one way or another. This was never difficult. He referred to me in many newspaper and magazine interviews as his 'closest male friend' and his 'best friend'. This description highlighted an omission. In wanting me as his friend, confidant and sometimes minder and adviser, he forgot that I was also his son. I am not sure if he ever appreciated the difference. Until I had children, I am not sure that I did completely myself. Between father and son, communication about feelings remained a one-way affair.

Work was always number one. As his career scaled new heights, he liked me to attend the prominent libel trials and a number of the less publicised cases, heard at the Royal Courts of Justice in the Strand. I was fortunate that the building was close to my London office. In the 1990s, many stolen hours and quiet afternoons were spent listening to him in full flow. He found this particularly important if he was at a low ebb. His need for support and encouragement was constant. It helped to sustain him. Greeting me with an enthusiastic outline of what was happening at every juncture of the current case, he continued to be excited by each development. Polished performances against Aitken, Grobbelaar, Hamilton, Sutcliffe and Taylforth were gripping to watch, but saddening once they were finished. For, beyond the courtroom door, his existence was deeply unsatisfying to him. Beneath the glittering veneer of an apparently crowded and successful life played out in the full glare of publicity, there was little sense of personal or spiritual fulfilment. The reality was profound loneliness – obvious to many who knew him well. George's private world marched to a solitary beat. Interviewees for this book have repeated the theme with a continued and powerful resonance.

Winning in court provided some sense of purpose. The fact that he was unfulfilled served only to focus his energy and enthusiasm on the next client, the next case, the next headline, the next victory. Reports of his achievements gave him a real buzz, proving that he was somebody of substance. In anticipation of an autobiography, which he had planned to write as far back as 1983, he asked me to collect and order all his press cuttings. Our cupboards remain filled with crowded boxes of fading newspapers, carefully sorted and indexed by date and subject over nearly twenty years. These have little value now that he has gone. They rest in silence alongside the Jeremy Thorpe brief and notes from various speeches that he'd given to me in 1994. But legal papers and notebooks do little to illuminate the life of a man or define his contribution to the world. This biography aims to explain the person who was my father, the flawed genius of the courtroom.

2
Roads to Freedom

Why do you whisper green grass?
Why tell the trees what ain't so?
Whispering grass, the trees don't have to know.
Why tell them all your secrets?
Who kissed them long ago?
Whispering grass, the trees don't need to know.

The Inkspots, 'Whispering Grass'
(recorded June 1940)

On 6 October 1929, George Alfred Carman entered a world about to feel the full impact of the Wall Street Crash. His father Alfred, better known as Alf, was an auctioneer. His mother Evelyn, a seamstress by training, had just opened her own dress shop. The Carman family were fortunate to thrive in the face of adversity, and for them the following decade ended noticeably more prosperous than it had begun.

George's parents had met nine years previously. After serving as a boy soldier in the trenches of France, Alf stayed on in the British army, crossing the Irish Sea in 1920 at the outbreak of Civil War. His father, also called George Carman, had been a regular army sergeant for sixteen years, serving throughout the South African campaign. As the son of a Boer War veteran, it was quite natural therefore for Alf to choose to join the Black and Tans, the irregular force so named because of the combined black police belt and khaki army battledress. A romance with Evelyn, the teenage daughter of a Dungarvon cattle dealer called Michael Moylan, appeared unusual in this climate of hostility. She was keen to escape the rural monotony of small-farm life in County Waterford. Alf represented her passport to a better future.

The couple moved to Blackpool, getting married in October 1923. Evelyn, aged nineteen, found work as a ladies' companion. Alf, by now twenty-three, embarked on a career as a furniture auctioneer. Although she was four years younger, it was Evelyn who dictated terms. Alf converted from the Wesleyan Church to Catholicism, remaining a devout Catholic thereafter. They travelled around the country for a while and moved to Folkestone when George's elder sister Joyce was born in August 1924. By the time George arrived five years later, the Carmans had returned to Blackpool. Here they were to make swift progress up the property ladder, buying the first in a series of brand-new houses, which grew in size and status.

Evelyn's shop, Madame Louise, was located in what was then a smart Blackpool shopping street, the Strand. Using terminology now forgotten, it was called a gown shop, specialising in smart dresses for the affluent professional and business classes of the Blackpool/Lytham area, and for performers visiting the resort for a long run at one of the local theatres. In the pre-television era, these were stars with money. They needed to look the part. Evelyn understood her customers' needs and aspirations. She pampered and flattered, encouraging them to spend as much as they could on sequinned evening dresses and elegant daywear with the latest fashion in pleated silk chiffon and crêpe de Chine from Paris and London. Glamour did not come cheap. Prices started at around ten guineas, going up to forty guineas or more at the top end – a small fortune in the 1930s, when the average weekly wage was less than £4. As with much of Blackpool trade at the time, many transactions were done in cash.

A feisty, frenetic woman, Evelyn was above all a perfectionist. Between parent and child, Alf formed the closer bond with Joyce, and Evelyn with George. But Evelyn's energies were divided. Madame Louise demanded considerable attention. The shop's great success was rooted in her superb salesmanship, determined hard work and an abundance of natural charm. She combined a tremendous eye for detail with strong creative flair. Highly strung and temperamental, she would sometimes wake with an idea at 4 a.m. Alf would at once drive her to rearrange the window display. Dedication paid off. In 1936, a second shop was opened.

Alf used to recall that the early years of married life passed in a whirl. He struggled to cope with Evelyn's volatile moods, nervous energy and restless ambition. But this gentle and thoughtful man worshipped her. Their contrasting personalities complemented each other well. The infant George's needs, competing with a thriving business, required the services of a full-time nanny. Miss Fish joined the two existing maids. By the age of four, George was throwing great tantrums over his mother's absences and howling bitterly when she returned to put him to bed. Their relationship, although very close, was partly flawed in her son's eyes because she could not devote more time to him. In short, he resented her working.

Proficient at the usual sibling trick of getting his sister into trouble, George transferred blame where he could for his own misdeeds. Much to Joyce's fury, her little brother was usually believed. On one occasion, Joyce, George and his best friend George Robinson tried to organise a dog show. They rounded up all the animals they could find, asking friends and neighbours if they could take their dogs out for a walk. Each animal was then shut in the Carmans' garden. The scheme was to charge people for letting them in to inspect the assorted breeds. Evelyn did not see the funny side of things when she returned to discover more than twenty dogs barking outside the house. Even George must have had some difficulty explaining how they had got there.

Domestic arrangements were quite regimented. Evelyn ruled the household and was pleased that her son seemed to share her obsession with hygiene. And young George was keen to imitate the adult occupations he saw in his Blackpool environment. As a tram conductor, he organised his parents into a row of passengers while he collected fares and dispensed tickets. Music was a key feature of their life, with his mother's favourites, 'Danny Boy' and 'When Irish Eyes are Smiling', played frequently on the gramophone. George was encouraged to learn the piano. He was given lessons twice a week by a farmer's wife and later by a Miss Annigoni.

Holidays during the 1930s were spent with Evelyn's family in Ireland. Alf took the Riley across on the ferry, driving on to Dungarvon, where a new car was a real talking point. The roads were cobbled, women wore black, and there was traditional Sunday lunch after Mass: roast beef and all the trimmings, followed by apple and rhubarb pie with custard. Afterwards, they would sit around the table singing Republican songs. Basic country living ('primitive' according to George), with cows in the field and pigs in the backyard, made a deep impression. So did his two uncles. One of them was a star in the All Ireland Hurley team. The other was 'simple' and had to be looked after. The success enjoyed by the Carman family in England was the talk of the Moylans in Ireland. But after the war, the two families rarely spoke.

To distance herself and her children from what she regarded as the backwardness of her Irish upbringing, Evelyn developed a strong compulsion for self-improvement. Despite not having had a formal education, she knew its value, and was determined that George should make the most of his ability. Just before his eighth birthday, he went to board at Blackpool's best-known Catholic school, St Joseph's College, or Holy Joe's, as it was often called. While most boarders had been despatched there for some fresh sea air from the industrial gloom of Manchester and Liverpool, George's home was only a ten-minute walk from the school gate. It made him different. This strange decision can be explained by Alf's and Evelyn's regular trips to London to buy new stock and by the general demands of their work.

Life under the Irish Christian Brothers at St Joseph's was every bit as horrific as reports in the 1990s of their teaching methods have suggested. Brutal physical punishment was routine. The twelve-inch leather strap, carried at the waist of each brother, was liberally used by some in response to any minor misdemeanour, or in anticipation of it. As Father Vincent Smith, George's classmate for four years at St Joseph's, and later at Upholland, recalls: 'They were certainly Irish, many were brothers, but the Christian element was definitely lacking in most of them. They believed they could beat knowledge or religion into anyone.'

George's first beating came as the result of refusing to eat lumpy porridge. He ran home in tears, only to be sent straight back by his mother. He was soon being teased mercilessly by other boarders for the combination underwear which she had bought him, and which earned the nickname 'Peem' after a cartoon character. Learning to tolerate the regime, he remained unhappy and would look forward to his parents' Sunday-afternoon visits, when they would take him out for a traditional high tea of ham, cheese, salad and cream cakes. A quick temper was to get him into further trouble. In the view of another St Joseph's contemporary, John Walton, 'There was a belligerent atmosphere at the school. The brothers were frustrated men, always on the look-out for anything wrong.' He remembers George 'getting into several fights with authority' and being strapped hard for 'arguing with brothers and answering back when reprimanded'. Another schoolmate says: 'He was clever and a bumptious little so-and-so. Every so often, his cocky manner got him into big trouble with the brothers.'

His first-year school report reveals a natural artistic bias. In English, he scored 90 per cent and in religion 85, while in arithmetic and geography the marks were 57 and 22 per cent. Overall, he was first in class. As an able sprinter, he also excelled on the sports field. Evelyn came to watch him in the eighty-yard race, impressing on him that there were no prizes for coming second and that winning was everything. She told him repeatedly: 'You must win, George.' Taking the lesson to heart, he reacted to her fierce ambition by getting very worked up, regularly fainting before races in what would now be called panic attacks. He was subsequently to suffer from vaso-vagal attacks, similarly provoked by anxiety. This phenomenon continued until his mid-thirties, causing him to pass out on several occasions before he went into court to make a speech.

Hard work and increased prosperity brought solid middle-class Blackpool living within his parents' grasp: a sizable detached house, servants and the new Riley motor car. Their prosperity remained largely undiminished when war broke out. At some point in 1941, George ceased to board. For three years he continued as a day boy, going home for tea, having an hour's piano practice and then returning to school for a couple of hours to do his homework, before going home again to bed. More often than not, he would discover both parents out and the maids finished for the day, and he began to find the isolation unbearable. He developed a passionate dislike for being in an empty house which lasted for the rest of his life. After the phrase came into fashion in the 1970s, he described himself as having been a 'latchkey child' from the age of twelve onwards.

News events were of intense interest. He became very excited when defeat at Tobruk was followed by victory at El Alamein. By the end of 1942, the tide had turned. Encouraged by Evelyn, George was developing a distinct snobbishness that made him dissatisfied with the family's position. When his father had to work in a local munitions factory as part of the war effort, he felt humiliated. They were never close. Alf's strong Northern accent and lack of a university education began to signal to his teenage son that he was beneath him, socially and intellectually. George would later describe him as 'easily satisfied, placid in temperament and fairly easy-going'. These were not qualities he admired, since they represented the antithesis of his own personality. Things became increasingly difficult at home. Briefly persuaded by Marx's logic encountered in extracts from *Das Kapital*, he accused his father of being a capitalist exploiter because he employed four people. Alf was taken aback. Despite being widely read, he was a man of few words, unable to deal with George's precocious talent for opinionated political argument. George would recall the *Das Kapital* incident to me as an illustration of his 'youthful naivety', and would laugh at the thought of this brief Marxist phase. But, to a degree, it characterised the underlying contempt he felt for his father's lack of drive and ambition. Jealousy may also have been at work. For contentment completely eluded George.

In reality, Alf was a moderately successful small businessman, operating very much in Evelyn's shadow. In addition to being an auctioneer, he ran a furniture shop. His background was without privilege. After winning a grammar school scholarship, he chose instead to run away to sea before returning from a seven-month absence to work in a Burnley mill. He was thirteen. During the Great War, like everyone else, he enlisted by lying about his age to become a sixteen-year-old barber and machine-gunner in the mud and blood of Ypres. Captured in 1917, Corporal Carman then escaped from a train behind enemy lines – a story he enjoyed telling me as a child – before making it back to his own line. The legacy of trench warfare never left him. As with so many of his generation, the battle went on.

Catholicism was everywhere in George's life. At St Joseph's, Hail Mary was said on the hour every hour. Religion guided the curriculum. There was Mass every Sunday, sometimes twice. So it was no surprise that the local parish priest, Father Atkinson, made George an altar boy, and later chief altar boy, at his church, St Kentigern's. In customary Irish fashion, Evelyn aspired for her son to be a priest. Just short of fifteen, he was sent to Upholland Seminary, near Wigan, home to 200 boys aged between eleven and eighteen in the junior seminary, and to more than sixty adults, studying theology and philosophy, in the senior seminary. Students were sub-divided into three groups by age: the Lower Line, Higher Line and senior seminary. Any fraternisation or talking between members of different lines was punished by mandatory expulsion. This zero-tolerance policy was intended to prevent homosexual relationships developing in a close, all-male environment. Physical punishment was however more benign than at St Joseph's.

Frank Slattery, who was to go on to become a monsignor in Windermere, left St Joseph's with George to go to Upholland in September 1944. He recalls that his contemporary was 'friendly and approachable, but he had a very fiery temper. He got into a fight in the toilets with a boy from the Isle of Man called Kipper Kinrade. I separated the two of them and they both turned on me.' Another Upholland contemporary was Sir Anthony Kenny, later Master of Balliol: 'I could not communicate with George when we were there, because of the rule about lines, since he was two years older than me. But I do remember him looking rather bored during the periods of meditation. Many years later, when I raised the subject of Upholland at a Balliol dinner, George changed the subject. He obviously did not want to discuss it.'

Their existence was Spartan. Meals were eaten in silence while religious texts were read aloud. For breakfast, students ate dry bread with tea, except on Easter Sunday when eggs and bacon were served. Lunch was the only proper meal of the day, with dry bread and water at teatime. More bread arrived for supper with cheese and fish paste. Communication with the outside world – including food parcels – was strictly forbidden. Boys were allowed only two visits home a year, at Christmas and in the summer. 'It was a very impersonal place, but very secure, structured and regular. You lived cheek by jowl with everyone else and we rejoiced in the routine of life,' says Monsignor Slattery, who spent ten years there.

The strict regime entailed rising at six for meditation, Mass at seven, and an edict that when passing one of the maids – 'specially chosen for their extreme plainness' – boys had to avert their gaze. Conversing with a maid was another instant-expulsion offence. George described the seminary education in interview as 'first class because the priests had been trained in Rome and at Cambridge. I had marvellous teachers, dedicated

men of broad culture and learning. The tremendous discipline
they instilled was of great value afterwards. When I told the
Rector I wanted to leave, he said, "What a pity, we were just
going to send you to the English College in Rome."' George
was very reluctant ever to discuss in detail the reason for his
sudden departure after a year. He would joke, 'I discovered
girls,' before outlining the serious doubts he had been having
about certain aspects of Catholic theology, namely birth control.
How he discovered girls remains unclear and the full story of
his Upholland experience is an unknown.

More certain was the prevailing conspiracy of silence at
St Joseph's, where he returned after his time at the seminary.
Conversation with a number of his contemporaries shows that
the names of those brothers who abused, physically or sexually,
are deeply engrained on their memories. One in particular, nick-
named Dracula or Drac, was widely known to detain boys for
his own pleasure in the science block, most afternoons. Another
was transferred elsewhere when his predatory sexual habits
became too obvious. Nobody talked. George's strong aversion
to discussing various aspects of his school years, supported by
some of his later behaviour, make it reasonable to assume that
he may, for a while, have been a victim of sexual, as well as
physical, abuse.

Though it is shrouded in mystery, an earlier episode stands
out that might lend possible support to this theory. For the
Easter of 1938, George went on a one-month school trip to
Rome. This was organised by Father (later Bishop) Pearson,
who ran the Catholic Boys Association and had lived in Italy
for a few years. The party travelled through Europe by train,
visited all the sights in Rome and were entertained generously
by nuns, by Vatican officials and by staff at the English College,
where the boys swam. Their visit occurred at an historic
moment. The Nazi Anschluss in Austria had taken place without a struggle only weeks before the boys arrived. On 2 May,
when they were still there, Hitler arrived in Rome to meet with

Mussolini at the new railway station, built as a monument to fascism. During the Führer's week-long stay, many of the city's streets were garlanded with flags, flowers and tanks. Large crowds cheered and celebrated the Axis leaders' public parades. Martin Quinlan, an older St Joseph's boy on the trip, recalls the whole experience as 'quite unforgettable'. George remembered nothing.

One has to look at the context to see why this is so odd. A devout Catholic boy, who later trained to be a priest, would have considered a trip to Rome of great personal significance. Yet he never once mentioned it to me, to any of his wives, or to anyone else I have asked. A group photograph taken overlooking the Eternal City shows him to be significantly younger than everyone else. While the other boys on the trip were aged between thirteen and eighteen, George was only eight – an unusual disparity. When recalling childhood journeys, he detailed at length the family boat trips in 1936 and 1937 to visit, as he termed them, his 'shockingly poor' relatives in Ireland. He also spoke animatedly when describing 'my first holidays in Europe' – his 1949 Paris visit and a hot Spanish summer the following year. For reasons that remain enigmatic, George's Roman holiday was evidently shut out of his mind, never to be discussed.

The return to St Joseph's in 1945 saw his talent recognised by Brother Woodhouse, or Woodlouse, as the boys called him, who had just succeeded Brother 'Polly' Moran as headmaster. In the words of a classmate, Pat Nolan, 'He found [in George] a boy with the ability and aptitude to do great things and was very proud of his prodigy.' Another contemporary, Max Armstrong, says that Woodhouse 'took George under his wing as his own personal gem'. Physically tall, slim and angular, he was more intellectual than most of his peers and taught history and Latin for Higher School Certificate. George studied both subjects. Woodhouse's star pupil later spoke about him with affection, recalling the dedicated and inspired teaching over many evenings of extra private tuition. Nurturing an interest in the English language, he was made to analyse leading articles in *The Times* (Alf took only the *Daily Express* at home). Woodhouse introduced him to literature. Wider reading was encouraged: Macaulay, Hazlitt, Pope, Lamb, Cicero and Milton. Favourites that he often mentioned to me included Cicero's speech, *Pro Milone*, and Milton's famous 1644 piece on press freedom, *Areopagitica*.

Nolan describes the impression made by George: 'I remember the headmaster bringing this rather small boy into the class, telling us that he had abandoned his studies for the priesthood and would be joining us. He was unusual. Most pupils in a school gravitate into one category or other. George did not. As a high academic achiever, you would have thought he would belong to the Swots. However, he also became a key player [George was scrum half] in the most successful rugby team that the school ever had. As such, you would expect him to join the gregarious roustabouts who met at the Winter Gardens on a Saturday night. He did not belong to these groups, although he could join in with either one. When it suited, he bubbled with charm and personality, but did not seem to like people; instead he liked to charm people.'

Charm's value was learned to good effect in one of George's summer jobs after the war, when he worked as a waiter at a kosher hotel, behind Blackpool's Golden Mile. The popularity of puddings with some of the larger ladies staying there astonished him. Hiding his disgust at their gluttony, he went out of his way to serve them enormous portions of trifle and gateau, always delivered with a smile. Grateful husbands rewarded him generously. Although he came to despise it, the attractions of Blackpool provided other valuable lessons. Besides illuminations and the sea, he watched for hours as star turns at the theatre and end-of-the-pier performers held audiences in thrall. The facial responses of spectators were of particular fascination – what they listened to, what they laughed at and how they reacted to surprises. Some of the techniques observed here were to find good use in front of many juries. At the other end of the pier, he was learning to spend his pennies on the one-armed bandits and assorted slot machines.

Common to his generation, George went to see endless films, which developed in him a romantic, Hollywood view of life. This never disappeared. Accompanying him to the Tivoli Cinema, and sometimes to church, was his first girlfriend, Mary Murphy. Now called Mary Williamson and living in Leicester, she recalls her two-year friendship with George very well: 'Although his height bothered him and he wanted to be taller, he was very full of himself, serious and always smartly dressed. He loved being in the limelight and being the centre of attention in any discussion. He had lots of opinions on everything, but would never reveal very much about himself and kept his secrets. When he ended the relationship, he wrote such a complicated letter that it took my sister and I more than an hour to look up all the words in a dictionary.'

George had a difficult childhood relationship with his sister. Neither acknowledged that their similar personalities created strong mutual intolerance. Joyce was naturally jealous of Evelyn's favouritism towards her brother. She increasingly disapproved of his personal habits, which started to emerge as he approached eighteen. Getting drunk and chatting up local girls was not the sort of respectable behaviour that she expected. In April 1947, she married a local accountant, John Blane, who had recently recovered after three years as a Japanese prisoner of war. An army officer captured at the fall of Singapore, he weighed not much over six and a half stone when liberated. She had made a good match. Evelyn was pleased that her only daughter had married into money. The Blanes were prosperous with interests in the Clifton Hotel and various other Blackpool properties.

Joyce remained a conventional housewife, dominant mother and devout Catholic, married to John until his death forty-three years later. They had two sons, Christopher and Nicholas. Both boarded from eight onwards and were later taught by the monks of Ampleforth. In a *Times* newspaper interview, given in July 2000, George made the following comments: 'I have always thought ever since she married him that accountancy is a dull profession. Their very respectable life was insular – revolving around the Rotary Club, Food and Wine Society and the golf club.' He maintained a safe distance from her in adulthood, wary of her disapproval and highly critical of her 'conservative, conventional attitudes'. Significantly, Joyce's birthday, 11 August, was the only one he ever remembered. A card and present were sent each year without fail until her death in 1993.

The smallest boy in the sixth form, George was also the cleverest. He took the role of prefect very seriously, 'always putting people on report for failing to wear a school cap', according to Nolan. Tony Whalley, five years younger than George at St Joseph's, remembers being punished by him in 1946: 'As a prefect, he got to wear a gold band on the rear of his school cap instead of the standard red one. I was nailed twice by him and required to attend the prefects' meeting. Once because, when late for school, I rode my bicycle up the College drive, and on the other occasion because I had misplaced my cap. He required me to write an essay about personal responsibility as a punishment and complimented me on the finished product. My mother informed me that George came from a very smart family, and I could do worse than be disciplined by someone who only had my best interests at heart. As I moved through the school, it seemed that George became the yardstick against which we were all judged.'

Becoming captain of one of the school houses, Layton, he set about organising an inter-house debating society. He began to work in earnest for the ultimate prize, which Woodhouse had in mind: Balliol College, Oxford. Evelyn warmly supported the idea, ever ambitious for her son to do well. Alf was against it, preferring that he go to Manchester University, because it was much closer to home. But George had been reading about the great advocates: Edward Marshall-Hall, Edward Carson, Norman Birkett and, his role model in adulthood, F. E. Smith, later Lord Birkenhead. He had decided that he wanted to join what the most famous advocate of that time, Sir Patrick Hastings KC, called 'the greatest profession in the world' and 'a glorious way of earning a living'. He was going to be a barrister. And the first step, he decided, was to go to Oxford and read law.

Woodhouse had a link with Balliol, well known for its strong Catholic connections, through the distinguished convert and theologian Ronnie Knox. He had been at the College and was Catholic chaplain at Oxford before the war. George was sent off to see the formidable Monsignor at the Manor House in Mells, near Frome, where he spent the last ten years of his life, finishing his translations of the Bible. This was the family home of another Catholic Balliol man, the Earl of Oxford and Asquith, whose daughter Lady Annunziata was the focus of George's attention more than thirty years afterwards. The present Earl remembers Knox as 'shy, but wonderfully considerate'. For George, he was an inspiration.

Beyond the demands of Higher School Certificate, he studied hard for the Oxford entrance exam in 1947. When it came to it, he had resolved to get in entirely on merit. He would recall with a satisfied smile the first essay question in the general paper: 'Architecture is frozen music. Discuss.' This was just the sort of topic his reading had prepared him for. Woodhouse's effort had not been in vain.

George believed strongly in fate and saw great significance in what happened next. Early one morning as he sat awaiting the arrival of the post at home, a single letter came through the letterbox and fell down a crack between the carpet and the door. Much to Alf's horror, he insisted they take up the hall floorboards near the front door. They shone a torch into the void and there was the Balliol crest on the back of the envelope. It was a letter offering him an interview in five days' time.

The Master of Balliol and the law tutor, Theodore Tylor, conducted the interview. George was terrified: 'I had not met academics before or people of such sophistication and subtlety.' They asked the title of the last book he had read. Points were scored with an immediate reply, *Language, Truth and Logic* by A. J. Ayer, who, as he well knew, had been a Christ Church scholar. Tylor said: 'So you want to go to the Bar. Do you have any connections, family or otherwise?' George replied: 'None.' Tylor said, 'Well, you'd better become a solicitor then.' George was furious. He felt humiliated and indignant, but more determined than ever. They asked him: 'How would you define sovereignty?' He gave a fumbling answer, which made the interviewers laugh. Tylor said, 'Are you aware that the Master of the College has written a book on this subject?' George replied: 'No, but perhaps I will have a chance of reading it when I come to this College.' Finally, they asked: 'If we grant you a place here, you know we expect excellence?' He told them that that was why he had applied to Balliol. Several weeks later, he was offered a place. His dream had come true.

Before going up to Oxford, there was the small matter of national service. George thrived on Aldershot basic training. Strict discipline and personal fitness were an extension of the ethos at Upholland and St Joseph's. After passing out as a second lieutenant in early 1948, he hoped to become a tank commander, as it seemed a glamorous job. This required undertaking various practical tasks and sitting several written papers. He failed nearly every test, giving up in despair when asked to reassemble the assorted parts of a bicycle pump. Anything technical or mechanical always caused him great problems. Cameras, mobile phones, fax machines and television remote controls would later prove to be totally beyond him and he never, to my knowledge, fitted a plug or changed a light bulb in his life.

Tanks were out of the equation. Young Lieutenant Carman was instead posted to a Guards regiment. He rather liked the sound of this. The problem here was money, as he found that the drinks bill – whisky sodas at the bar and vintage wine with dinner every night – was more than his monthly pay. In a Guards officers' mess, where fellow officers were the affluent sons of landed gentry and generals, you were expected to have private means. He put in for a transfer after two months. The automatic army solution for this bright young man with a shortage of funds was education.

Shunted off to spend time at the other end of the social spectrum, George was sent to train illiterates how to read and write with the Royal Army Education Corps. This exposed him to young men of his own age who came from a background of real hardship and poverty. It also gave him a sense of purpose. He set about teaching the basics in life to people from the poorest and most deprived sections of society, starting with cleanliness. If a soldier had failed to wash properly and turned up for inspection dirty, he would have him stripped down and scrubbed from head to toe by a sergeant using a bucket of hot water, soap and a large scrubbing brush. This would be done in front of all the other soldiers. It soon raised the levels of hygiene. His teaching methods were similarly effective. Men were given basic lists of words and short sentences to copy again and again. In between they had to read short paragraphs aloud from the *Daily Mirror*. The idea was that by the end of eight weeks each man should be able to write a short, simple letter home to his mother and read a story from the newspaper. Most of them could. These achievements gave George enormous satisfaction.

One former St Joseph's College boy, Jim Callagher, was a sergeant in the same regiment and posting. George approached him one day and asked if he could borrow some cash until pay day. Callagher lent him ten shillings. Spotting George soon after pay day, he chased after him to ask for the money back. George repaid it and then said: 'Thanks, Jim. Better be off now. Wouldn't do to be seen talking to other ranks.' His sense of status and position had grown with commission and promotion. By the time he left the army, Captain Carman hung up his Sam Browne, his gloves and his swagger stick with some reluctance.

The autumn of 1949 – the start of what has been called by many a golden period at Oxford – found the Blackpool boy arriving at Balliol with high expectations and keen to put thoughts of his home town's most famous son, George Formby, and his ukulele well behind him. Every generation may choose to see their undergraduate years as special in some way. George was no exception, frequently describing this period as the happiest of his life. Ten years before he went up, John Betjeman had written: 'Balliol produces more distinguished men, in politics and literature, than any other college. Its famous run of scholars in the nineteenth century causes one to look at its hideous Broad Street façade with superstitious air.' In starting out, the young law undergraduate was determined to become one of those distinguished men – in his case, a distinguished barrister. As Professor George Steiner, the renowned academic, later said of his close Oxford contemporary, 'George already gave the maximum yield of efficiency in whatever he said or did, which is rare in young people. There was no flap or flip or flop. He symbolised the much more ruthless, much tougher, much more professional world that was to come.' Dick Taverne, also an Oxford friend, remembers that 'George had a wonderfully caustic, irreverent approach to life with a dry sense of humour. He was quiet and, although very clever, gave no indication that he would become a great advocate.'

Balliol had an unrivalled reputation for academic excellence, frequently coming top of the Norrington Table (which ranks colleges according to performance in undergraduate finals) and repeatedly securing more firsts than any other Oxford college. (Balliol's return to the top slot in the July 2001 table after an absence of thirty years would have delighted George.) As one of his friends commented: 'Many people arrive at Balliol with an inferiority complex; few leave with one.' Its unique characteristic was diversity. Commonwealth students from Africa and

India had long been part of the culture, as were a fair sprinkling of Rhodes Scholars from the US. A glance through the College register shows a much wider geographic intake at Balliol than elsewhere. It also reveals the extraordinary range in the ages of undergraduates. Because of the war, many had returned to or started their studies late. Accordingly, in addition to the usual clutch of bright teenagers, many were in their early and mid-twenties, providing a rather more worldly feel. At twenty, George was more than a provincial innocent abroad. But he was well placed to benefit from the maturity and greater experience of contemporaries who had seen something more of life.

Sir David Lindsay Keir, the strait-laced Master of Balliol, who had arrived at the same time as George, was a remote figure. A constitutional historian, he is described in the history of Balliol by John Jones as leaving 'a memory somewhere between luke-warm and adverse behind him'. George certainly did not care for him. It was the undergraduates who mattered. Three were reading law in his year at Balliol, including Patrick (Paddy) Mayhew, later Conservative Attorney General and Northern Ireland Secretary. Another, Stanley Brodie QC, remembers that 'George was a very good self-promoter. He liked to put himself about and take whatever opportunities were available. He used his Catholic connections to get himself noticed.'

George was still a declared Catholic. Active in the Newman Society (a forum for Catholic undergraduate debate), he was defeated for the office of president by Bruce Kent, later a monsignor and active nuclear disarmer. Undeterred, he decided to start a liberal Catholic journal, *Profile*, with a Brasenose co-religionist, George Bull. The idea was to present opposing views on topical issues. They attracted contributions from eminent Catholics: Lord Longford, Graham Greene, Evelyn Waugh and Father Martin D'Arcy. The birth-control pioneer Marie Stopes was invited to write alongside the aggressive polemicist Dr Halliday Sutherland, who had been involved in bitter litigation with her in the 1920s. George wanted to renew the debate. Sutherland declined, threatening to denounce him to Rome as 'a dangerous man'. *Profile* folded after its second issue through lack of money. George wrote to Bull: 'I feel that I had just better stick to law and politics and leave journalism to those who want broken hearts . . .'

For a year, he shared rooms with a small pugnacious American, George Carver, who coxed the Oxford boat that famously sank in the 1951 boat race. Twenty-five years later, the diminutive rower was to show steadier judgment in becoming number two to future US President George Bush, as deputy director of the CIA. Of the other bright young Balliol men with a glittering future, William Rees-Mogg, later editor of *The Times*, was the one who stood out in George's mind as a possible Prime Minister. Rees-Mogg also recalls George: 'He was a good speaker in debate, but, like me, had to work at it. He was not a natural, like Jeremy Thorpe or Robin Day.' Both Thorpe and Day were to join Rees-Mogg as presidents of the Oxford Union, the traditional platform for greater things in public life.

George's obvious intellectual ability was no match in debate for the over-brimming self-confidence displayed by the Union giants. Without public school education or a natural ebullience, he felt at a disadvantage. Indeed, outside the courtroom, an arena that he made his own, George would remain reserved and often socially diffident throughout his life – a surprise to many of those who met him. Before going to Oxford, he had made his first attempts at public speaking, arguing when aged nineteen for the Catholic Evidence Guild at Speakers' Corner in Hyde Park. But the Union was the place where George's desire to perform found a more natural outlet.

Becoming known for substance rather than style, he turned to one of the better performers for help on presentation. Jeremy Thorpe's Oxford arrival had been smoother than his silk brocade waistcoats. Certain that destiny would offer him great things, the Old Etonian turned Trinity law undergraduate overflowed with charm, wit, panache and a ruthless determination to become president. In January 1951, he succeeded. In contrast to his Balliol neighbour George, his ability was a triumph of style over substance based on apparently effortless superiority and limitless self-belief – valuable commodities in the Union. At the same time, the gregarious Union star was struggling with his constitutional law studies. So the two students did a deal. George wrote a few of Jeremy's more demanding law essays, while the leading Young Liberal helped George draft some of his Union speeches. It worked. For the motion in one particular debate, 'The Labour Party has lost its soul beyond recall', George – a sometime member of the Labour Club and politically to the left – delivered his most successful speech, almost entirely with Jeremy's guiding hand. Thorpe remembers George as 'noticeably small, but a good, clear speaker with a serious manner'. Other fellow law undergraduates included Vivian Price, soon to be best man at George's first wedding to Ursula Groves. Like Thorpe, he would later turn to his Balliol law chum for professional help in the courtroom.

George was a late riser, lunching at the Kardomah café around midday. He began a lifelong love affair with Indian food, working his way at night through the Taj Mahal restaurant menu. In between, Brodie remembers, 'George did a very good job enjoying himself.' Drink depended upon the occasion. Sherry parties were in vogue. Gin and tonic, whisky, wine – whenever it was going – and champagne – on any occasion – were all consumed. Failing those, anything else would do (except beer, which was thought of as inferior). Apart from law, George was intellectually questing and questioning. He enjoyed discussion and argument, read some Wittgenstein, went to see *The Third Man* at the cinema several times and had the occasional night out in London clubs. It was a typical leisurely undergraduate existence of the period.

George's accent – the source of much comment since – was not broad Lancastrian at this time, as some have suggested. His Oxford friend Basil Stein insists, 'He spoke very clearly and carefully, without any accent.' Nevertheless, his voice seems to have undergone some transformation, as he indicated in an interview: 'I made a conscious effort to divest myself of a regional accent as soon as I realised I wanted to go into public life.' Elsewhere he said, 'I think I was always careful to speak in a decent way,' and, more revealingly, he told the *Sunday Express* magazine over a Savoy Grill lunch in 1992: 'I decided in my teens it would be an advantage to speak without a regional accent. It wasn't snobbish, more to do with getting a job. I don't fit easily into any class.'

In fact, George developed several accents. First was his normal speaking voice, for which he employed neutral Received Pronunciation. In tone, this was deep, gravelly and well modulated, except for certain words that always caused him problems, such as 'difficult' (he emphasised the '-cult' ending), 'lorry' (he tended to say 'lurry'). He also mispronounced surnames at will. Jan Tomalin, the in-house lawyer at Channel 4, and Roger Courtiour, a journalist investigating the Thorpe case, were both innocent victims of this phenomenon. For his court voice, he adopted a fusion of oratorical styles, part actor, part advocate. In performance, there were elongated vowels and an exaggerated drawl – for example, 'reaaaally', which would be delivered as an incredulous theatrical response to a witness in cross-examination. Finally there was his establishment voice. This was reserved for certain interviews, smart social functions and the Court of Appeal. A slightly grander version of his normal voice, it echoed the intonation and style of the better class of High Court judge.

For law tutorials, George was fortunate to have the famous blind don Theodore Tylor, who had teased him in the interview. Tylor's mother was a member of the Cadbury family and his father was the architect of Bournville village. A bachelor who lived with his sister, he was a bad lecturer but an excellent tutor. His handicap was offset by a phenomenal memory, which enabled him to become an outstanding chess player of international calibre. He had thoroughly mastered every book in his extensive library. George would be asked to retrieve a particular volume from a specified shelf and told to open it at a certain page. There he would find the relevant point or judgment they had been discussing. Tylor's blindness was not, however, total. He could distinguish between light and shade. This was unknown to one of George's fellow tutorial students who thought it would not matter if he turned up wearing tennis kit instead of the required jacket and tie. He was stunned when caught out.

Towards the end of his first year, George became very close to a Somerville undergraduate, Anne Mueller, who was reading politics, philosophy and economics. In the 1980s, she would become Dame Anne Mueller, the most successful woman civil servant of her generation as second permanent secretary in the Cabinet Office, and subsequently at the Treasury. The relationship 'was very intense', according to Stein, who knew the couple well. A pretty girl, Anne was small, serious and clever – not dissimilar to George. 'She was a little curious and slightly inhibited,' adds Taverne. Her English mother had married a German businessman in Bombay in the 1920s. This made for a difficult wartime childhood at Wakefield Girl's High School. She met George at an Oxford party. The couple soon hit it off, deciding to go on holiday to Spain together in the long vacation. They visited Granada, Seville and the El Greco museum at Toledo. Lying on their backs to watch the stars, they talked for hours. By Christmas 1950, George had proposed. Anne accepted. Brodie comments that 'It was very unusual for undergraduates to get engaged, and their relationship was somewhat frowned upon because they were so young.'

Things changed the following year. George chased various other women, mostly local nurses ('He was always interested in pretty girls,' says Brodie). The problem for Anne was his much less public bisexuality, as he developed at least one intimate relationship with a fellow male undergraduate. Oxford at the time had 7,000 men and only 700 women. Many had come from public school backgrounds where fumbling in the dormitory was routine and full-blown homosexual relationships not un-common. But this was 1951 and these were still criminal acts. Things were kept very much in the closet and George preferred to keep it that way. Whatever the detail, it was more than Anne could tolerate. She broke off the relationship, writing to George that she could 'no longer accept his aberrations'. Determined to win her back, he made every effort to persuade her to change her mind. But things never returned to an even keel. They continued to see each other on and off after Oxford until late 1952. George became a nuisance, pestering her to continue as before. Eventually, she instructed solicitors, who threatened legal action to restrain him. This did the trick and he never saw her again.

Against a background of emotional turmoil, his studies suffered. Following a poor showing in law mods (exams) in his first year came tutorial efforts that were distinctly below expectation. He got a final-year invitation to see the Master. The College was very keen in exercising strong influence over its students. Lindsay Keir was unambiguous, telling George that he was a bright young man who had the ability to get a first. Indeed, Balliol expected it. The message hit home that he should do his duty. Three years of indolent fun and self-indulgence gave way to three months of hard graft. George would recall that in the following weeks he worked harder than at any time in his life, before or since.

When William Rees-Mogg, Dick Taverne and Robin Day sat down before leaving Oxford in 1951 to predict the future stars of their generation, they took the view that the charming and flamboyant Thorpe would 'come to a sticky end'. They could not have foreseen quite how things would turn out. Steiner had suggested that George would become Lord Chancellor, but the three wise men did not envisage such a glamorous and high-profile future for him in politics or the courtroom. 'He seemed more conventional, quiet and academic,' according to Taverne. 'We could never have predicted that he would become a future Patrick Hastings.'

First-class honours degrees at university were much rarer in the mid-twentieth century than today. The brilliant Rees-Mogg, widely expected to get a first, had achieved a second. In 1952 Jeremy Thorpe got a third, whilst at the same time George, like Dick Taverne before him, secured the treasured first. But, more than that, he got an unvivaed first, one of only two given for law in that year at Oxford. The other went to his Magdalen contemporary Nicolas Browne-Wilkinson, later a Lord Justice of Appeal. This was without doubt the single personal achievement in George's life that made him most proud. Now armed with proof of his ability (even though he would never return to Oxford formally to graduate), nothing, he believed, would stop him from flying as high as he wanted in searching for what F. E. Smith had called 'the glittering prizes of life'.

3

From Balliol to the Bailey

There is always room at the top.
Daniel Webster, when advised in the 1820s not to become a
lawyer as the profession was overcrowded

The euphoria of a Balliol first gave way to a further year of study for the Bar finals. Moving straight to London in the autumn of 1952, George joined Lincoln's Inn (each barrister has to belong to one of the four Inns of Court). His new home in Emperor's Gate, South Kensington – a fashionable part of town – gave him a room, breakfast (fresh grapefruit and boiled eggs) and laundry for fifty shillings (£2.50) a week. The landlady was an artist's widow and her son wrote travel guides. Studying by day and enjoying London by night, George entertained Balliol friends such as George Steiner and Basil Stein, and partied in smart clubs. He also socialised briefly with Ken Tynan, the brilliant drama critic. Money was an issue. Stein remembers that 'George would often complain about being hard up and that his father did not give him enough to live properly in London.'

A £10 weekly allowance was supplemented by sporadic part-time work: libel reading for the *News of the World*, washing up in Lyon's Corner House and teaching American servicemen at Brize Norton. The airmen gave him free boxes of cigarettes – the start of chain-smoking consumption that evolved as a lifetime habit. Unable to comprehend a career without immediate income, Alf did not appreciate that his clever son was entering a largely rich man's profession. All he saw was a permanently broke twenty-three-year-old in need of extra handouts. George knew that subsidy would be needed for several years ahead. He came up with a wheeze for making money quickly. On a visit to the Swallow Club with a friend, he got chatting to one of the dancers about working as a masseuse. She was set up in a flat near Great Portland Street. Disaster inevitably struck when visitors soon wanted more than a massage. The girl disappeared. George and his partner were left out of pocket, having paid two months' rent in advance.

The week after Queen Elizabeth II's Coronation, in June 1953, George was awarded a certificate of honour in the Bar finals, coming first in the exam. From Lincoln's Inn, he received the King George V Coronation Scholarship, presented to him by Lord Denning. Now all he had to do was find a good junior to take him in pupillage – a legal apprenticeship that remains a requirement for all young barristers. In essence, this involves shadowing a more experienced colleague in and out of court. Tylor had connections. The Balliol law tutor helped George get a place in the Temple as the pupil of Neil Lawson, later chairman of the Law Commission and a High Court judge. 'I shouldn't give away secrets but I was very impressed [by Tylor's connections],' George revealed to one interviewer. The forty-five-year-old Lawson was a workaholic with a good paper practice. George would reflect on this period: 'None of the work was of direct value to you for the next five or ten years because you never got work of that complexity, but it was something to put in the storehouse.' It also meant another year with virtually no income. Alf was not amused at having to find a further 100 guineas for the pupillage fee. Lawson gave his young pupil three pieces of advice: never accept as accurate a solicitor's instructions, return all paperwork within seven days, and don't forget to turn off the gas fire before you go home. George took the first to heart. Much of his professional life was spent complaining about solicitors, their poor preparation of briefs and late payment of fees.

His father wanted him to transfer to Manchester or, better still, to give up the Bar altogether and become a solicitor or earn a living elsewhere. This was similar to Tylor's unwelcome advice at George's Oxford interview. In December 1953, he was still awaiting the scholarship money. Reluctantly agreeing a return to Blackpool, he applied to Manchester chambers. His mother had become unwell, complaining of severe pain. Alf thought he should be at home to help. As Evelyn was forty-nine, her problems were dismissed by the doctors as menopausal. Over Christmas, she deteriorated rapidly. Ovarian cancer was diagnosed, too late. It spread rapidly throughout her body. Within six weeks, she was dead. George had given her the final morphine injection. He was naturally devastated, though also relieved after hours spent watching her endure terrible pain. His views on many things, including quality of life and euthanasia, were transformed. Much later, it strongly influenced his conviction that he was on the right side in cases such as that of Dr Leonard Arthur, the paediatrician charged with the murder of a Down's Syndrome baby, and that of the crime writer and Samaritan Charlotte Hough. She was given nine months in prison for the attempted murder (assisting in suicide) of the eighty-four-year-old Annetta Johnson, following an investigation into her death by the *Evening Standard*.

But, at the time, the most important figure in George's world, and probably the only person whom he ever really trusted, was gone. Badly shaken and unable to come to terms with his grief, he tried for some months to make contact through clairvoyants. Never fully able to accept that his mother had left him when still so young, George always thereafter talked about her in hushed tones. He continued to feel the pain of Evelyn's early death for many years.

Homosexuality, referred to in an intimate letter from one London friend as 'the ever interesting topic', retained a place in the young barrister's thoughts in his mid-twenties. Evident from correspondence is George's support of the 'War' – the campaign for the legalisation of homosexuality. Another letter written to George in December 1953 talks of a mutual male friend planning the seduction of another man (then a newspaper editor) and refers to a covert gay venue in Chelsea: 'an outsider would not notice that it was different from any other club. But it is.' There is joking about 'RSPCQ' (the Royal Society for the Prevention of Cruelty to Queers) and about a 'special vocabulary – code words, the argot of a massive underground'. The letter continues, 'Item: Gielgud had 12 curtain calls here on first night.' The great actor had recently been prosecuted for soliciting in a public lavatory and was making his return to the London stage. The letter concludes with 'Have a madly gay time.'

But the move to Manchester concentrated his mind on work. After several interviews, he was offered a place at 60 King Street, which at that time was a predominantly Jewish set of chambers. His fellow pupil Ben Hytner QC recalls: 'George had gone to see a man called Tommy Backhouse, the head of chambers at 43 King Street. He said to George: "We've no room. I think you should try Godfrey Heilpern at 60 King Street."' Heilpern assumed from George's story and from his colouring and features that he was Jewish. This impression was supported by George mentioning in conversation his Balliol friend Stanley Brodie, who was a nephew of the Chief Rabbi, Israel Brodie. According to Hytner, Heilpern told the younger members of chambers, 'I can't see a Jewish boy on the street. I've got to take him in.' Some months later, George was asked by his clerk if he would be off the following Monday for the Day of Atonement. 'What's that?' he replied. The truth was out. George was a Catholic.

In a set of chambers containing twelve barristers, he competed with Hytner for the same work at the bottom end. It was definitely not establishment. The gifted former head of chambers Henry Burton QC had been one of 112 fatalities in the Harrow & Wealdstone train crash of October 1952. Heilpern, an accessible and approachable man, had just taken over. George learned much from him, doing his paperwork in chambers (or devilling, as it is called). Intellectually conceited with an Oxford first, he was however socially nervous among his more privileged colleagues, having himself come from a poverty-stricken background. Hytner recalls that snobbery and significant anti-semitism were in many solicitors' minds when they decided where to allocate work. Some insurance companies preferred to use the non-Jewish chambers at Chapel Walks, where Fenton Atkinson and Joe Cantley, later the presiding judge in the Thorpe trial, were heavy hitters.

Overdraft and debt were established as part of George's life. In the magistrates' court, he struggled to make a living, later summarising this period as 'Going to a court I couldn't find, for a case that did not matter, for a fee I never got.' Travelling to local towns – Blackburn, Bolton, Bury, Chesterfield, Preston, Rochdale and Wigan, places where, as the phrase goes, palms were hairy and Proust was seldom read – he defended motorists on careless-driving charges. Before getting his own car, he sometimes hitched a ride to court from passing lorries. The fee would be three guineas for the appearance and one guinea for the conference, typically settled twelve to eighteen months afterwards. Barristers had no right to sue solicitors for outstanding fees and, at that time, no other recourse to obtain payment. From his travels, George learned courtroom manners, effective presentation and how to cultivate an advocate's style. He also became very skilled at standing up robustly for his client.

Legal aid did not exist in the 1950s. Work for young barristers was scarce. Empty days in the diary gave him an opportunity to watch the better silks in action. In particular, George admired the maverick approach and commanding presence of Danny Brabin QC, an outstanding advocate who later proved to be a disastrous High Court judge. From Brabin, he developed some of his own cross-examination methods and other techniques – speaking slowly, always looking at the jury when the witness answers a question and using silence to full dramatic effect. Sir Basil Nield, the Recorder of Manchester, also took an interest in George, entertaining the young barrister at the judge's lodgings.

To support his meagre income, George taught basic contract law to banking students at Bury Technical College for ten shillings (50p) an hour. In his fourth year at the Bar, he was fond of saying, his earnings in a year were as much as those of a Manchester bus driver without overtime. This is true. His lifestyle however was somewhat different from theirs. Indeed, there were few bus drivers buying rounds of drinks in the city's nightclubs with the same regularity as George. Through financial hardship, the dream of being a High Court judge kept him going. This was the long-term aim, the ultimate badge of respectability. His real fear was having to leave the Bar and get a salaried job, as some of his colleagues did. That would have meant failure.

Following his mother's death, George lived at home for a short while. Constant arguments with his father ended this arrangement. Unable to forgive Alf for making him leave London, he went to live in Manchester, spending some of Evelyn's legacy to subsidise his lifestyle. In the autumn of 1954, he was introduced to Ursula Groves, daughter of a wealthy brewer and local Conservative grandee. There was a bond. She had also recently lost her mother to cancer. Given her apparent wealth (Groves senior owned more than a hundred pubs) and family political connections, this had the potential for an ideal union. It would assist George in his newfound ambitions to be an MP. There was generous financing from both fathers when the wedding was announced for July 1955. They bought a house in the Manchester suburb of Sale.

With Groves's help, George was shortlisted to fight the Salford constituency in the next General Election. As in any first-time contest, it was a no-hope affair. But when attending a Conservative candidates' weekend he was dismayed by some of his fellow aspirant politicians, especially Basil de Ferranti, to whom he took an instant dislike. Inherited privilege was anathema to George. He stood down from the seat. The opportunity of becoming a Labour candidate had arisen when he was still at Oxford. Dick Crossman, the brilliant don and future diarist of Harold Wilson's Cabinets, had asked him to consider standing for parliament but the offer had been declined. George was to remain a political butterfly, socially conservative on the outside, yet unmoved by party dogma or principle and committed only to meritocracy.

His attention was now focused on arrangements for the wedding. A former schoolfriend recalls: 'George told me he was getting married. He said that, after speaking to the Bishop at the Catholic Cathedral in Salford, he had discovered a problem: the interior was being repaired and it was completely scaffolded. George asked to have the scaffolding removed before the wedding. The Bishop refused. George responded: "Do you know whom I am to wed? Her father is very important and I do not intend to get married surrounded by scaffold poles!"' George chose to switch venues instead and the ceremony was held at St Anne's, a fashionable Protestant church in the centre of Manchester. When Brother Woodhouse, St Joseph's headmaster and head of the Old Boys Association, heard that his favourite old boy had decided to marry outside the Catholic Church, he was so upset that he cancelled the Old Boys' Dinner.

The marriage would last for only three years. Ursula had been supporting them working as a canteen manageress. George had pawned and then sold her engagement ring and other heirlooms, including valuable jewellery from Asprey's. Their house had also been sold at a loss because money was so tight. When they separated they were living in a rented flat in Wilmslow. George told several people soon after separation that he had decided to end it when his father-in-law married his secretary Anita, who was in her twenties. Realising that Ursula was never going to solve his financial problems, he therefore opted for divorce. Her affair with another man was a more immediate catalyst. George paid Ursula £5 a week for a few months after separation and then stopped.

In October 1958 he met his second wife. Celia Sparrow, a pretty twenty-year-old, was unexcited by her brief cabaret booking as a singer at Manchester's Piccadilly club. Trained as a classical actress, her singing had attracted the attention of producer Jack Good, who had booked her on to the television programmes *Oh Boy* and *6–5 Special*, and earlier she had cut a record with Beatles producer George Martin and toured with Cliff Richard. But that night George saw her sing and romance blossomed. She returned to Manchester when George, wooing her with his customary zeal, got her a slot at another club where he knew the owner. He became their pianist for a week while Celia sang on stage. As a divorced man seeking dispensation to remarry in a Catholic church, he needed to pull some strings. This he did, and in July 1960, as soon as the divorce from Ursula came through, a Catholic wedding took place in London. They bought a Wimpey bungalow in Woburn Drive, Hale, near Manchester, and within three years moved near by to a substantial five-bedroom Edwardian house in Park Road.

George had been busy at the local quarter sessions and assizes, doing a range of robberies with violence, burglaries, woundings, inquests and grievous bodily harm cases. In his hometown, he appeared in front of Sir Robertson Crichton, Recorder of Blackpool in the 1950s and of Manchester the following decade. A former Balliol man, he became an early champion, singing George's praises widely. Local solicitor John Budd also recognised his ability. The first of many five-guinea briefs arrived from him. Continued instructions in a range of criminal cases followed over the next twenty years. Samuel Lee, who joined Budd's firm in 1958, remembers: 'George immediately stood out as a brilliant young man, who knew what he was doing and really enjoyed himself when winning. He was very friendly and approachable, often drinking with the guys from the press in the Embassy Club after court.' In 1995, Lee asked George to defend his former St Joseph's College contemporary, the property tycoon Owen Oyston, who was charged with rape. Other commitments obliged him to decline. Oyston was convicted and sentenced to six years.

Other Blackpool links dwindled. His father sold off the shops one at a time and effectively retired by the early 1960s, travelling on cruises and holidaying in Australia and New Zealand. George said he was lazy, living off the capital which Evelyn had largely been responsible for accumulating. He saw little of Alf and rarely spoke to him on the phone except to make calls for money after heavy casino losses. Joyce was displeased at the divorce. She consoled herself with the thought that at least he had married a Catholic second time round. For the most part, brother and sister remained at a safe distance from each other.

George's career really took off in the 1960s as the quality and complexity of work grew. Unlike legal practice now, which is increasingly specialised almost from the word go, George's generation of barristers was much more generalist, spreading their talent widely across different areas of law. In addition to crime, he did contract and commercial, licensing, medical negligence, insurance, planning, landlord and tenant and even some banking cases, acting as junior to many of the leading silks. Apart from Heilpern, who was generous in using him, Gerald (later Lord) Gardiner, Leonard Kaplan and Robert McCrindle also led George. Jack Nahum QC, brother of the society photographer Baron, was another leader. Lee describes Nahum as 'a great ladies' man and very fond of gambling at cards'. George talked of him as 'a man after my own heart'.

A lucky break occurred in a 1964 Appeal Court case relating to the Barton Bridge inquest following the deaths of several men carrying out a Lancashire construction project. Heilpern was ill. At the last moment, George stepped in to do it, and did it successfully. It got him noticed. In April 1966, Heilpern defended his most notorious client, Myra Hindley, charged with the abduction and murder of two children. Although not involved, George listened with others in chambers to the horrific tapes of torture made by Ian Brady and his peroxide-blonde partner.

The largest single area of George's practice by this time was personal injury (PI), with factory accident cases being the principal breadwinner. As a junior, he acted for plaintiffs, instructed mostly by the trade union solicitors Thompsons. Between 1966 and 1971, they provided over half of all his work. The Thompson brothers, Brian and Robin, were champagne socialists, brought up in comfortable bourgeois affluence on the edge of Hampstead Heath. This did not affect their close links with traditional left-wing and communist trade union leaders. Nick Carter, who set up the firm's Manchester office, was impressed. 'Underneath George's charm, there was steel. He was a determined fighter and a very tough negotiator, battling hard for his client, always ensuring that his man would give exactly the right answers by checking with him carefully beforehand.' He recalls that George was particularly skilled at getting expert witnesses from each side together in the corridor to try and do a deal before going into court. If this did not work, it had already afforded the opportunity to test the other side's man before questioning him in the witness box. These were clever tactics. Carter often socialised with his number-one barrister: 'He could be good fun. I liked him but tried to forget about the "darker side" of his behaviour.'

A large paper practice (giving detailed written opinions on claims) was integral to success in PI work. George hated doing it, particularly anything that involved technical descriptions of machinery or complex points of law. Forgetting the second part of his pupil master's earlier advice, he did not always return papers as quickly as he should, losing some work as a result. Regarding the composition of opinions as 'monumentally tedious', he much preferred the excitement of being in court. Nevertheless, he had to buckle down and draft the pleadings (statements of claim, defences and so on). At the same time, his High Court work in London began to increase, with three or four cases a year in the capital.

Crucial to any barrister's success is a good clerk, effectively the broker of a barrister's services to solicitors, negotiating fees and terms for each case. Tall and blessed with laconic humour, Fred Turner, the juniors' clerk, understood his barristers well. George, who ate small portions of any meal, was amazed at

Fred's capacity to consume two T-bone steaks and chips at lunchtime. He would imitate his Salford accent when chasing fees from slow-paying solicitors: 'Hello, John, it's bucket and spade time. Mr Carman wants to take his family to Scarborough on holiday. Now can you please do something about the outstanding fees?' Fred did not need to sell George too hard. He was doing a very good job selling himself.

Instrumental in helping him on the way up was John Gorna. A successful and well-connected solicitor, he had made money in property development, linked to the post-war boom given impetus by Charles Clore and Jack Cotton. He had much in common with George. His father had been a hard-working Italian immigrant who became head waiter of the French restaurant at Manchester's premier hotel, the Midland. He was also a leading figure in what his barrister daughter Christina describes as the 'Catholic Mafia', becoming a papal knight for his efforts. He tried hard to help with George's gambling problem, holding back fees and directly repaying some of his debts with the money. He became my godfather. The advice he gave to George led to intermittent quarrels between the two men, an inevitable consequence perhaps of their strong personalities and quick tempers. Gorna would occasionally order him out of the car when he was giving him a lift home.

Recognition of George's talent – 'the best he ever saw', according to Christina – came with quality High Court briefs. By the late 1960s, a flood of work for Manchester United, of which Gorna was a director, brought George his first taste of national prominence. He regularly advised the club's then chairman Louis Edwards and, on one occasion, his nineteen-year-old son and successor Martin. In 1969 it was George Best's turn, and the case made legal history. Then at the top of his United form, he was sued by a twenty-one-year-old Danish au pair, Eva Haraldsted, for breach of promise to marry – an anachronism of civil law long past its sell-by date on the statute book. This was the last such action in England, as the relevant act was repealed shortly afterwards. The blonde Haraldsted, dubbed 'the striking Viking' by the press, claimed that Best had proposed marriage to her in Manchester only weeks after they had met in Copenhagen. She had accepted, flying back to announce the happy news to her parents and a few dozen journalists in Denmark. On sober reflection, Best changed his mind when she took him furniture shopping for their future home together. He broke the bad news to her. After consulting solicitors, she sued for damages. On the direction of Gorna and the United manager Sir Matt Busby, George was retained. Fleet Street prepared for a field day in court. But George settled the case quickly, with Haraldsted being given £500 and a one-way ticket to Copenhagen. Best was phlegmatic: 'I fell in love with a pair of knockers, which can happen to anyone.'

The matter did not rest there. In early March 1970, Best went out drinking at Blinkers, Manchester's smartest nightclub, with his United teammate and Scottish international Pat Crerand. Haraldsted had stayed on in Manchester and was in the club that evening. She chose the record 'I'm Leaving on a Jet Plane' by Peter, Paul and Mary. Not to be outdone, Best responded with 'Get Back' by the Beatles. It was a game they had been playing for two months. On this occasion the 'childish exchange of courtesies' through pop songs led to blows. There was soon the sound of street-fighting men on the pavement outside and a twenty-three-year-old friend of Haraldsted sustained a broken jaw. Crerand was charged with grievous bodily harm. In April that year, George defended him. After a two-day hearing, he persuaded the stipendiary magistrate that his client had been acting in self-defence. Many nights of celebration at Blinkers followed as the two Georges toasted each other with champagne.

In the same year, George did his first defamation case in front of a jury. He acted for Sammy Betesh, a small, moustached Manchester solicitor who had gone into a local shop to buy a coin magazine. The shop owner accused him of not paying. After another two-day hearing, the jury awarded Betesh £1,000.

'It was a masterful piece of advocacy,' recalls instructing solicitor Ted Gee.

Another solicitor who knew him well states that 'Given his enormous ability, George made a relatively slow start professionally, because he was having such a good time in the 1950s and 1960s. He cared passionately about his clients, but not at all about convention. He would discuss the detail of his latest case with anyone, in any bar he walked into, always willing to listen to their opinions.' While everyone knew about George's drinking and gambling, few realised the extra dimension these habits gave him in court. After a public school and Oxbridge education, many barristers continue to live an ivory-tower existence, largely isolated from the thoughts and feelings of people less affluent or less educated than themselves. Never George. 'The life of the law is not logic but experience' – an aphorism of the famous American jurist Oliver Wendell Holmes – was his motto. Bringing rich experience of life to the law, he conversed with all sorts in the pubs and bars of Manchester before moving on after closing time to spend the small hours exploring the city's illegal drinking clubs, shebeens and private bars. Some, like the Nile Club in Moss Side, a post-casino favourite, could be dangerous. This only added to the thrill. As one of the few white customers, he would be asked by the bouncers to remove his tie before going in. Others, like Russian Dave's, were filled with girls looking for punters and vice versa.

Mixing with club owners, barmaids, villains, taxi-drivers, prostitutes and assorted inhabitants of this twilight zone gave him freedom to be himself. Like Toulouse-Lautrec or Jean Genet, he kept his creative finger on the pulse, communicating with fellow drinkers as equals and drawing from their experiences in his work. In this environment, he did not patronise, but remained a detached observer. By understanding what made them tick, he kept himself on an equal footing with some of the real people who make up juries, rather different from the privileged and exclusive elite who still compose the majority of barristers and judges. After-hours George found his way to many a juror's heart by preserving the common touch. He never forgot his role in court as a standing passenger on the Clapham omnibus. An echo of this approach was noticed by Susan Aslan, a solicitor at D. J. Freeman who instructed George in the Al-Fayed case among others: 'He was fascinated by the human condition and very interested in people. In a [1999] libel defence for Channel 4 brought by Inspector Gladding, one of our potential key witnesses was a black drug dealer called Neville. He and George had got on terribly well during the case. They ended up drinking together in Daly's. What a couple they made. George said to him: "Why don't you go straight?" There was no professional need to cultivate Neville at all. He just liked him.'

But he did cultivate a reputation as a womaniser, often seen about town at night with a succession of young, tarty girls on his arm. These were frequently paid companions: hired escorts from model agencies, picked up in clubs or specially selected for him from behind the make-up counters at Manchester's premier store, Kendalls. They gave him an insight into the life of what the ordinary girl or woman on the street was thinking. He liked to be seen with what he thought were attractive young girls. They helped to present an image of him to the world as a ladies' man. It was another mask. Most people bought it at face value. The truth was a little different. For while he definitely enjoyed, indeed preferred, the company of women, he often had no sexual relationship with those whose time and companionship he bought. 'He would sometimes come in with some very scraggy-looking women and say "Give my princess a drink,"' recalls Phyllis, who admits that she thought his attitudes sometimes seemed 'very odd'.

Being seen as much as he could with a string of different girls was in part an elaborate charade to cover a confused sexuality. George worked hard to keep his other side well hidden. A spasmodic double life, in which he dabbled with the occasional gay relationship, was kept completely secret from virtually everyone who knew him. The passionate relationship with a younger man that developed in the late 1960s and continued on and off for some years thereafter was never flaunted, except to the privileged few. Repeated instructions to me – never trust anyone – made little sense. That advice was the product of a life spent looking over his shoulder. Those who knew have told me that he lived in constant fear of being found out. He was indeed, as his first teenage girlfriend Mary Williamson said, 'a man of many secrets'.

By 1970 George was anxious to apply for silk, a shorthand term for becoming Queen's Counsel, so called because of the silk robes which QCs wear. At that time, there were only 400 silks in practice, compared to more than 1,000 today. It was also harder to be appointed. Aged forty and with a very healthy, predominantly civil practice, George applied confidently to the office of the Labour Lord Chancellor, Lord Gardiner, who had led him in several cases. The application was refused. At the same time, that of his main chambers rival, Ben Hytner, was accepted. Most first-time applicants are inevitably disappointed. George was particularly despondent. Worried that some aspect of his private life debarred him, he arranged to see his Oxford contemporary, then Financial Secretary to the Treasury, Dick Taverne, who had worked closely under Gardiner on the Family Law Reform Committee, and was himself a QC. Rushing off to the House of Commons only weeks before the 1970 General Election, he was offered tea and sympathy by Taverne and told not to worry.

Celia had a brief affair that autumn with a lecturer called Keith Sagar, the author of several books on D. H. Lawrence. She told George shortly afterwards. He went wild and responded by enlisting the help of Sidney Almond, a large, muscular man who lived near by. They drove across the Pennines to 'sort Sagar out', taking me with them. I was nine and excited by the idea of a chase. It came to nothing. There was no sign of Sagar or of his car of psychedelic colours – a 1960s hang-over. After waiting for an hour in a quiet Yorkshire street, we turned round and drove back to Manchester.

In 1971, the year he finally took silk, George was earning nearly £20,000, a considerable income then. On appointment, he was immediately offered a place in the London chambers of Sir Peter Rawlinson QC, recently appointed Edward Heath's Attorney General. This was a great opportunity, but one he genuinely could not afford to take. With no capital and largely unknown in London, he considered the risks too great. 'You would rather be a big fish in a small pond,' Fred Turner told him. George reluctantly agreed. Becoming a QC meant no more paper work and an increase in heavy crime – murders and armed robberies. George continued to hold his own in personal injury work, which was much more highly competed for among silks. Having spent much time as a junior doing plaintiffs' work, he now found that defendants' solicitors started to instruct him. Prominent among these was the charming and wonderfully genial Fabian Williams of James Chapman & Co. George later became godfather to his son Sam.

The silks' clerk was the legendary Ronnie Lynch, doyen of Bar clerks in both London and Manchester, who had been in the job since the 1920s – a small and bespectacled man in his sixties with large ears, a permanent smile and a warm heart. Although his decades of success had brought him substantial wealth – he commuted between his Weybridge and Salford homes – he dressed scruffily, resembling an old-fashioned trade union leader or a bookmaker. This was appropriate since he ran several bookmaking businesses on the side. Ronnie knew everyone and everyone knew Ronnie. An outstanding salesman of great subtlety and roguish charm, he was a superb negotiator, often getting higher fees than the 'Boss', as he always called George, had expected. When arguing over fees one day in the 1970s, Ronnie said that George would prefer to earn £50,000 a year provided others in chambers were earning less, rather than earn £60,000 a year if everybody else was earning more than that. The Boss admitted that it was true. He wanted to be top dog.

As a matter of etiquette, barristers did not listen when their praises were being sung by Bar clerks on the phone. George knew he was in good hands. Ronnie strove to get him the quality work he deserved. Apart from negotiating on his behalf, he looked after the man he was later to describe as 'the most able but most demanding silk' he had ever clerked. He helped him as a friend and confidant in his domestic problems. Beyond drinking with him at the Fifth Inn, he sometimes went to retrieve him from the casino, or bar, where he was otherwise occupied, to get him into court. Since he knew most of the Manchester judiciary, he also pulled strings on occasion to secure an adjournment when the Boss was too tired and emotional to get on his feet. Ronnie helped to make George and to keep him going.

A year after he took silk came his appointment as recorder, a part-time judicial role and the first step on the ladder towards the High Court bench. Sitting for twenty days a year, George treated his duties very seriously, always anxious to be seen to exercise sound judgment. When presiding, he sat with a note in front of him that read: 'Keep your mouth shut' – a reminder not to intervene. Finding some decisions difficult, he always tried to be scrupulously fair. In one case, he sentenced two Manchester City football hooligans to three years in prison for brutally attacking a passer-by with a brick wrapped in a sock. This was at the top end of the scale and George was delighted when the sentence was upheld on appeal.

On another occasion, he showed great compassion in dealing with a young man who had been a persistent burglar. The offence being tried, taking account of the defendant's record, demanded a custodial sentence. George decided to show great leniency and gave him a suspended sentence. He had been very impressed by the man's evidence and that of his pregnant girl-friend, by whom he already had a child. On leaving court that cold winter's day, he was alarmed when someone jumped out from behind a bush. It was the same young man, who had waited several hours to thank him personally for giving him another chance. George felt that the risk might well have paid off. This was what he liked to think of as justice in action.

His drinking and gambling continued unabated. Some of this was with Manchester's other well-known 'good time George', Mr Best, who visited our home in 1972, just before another hearing where George was representing him. The United number eleven played football with me in the garden. Within weeks, he had begun an affair with Celia. My parents had for years slept in separate rooms and led increasingly separate lives. The Best episode was to end their marriage.

I was made fully aware of what was going on when Celia told me why Best's distinctive red E-type Jaguar, clearly visible from my school playground, was parked directly outside our house in the afternoons. When he found out, George went round discussing the detail with anyone who would listen, including Manchester United management. They took a dim view. Best was missing training sessions to see my mother. Everyone at school soon seemed to know. In a life of constant drama, George enjoyed his crises. A role as the injured husband put him centre stage.

Divorce still carried a certain stigma in the early 1970s. It made him fear that his chance of becoming a High Court judge would be damaged. But, after Celia's affair, he felt that things had passed the point of no return. He began proceedings on the grounds of her adultery. For the rest of his life, he refused her requests to make a one-off lump-sum payment, preferring instead to pay a modest maintenance of a few hundred pounds a month – a sum which did not keep pace with inflation. It was another form of retaining control. Ursula had been deliberately omitted from his first *Who's Who* entry, in the naive belief that this first marriage would be forgotten. Celia could not be removed so easily. Occasional revisionism is a feature of life. George's disposal of the past was a constant process. When reminded during a *Times* interview in 2000 that he was seventy years old, he made a telling joke: 'I don't like the age anyway. I think I'll take it out of *Who's Who*.'

Frances Venning was a talented and committed chef who had worked in many good restaurants after starting out aged seventeen at the famed Boxtree, near Ilkley. She met George in Scotland over Christmas 1973. They lived together while my parents' divorce proceedings went ahead. Things didn't change. The relationship was volatile from the outset. Frances suffered from epilepsy, the delayed result of a childhood injury, which was controlled by strong medication. Disturbed sleep could trigger an attack. George's lifestyle did not help. Late-night arrivals and violent arguments caused her to have many unnecessary attacks. These were clearly very traumatic.

Using her considerable culinary skills, she entertained solicitors and his chambers colleagues, as often as he would allow, with superb lunches and buffet parties. There was even a memorable champagne breakfast in 1975 – still recalled fondly by those who attended. Yet he belittled her tremendous talent and prevented her from working as a chef because it was 'a demeaning occupation'. Faced with the near impossibility of creating a stable home, Frances battled on. She stayed with George, marrying him in March 1976. 'I can't help it, I'm doing it again,' he joked with best man Pat Russell at their Bradford registry office wedding.

Although drink took him to the edge of disaster in the 1970s, George somehow managed to exercise just enough self-control to avoid going over the edge. A number of those around him worked hard to prevent his self-destruction. Many juniors had to cover and make excuses. Typical of the reactions of those who worked with him is the comment from one barrister: 'For many years, waiting for him in court in the morning, one would always be on tenterhooks as to what state he'd be in and would he be there at all. It was amazing how he managed to control the problem more effectively in time in the way that he did.'

Frederic Reynold QC was a London chambers colleague for

twenty-nine years. When George became head of those chambers in the 1980s, Reynold chaired the management committee, running day-to-day matters. He also acted as his junior in two big cases. One of these was the February 1977 dispute of *QPR* v *Sheffield Wednesday* concerning the sale of a player with an injured knee. Reynold remembers that 'George had an irresponsible attitude to his work at that time because of his heavy drinking. I was in the absurd position each day of not knowing whether he would appear the following morning. Sometimes, I had to carry on by myself without warning. On one occasion, he advised the solicitors to settle because he did not feel like going on. I had to countermand the instruction. Amazingly, it all worked out in the end. When judgment later came through in April, he sent me a telex on board the ship where I was on a cruise with my father. It read: "QPR 0 Sheffield Wednesday 2. Love George."'

In a eulogy read out in court after George's death, the Recorder of Manchester Sir Rhys Davies made a similar observation: 'I remember the exchanges we occasionally had with Manchester taxi-drivers. As we climbed into the cab they might ask, "Are you in the law then?" If we gave an affirmative response, we might get the rejoinder. "Here, I had that Mr Carman in my cab last night." As an anxious junior, when one eyed the court clock as it crept towards 10.28, one would have rather wished that he had had him in his cab that morning.' As another colleague points out, George was effortlessly able to get what he wanted: 'There was an old-fashioned retired police sergeant, John Cooper, who looked like a bulldog, with a silver-topped wooden cane. He worked at the Manchester courts. After drinking all night, George would summon Sergeant Cooper, saying "Drive me home", and he would take him off to Didsbury.'

In October 1976, George bought a brand-new detached house in Altrincham. Fresh casino losses meant things were on a tight budget, and Frances, just like Ursula, was made to sell her emerald engagement ring to help pay for the kitchen she wanted.

(Celia's engagement ring had gone missing from her dressing table in 1971.) Our next-door neighbour was Willy Morgan, recently retired as captain of Manchester United and Scotland. His house had a room devoted to Elvis Presley with photographs and paintings of the King adorning the walls. The grand Victorian house on the other side, complete with croquet lawn, was owned by solicitor John Elliot, the son of Charles Elliot QC. A large, genial and prosperous man who drove a grey Rolls-Royce, he was also a hearty drinker. The two legal neighbours shared a number of good evenings together.

Day to day, George spent many hours negotiating for financial justice in the corridors of Manchester High Court in Crown Square. His principal adversary and colleague in PI cases was Patrick Russell QC, later an Appeal Court judge. Both enjoyed the engagement of battle. Pat Russell, six foot three and a Lancashire cricket fanatic, went in to bat against Carman, five foot three and a professional chain-smoker. They negotiated the level of damages paid out by insurance companies to victims of industrial accidents or of health authority blunders, and learned each other's game well. Their strong mutual respect meant they never had a cross word. 'I liked George enormously, but I knew when he was going to have a difficult case, because he would arrive wearing red socks,' Russell recalls. 'He was always highly strung, but never showed it in court. He was the consummate professional doing the best for his client.'

George was especially thrilled to win large awards. He secured a record £310,000 for a paraplegic man called Hutchinson. Winning significant damages for injured victims gave him great satisfaction. It was worthwhile work with real social value and a tangible result. He continued to do PI work up to the mid-1980s and in his last action won £550,000 from Berkshire Health Authority in 1987 for a fourteen-year-old girl, Olivia Graham, who had suffered serious permanent injury after falling out of her parents' car as a six-year-old in the grounds of Eton College. An eight-year wait before the conclusion of such a case is regrettably not uncommon.

In 1973, George had been instructed in a criminal case by John Gorna to defend James Hogan, the manager of the Battersea funfair, situated near the River Thames. He was charged, alongside the fair's owners and its consulting engineer, with the manslaughter of five children by reason of gross negligence. The children had been seated in three carriages on the Big Dipper ride on 30 May 1972. After reaching the top of the forty-five-foot incline, they slid backwards instead of forwards. The brakes and safety mechanism failed and the carriages became derailed before crashing. Death and injury followed. Given that the largely wooden structure was over fifty years old and in poor shape, Henry Pownall, the lugubrious prosecutor, was right to open the case by calling it a 'death trap'.

Roger Lane-Smith, a solicitor from John Gorna's office, stayed in London with George for the duration of the case, attending most days of the Old Bailey trial in November 1973. They spent many evenings together. Lane-Smith remembers: 'The night before George's closing speech, we went for dinner and then continued drinking whisky. It was well after midnight. I took George back and virtually poured him through the door and said: "For Christ's sake, George, it's the biggest day of your life tomorrow, you'd better be on form." Sure enough, he was as bright as a daisy.' George got to his feet in court and began: 'It was a sunny May morning in 1972. Children had come to Battersea to enjoy the day.' He went on to say that there were four parties responsible for preventing tragedy: Parliament, the Greater London Council, Festival Gardens Ltd and the owner of the Dipper. He added: 'It was astonishing to learn that it was left to Mr Hogan alone to refurbish it and do the best he could in putting it in running order.' After listening for awhile, another solicitor was impressed and asked Lane-Smith: 'Who is George Carman?'

That question came from the country's best-known criminal practitioner, David Napley, who had personally represented the consulting engineer Frank Etches at the committal. He took a close interest in the trial. It was the first time he had seen George on his feet. Chris Murray, Napley's partner at the firm Kingsley Napley, attended the proceedings throughout and describes his reaction: 'I had not come across George before. The real impact for me was his jury speech, which was phenomenal. It was unexpected. It was one of those spine-tingling episodes that happen very rarely in professional life, where suddenly you lift your head up and listen to an advocate for the first time and think gosh, this is something really special. He showed a wonderful ability, by instinct, to pick the right word and the right phrase, seemingly out of the air. He had a fabulous facility with words and a very attractive speaking voice.'

Human tragedy made the case a high-profile one, with press and television attending in force. The manager clearly had responsibility for the condition and safety of the structure. George's only line of defence was incompetence – that the manager did not know what his job was and should never have been employed to do it. He appealed to the jury's mercy by highlighting his client's conscientious approach and limited capabilities. As Napley recalled in his 1982 autobiography, *Not Without Prejudice*, 'It seemed to me the jury were mesmerised.' The manager was acquitted after the jurors had deliberated for four and a half hours. And with that success, the role of kingmaker in George's career passed from John Gorna to David Napley.

For when Murray and Napley stood in the well of the Old Bailey court afterwards, they agreed that George was outstanding and that the firm should instruct him. They did. Over the next few years, he was used in a variety of criminal and commercial cases. But it was not until Jeremy Thorpe's arrest in 1978 that a really big client would emerge and allow his skill to attract wider public attention. This would see him return to the Old Bailey to defend the case that would eventually help to make George Carman the barrister everyone wanted.

4
Trial of the Century

They hang a man first, and then try him afterwards.

Molière

It was 4 August 1978, a hot Cornwall afternoon. George stood in my bedroom at the Tresanton Hotel in St Mawes, puffing on a cigarette. He listened eagerly, waiting for the pips that signal the news headlines on Radio Four. When the announcement came that Jeremy Thorpe had been arrested and charged, he turned to me with a smile and said: 'I can do it. I can get him off.' After twenty-five years at the Bar, this was the watershed in George Carman's professional career. And he knew it. For most of the next year, the case totally consumed his life. Every waking moment of every day, he seemed to talk of nothing else. His thoughts focused on winning what the press soon dubbed the trial of the century.

Jeremy Thorpe was forty-nine. He had been North Devon's Liberal MP since 1959, leader of the Liberal Party between 1967 and 1976 and a Privy Councillor. Both his father and grandfather had been Conservative MPs. His father had also been a successful barrister. A popular, energetic and witty figure, Thorpe had almost single-handedly orchestrated an electoral renaissance as Liberal leader, taking the party's aggregate vote from two and a half million in 1970 to more than six million, or 19 per cent of the total, by the General Election of February 1974. That election produced a hung parliament and after talks in Downing Street, the flamboyant Thorpe nearly earned himself a Cabinet place in a coalition government under Edward Heath. But some of his Liberal parliamentary colleagues opposed coalition. No deal was reached and Harold Wilson crept back into Number Ten.

The serious charge facing Thorpe was conspiracy to murder Norman Scott, a former male model, between 1 January 1973 and 18 November 1977. The other alleged conspirators were David Holmes, a financial consultant, who had been a homosexual friend of Thorpe's at Oxford and was best man at his May 1968 wedding to Caroline Allpass, tragically killed two years later in a car crash; George Deakin, a Welsh club owner; and John Le Mesurier, a Welsh carpet dealer. In addition, Thorpe alone was charged with incitement to murder, by endeavouring to persuade David Holmes to murder Norman Scott, between 1 January and 30 March 1969.

George had been retained by Napley in the event of charges being brought. This happened in June after Thorpe had changed his solicitor from Lord Goodman to Sir David. The impression made by George in the Battersea case four years earlier remained. Christopher Murray, the Kingsley Napley partner who was closely involved throughout the trial, recalls the discussions that he and Napley had about appointing a barrister: 'Thorpe himself had no input when we chose leading counsel. Our first choice was going to be John Matthew QC. But David Freeman, who was acting for David Holmes, had already retained him. Because Thorpe had, in effect, been tried and convicted by the media, it was crystal clear that this case was going to rely upon tremendous powers of cross-examination and, above all, an excellent jury speech. When David and I discussed it, we reached the conclusion that whoever was retained would become a household name. And we made the decision to retain George very quickly.'

In November 1978, George was stopped on the motorway near Manchester. The decision six months earlier to end a self-imposed ten-year driving ban had resulted in his new gold-coloured Mercedes hitting several traffic bollards. He had been drinking gin and tonics on the train from London after meeting with Napley and Thorpe. Wisely, he declined the breathalyser and refused to give a sample. His solicitor Ian Burton was called.

He remembers the scene at Platt Lane police station. George said to the police sergeant: 'Do you know who I am?'

'No, sir.'

'I'm standing counsel to the Chief Constable of Greater Manchester. I am George Carman.'

'Oh I see, sir.'

'Get the Chief Constable on the phone.'

As Burton relates, 'The idiot in the police station obviously didn't realise that he was in the ascendancy and George was in the embarrassing position. He got on the phone to Mrs Chief Constable. She thought it was a terribly important matter. Mr Chief Constable [James Anderton] was at a dinner. She got hold of him. The Chief Constable sent a superintendent in a dinner jacket down to Platt Lane to find out what was going on. George had meanwhile been leading this poor police sergeant a merry dance telling him: "I want to make sure you follow procedure. Please make a note of this and a note of that." He even had them running round the police station, bringing him tea. Normally speaking, you have to sit in a cell with the cell door open.'

Burton then represented George at the magistrates' court in October 1979. They discussed tactics. 'What am I going to say in mitigation, George?' His client replied: 'I'll tell you precisely what you're going to say. I'm going to write your speech for you. This is what you'll say.' He wrote it down: 'Your Worships, I appear on behalf of Mr George Carman. He wants me to say that he is extremely sorry to find himself in this position.' 'And then sit down,' George added. 'Tell the clerk of the court that we don't intend to be rude but we don't want to add to the agony.' In the event, his guilty plea to drink-driving led to a fine of £150 and a one-year ban. He went off for a weekend by himself to Amsterdam 'to escape the publicity'. The thought of any adverse comment about his personal life always petrified him. A look of terror would cross his face in anticipation of what might be written. On this occasion, press comment was fairly modest.

The two undergraduate contemporaries who had traded

George, aged eight, altar boy at St Kentigern's
Catholic Church, wearing cap of St Joseph's
College, Blackpool, 1938.

George with unknown dog near
Dungarvon, Ireland, 1934.

George with elder sister Joyce in
a Blackpool street, 1932.

School holiday overlooking Rome, Easter 1938, organised by Father Pearson
(*standing centre*). George standing with walking stick (*far left*) and Martin
Quinlan (*seated third from right*).

Carman family group, 1948.

Back row: George's father Alf and grandfather George.

Front row: George's grandmother, sister Joyce holding baby Christopher Blane and mother Evelyn.

St Joseph's College. Rugby 1ˢᵗ XV, 1947. George (*seated, bottom right*), scrum half; Pat Nolan (*standing, fourth from left*).

George standing in front of Riber Castle, near Matlock, Derbyshire, August 1945. Note written on back reads: 'Me looking horribly ill at ease'.

(*Below*) Oxford 1951: Balliol Younger Society. George (*second row, third from right*). Stanley Brodie (later QC) standing to George's right and Vivian Price (later QC) next to Brodie. Theodore Tylor, Balliol's blind law tutor (*front row, second from left*).

Ursula Groves, George's first wife from 1955 to 1960 (*top left*).

Celia Sparrow (author's mother), George's second wife from 1960 to 1976 (*top right*).

George's first star client, George Best, with Eva Haraldsted, August 1969. Best later said: 'I fell in love with a pair of knockers, which can happen to anyone.' (*left*)

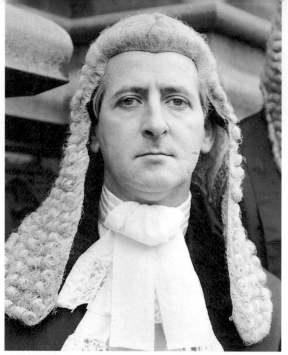

George fulfils ambition of becoming a QC in 1971.

George relaxing with cigarette outside Knightsbridge Crown Court.

Peter Bessell, former Liberal MP, chief prosecution witness against Thorpe, arrives at court.

Norman Scott, former male model, described by George as 'sad, mad or bad, or a combination of all three. I care not.'

22 June 1979: the day that changed George's life. Jeremy Thorpe salutes crowd outside Old Bailey after his acquittal for conspiracy to murder Norman Scott. George standing (*left*) next to Frances Venning (his third wife 1976–83).

Peter Adamson, a.k.a. *Coronation Street*'s Len Fairclough, acquitted on charges of indecent assault against two eight-year-old girls, July 1983. He later admitted to the *Sun* that he had been guilty.

Double act of Carman and Dodd: straight man and funny man. After Dodd's acquittal for tax evasion, Liverpool Crown Court, July 1989.

essays for speeches were never close Oxford friends. George had suspected that the Old Etonian Union president might be homosexual and was not entirely surprised when in 1976 the *Sunday Times* first printed an intimate letter written by Thorpe to Scott in the early 1960s. This referred to Scott as 'bunnies' and contained the phrases 'I miss you' and 'yours affectionately, Jeremy'. But by the summer of 1978 he was as shocked as everyone else when a prosecution was launched for conspiracy and incitement to murder.

Although delighted by the prospect of such an important case, George was very anxious about the financial position. As he had expected, the fee on offer was far from generous, given the huge amount of work involved. Thorpe, the story went, was hard up and George's clerk Ronnie was presented with a *fait accompli* by Napley on fees: £15,000 all in for consultation, preparation and trial. Effectively, that meant doing the case for less than the legal aid rate and required taking a significant drop in earnings. There was no room for negotiation. 'It will be worth more than £100,000 in publicity to Mr Carman,' was Napley's automatic response when Ronnie asked for more. Ronnie knew this was right and accepted without a struggle.

It was then unknown to George that the lawyers' bills were being partly bankrolled by the tycoon Sir James Goldsmith. That explained why he met the Marmite King more than once over dinner at Orme Square, the Thorpes' grand London home. Crowded with precious antiques and Thorpe's Chinese ceramics collection, this splendid house had been given to Jeremy's second wife Marion, a former concert pianist and good friend of Benjamin Britten, as part of her 1967 divorce settlement from the Earl of Harewood. Jeremy and Marion had married in March 1973. Her tremendous support for him during his ordeal would later earn her widespread admiration.

Before the trial, there was a three-week contested committal hearing at Minehead in Somerset which began on 20 November 1978. The objective was to get evidence on the record. It was treated as a dress rehearsal for the trial. There was an upside. A committal provided an opportunity to test the prosecution case and, more importantly, the chief Crown witnesses. First among these was Peter Bessell, former Liberal MP for Bodmin and Thorpe's principal confidant in the Scott affair. He would say that Thorpe, in his presence, had incited David Holmes to murder Norman Scott. The other chief witness was the victim of the alleged conspiracy, Norman Scott. He claimed to have had a homosexual affair with Jeremy Thorpe for two years between 1961 and 1963. The alleged murder attempt took place on 24 October 1975 when Andrew Newton, a former airline pilot and also a prosecution witness, shot dead Scott's Great Dane Rinka on Porlock Moor, part of Exmoor. The prosecution would argue that his subsequent attempt to shoot Scott failed when the gun jammed.

According to Murray, 'Napley knew he'd get it in the neck from the Bar if he did the committal.' Certainly, he was right to think that many London barristers disliked his intrusion into the courtroom. That was their territory. As London's premier criminal solicitor, he may have called the shots when instructing counsel but in court, Murray says: 'Many regarded him as an amateur trying to do a professional's job.' However, the former Law Society president was very experienced in committal work and a great believer in improved rights of audience for solicitors. This was a golden opportunity to put into practice the advocacy skills outlined in his book *The Technique of Persuasion*.

Napley therefore decided that he would go ahead and do it himself. Thorpe's three co-defendants were represented by barristers. In his autobiography *Not Without Prejudice*, Napley justifies this decision and his subsequent conduct of proceedings at length, saying that his conscience was clear, even though he admits to making mistakes. The immediate reaction of the press and *Private Eye*, in particular, was less favourable. Things were not helped by his appearance at Minehead in a copper-coloured Rolls-Royce, soon referred to by the hacks as 'gold plated, like his fees'. For George, not being in control, or even in action, in the biggest case he had ever had was deeply frustrating. Uncharacteristically, he had to hide his feelings and keep his thoughts to himself. He needed to remain on good terms with such an important instructing solicitor, for whom, it must be said, he always had enormous respect outside the courtroom, whatever their differences of opinion on the conduct of individual cases. Nevertheless, an underlying tension remained between the two men, though this was never detrimental to their professional relationship.

Everyone at Minehead assumed that there would be no press reporting allowed. Deakin's counsel, the thirty-eight-year-old Gareth Williams, then a newly appointed QC and later Labour Attorney General and Leader of the Lords under Tony Blair, had other ideas. He was 'very cunning', according to Murray, and, contrary to everyone's expectations, successfully applied on the first day of the committal hearing for reporting restrictions to be lifted. Lord Williams still firmly believes that 'My client's interests were completely different to the others and it worked out well in the end.' At the time, his enthusiasm was not widely shared by the defence team because Bessell, Newton and especially Scott were set to enjoy the full oxygen of national publicity. Over the next three weeks, as Napley talked tactics and reviewed the day's events in lengthy evening phone calls, George's frustration grew.

Napley made reasonable progress with Bessell and Newton, exposing some of their dishonesty and duplicity. Scott was more problematic. Many people had underestimated the former male model. Napley fell into the same trap, finding him a tough witness over a day and a half. Twisting his way through hostile questioning Scott gave a good performance. Further fresh 'evidence' of his intimacy with Thorpe was suggested by the mention of warts and nodules on the Liberal leader's body. The denouement came when Napley quoted Congreve at Scott, 'Nor Hell a fury, like a woman scorn'd,' to which he had a quick response:

'I am not a woman.' On 14 December 1978, the magistrates set the trial down for 30 April the following spring.

In the intervening months, there were countless meetings, or consultations, as lawyers call them. George respected Jeremy (it was always 'George' and 'Jeremy' from the word go), finding him courteous and polite and, to some degree, the model client. He had great admiration for his achievement and position in public life. More than anything, he was impressed by his resilience and continued good humour. Thorpe's legendary skill as a mimic kept everyone entertained and helped relieve the tension. However, it was not all plain sailing. His reluctance to confront some of the more thorny issues and deal with the allegations head on created difficulty. It was essential for George to have full instructions on each prosecution point. This meant leaning heavily on his client to get proper answers and to prevent him going down the wrong road.

Thorpe had qualified as a barrister. Before being elected to parliament, he had practised for five years in the magistrates' courts of the West Country. As the phrase goes, a little knowledge is a dangerous thing. Proceeding on the basis that the case was going to be a partnership with his barrister, he discovered fairly quickly that it was not. Although he came armed with an out-of-date copy of Archbold (a criminal law practitioner's book), Jeremy's presumed legal expertise was clearly deficient in arguing points of law. Politely but firmly, George had to put him right. He knocked him into shape, showing that he was in charge, even if instructions were formally given the other way round. According to one observer of their meetings, 'George was very much on stage in consultation. The whole thing was a performance. Very formal. Everything was very carefully planned and laid out. The clarity of thought and depth of recollection was tremendous and the way he was able to marshal facts and propositions was very impressive.'

Lord Widgery, the Lord Chief Justice, agreed to George's application to change the date of the trial to 8 May 1979, after the Prime Minister James Callaghan announced that the General Election would be held on the 3rd of that month. Jeremy had decided to fight his corner as the Member for North Devon. And there was a return visit to court as the writer and *Private Eye* contributor Auberon Waugh decided to stand against Thorpe for the Dog Lovers' Party. It was thought that a leaflet carrying his election address might prejudice a jury at the trial. George applied for an injunction to prevent circulation.

'Your father tried to send me to prison,' Waugh once told me when he was editor of the *Literary Review*, at the entrance of the Andrew Edmunds gallery, shared by the magazine in Lexington Street, Soho. He recalled, with feigned relief, that the Lord Chief Justice had refused George's application in April 1979, agreeing with the arguments put forward by Waugh's counsel Desmond Browne (later George's opponent in the *Hamilton* v *Al-Fayed* libel case). Unperturbed, George rushed off down the corridor to the Court of Appeal, where the Master of the Rolls, Lord Denning, was sitting with two other judges. Not for the first time, Denning overturned a decision of the Chief Justice, agreeing that two issues in the election address – who shot Rinka and did Thorpe have a homosexual relationship with Scott? – were seriously disputed by Thorpe and were significantly prejudiced by Waugh's address. The Dog Lovers' Party candidate avoided prison and agreed to tone down his election rhetoric.

The 1979 election saw a significant swing to the Tories as Margaret Thatcher was swept into power for the first time with a majority of forty-three seats. The Liberal vote was down on October 1974 at 12 per cent and two seats were lost. Their most prominent casualty was Jeremy Thorpe himself. He gave way to the Conservative candidate by a majority of 8,473, but still managed to secure 23,338 votes – quite an achievement given the enormous adverse publicity and virtual ostracism by the Liberal Party establishment. Auberon Waugh won seventy-nine votes for the Dog Lovers' Party. As Thorpe contemplated electoral defeat on the morning of 4 May, his thoughts must have focused on the more significant task of achieving courtroom victory at the Old Bailey four days later.

The case was conducted over six weeks in the cavernous oak-panelled Number One Court. What follows is by necessity only a précis of the important highlights. A full analysis would, in itself, fill an entire book.

The prosecution was opened by Peter Taylor QC, who later chaired the Hillsborough disaster inquiry and became Lord Chief Justice between 1992 and 1996. The son of a doctor and a product of Newcastle Grammar School and Pembroke College, Cambridge, Taylor had a professional background similar to George, practising personal injury and crime on the North-Eastern Circuit. In appearance, he was tall and solid with an aquiline profile. His style of advocacy was methodical, deadpan, courteous and moderate. Like Marion Thorpe, he was an outstanding pianist of concert standard. George had a formidable opponent.

Taylor laid out the prosecution case before the jury of nine men and three women. It can be summarised as follows. When they met at an Oxfordshire stables in 1960, Jeremy Thorpe was a bachelor MP of thirty-one and Norman Scott was a twenty-year-old groom, then calling himself Norman Josiffe. Scott went to see Thorpe in the House of Commons in 1961. For the next two years, they had a homosexual relationship. (It should be remembered that homosexual acts between men were a criminal offence in England until the law was changed in 1967.) Thereafter, Scott became a danger to Thorpe's reputation and career, continually pestering him for help and money. When Thorpe was chosen as Liberal leader in 1967, Scott became an even greater potential threat to his ambition. For Thorpe, anxiety became an obsession, and his thoughts grew desperate. Early in 1969, he incited David Holmes to kill Scott. His fellow Liberal MP Peter Bessell was present. Holmes and Bessell successfully dissuaded Thorpe from this plan over a period of time. Instead, the two men bought some of Scott's damaging letters, paid him money and tried to get him a job.

Shortly before the General Election of February 1974, Scott went to stay in Thorpe's constituency and began to talk openly about his relationship with the local MP. Holmes became convinced that Thorpe was right: Scott should be killed. Holmes had connections in South Wales, in particular John Le Mesurier, a carpet dealer, who introduced him to George Deakin, a club owner and dealer in fruit machines. A plot was hatched to find a hired killer. Deakin recruited Andrew Newton, whose reward was set at £10,000. Failed attempts were made to lure Scott to his death. Eventually, in October 1975, Newton met Scott in Devon, gained his confidence and drove him to Exmoor with his dog Rinka.

Newton produced a gun (a 1910 Mauser) and shot the dog, but failed to shoot Scott because the mechanism jammed. Newton was arrested, tried and in March 1976 sentenced to two years in prison. When he was released in 1977, Le Mesurier paid him £5,000, half of the fee. To finance this, Thorpe had persuaded Jack Hayward, a wealthy Bahamas-based benefactor, to make a substantial contribution to Liberal campaign funds. This money was diverted by Thorpe to Holmes's bank account in Jersey, so that payment could be made to Newton.

That was the nucleus of the case against Thorpe and his co-accused.

Before the first witness, Peter Bessell, gave evidence, the trial judge, Mr Justice Cantley, intervened to warn him: 'You have been given an extensive immunity and I want to make it perfectly clear that the immunity does not extend to perjury in this trial.'

'Know your judge. Look him up in *Who's Who*' was one of George's favourite tips to young barristers. Joe Cantley was a man he understood very well. George's ability to imitate his mannerisms and chuckles came from twenty years' personal experience of him as leader and presiding judge on the Northern Circuit. Like Peter Taylor, Cantley was the son of a GP and a grammar school product, in his case Manchester, followed by Manchester University. Widely regarded as a snob with establishment pretensions, his decision to marry for the first time at the age of fifty-four had taken the Manchester legal community by surprise. Lady Cantley, fifteen years his senior, had been his pupil master's widow. Despite Cantley's awkward nature and a fondness for laughing at his own jokes, George was happy to have a mostly fair and responsible judge who took pride in disclosing his prejudices.

The walnut-faced, suntanned figure with obviously dyed hair who stood in the witness box may have been Bodmin's Liberal MP from 1964 to 1970, but the fifty-seven-year-old Peter Bessell had more the appearance of a gaunt and shifty Richard Nixon. Indeed, he lived near the former American President, having made his permanent home in Oceanside, California. His return to Britain to give evidence was undertaken only on the basis of a wide-ranging immunity from prosecution. Throughout his life, Bessell, a sometime Methodist lay preacher, had a string of affairs with different women and was involved in a series of financial crises and disastrous, often crooked, business dealings. Under questioning from Taylor, he spoke in a deep, croaky voice. This is the evidence he gave.

Bessell had known Thorpe since 1955, becoming his parliamentary colleague in 1964. The following year, Thorpe confessed to him that he was a homosexual, showing him a letter Scott had sent to his mother Ursula. Bessell met with Scott in Dublin. He learned of a bundle of incriminating letters sent to him by Thorpe in the early 1960s, which were in a suitcase in Switzerland. Bessell obtained the suitcase, removed the letters and forwarded it to Scott. To check the likelihood of a police investigation into Thorpe's relationship with Scott, Bessell spoke with a Parliamentary Under Secretary at the Home Office, George Thomas, later Speaker of the House of Commons (and a closet homosexual), and to Sir Frank Soskice, Home Secretary. He was told there was not a problem.

After Thorpe became Liberal leader in 1967, Bessell paid 'retainers' to Scott of between £5 and £7 a week. He mentioned to Thorpe that Scott claimed there were further letters. In late

1968, Thorpe started to talk of getting rid of Scott and suggested ways of disposing of the body: by burial, by dropping it in a river with weights attached and, finally, by dropping it down a disused Cornish tin mine. When Bessell objected, Thorpe replied: 'It's no worse than killing a sick dog.' In February 1969, Bessell met Thorpe and David Holmes in Thorpe's room at the House of Commons, where Thorpe discussed a further plan to kill Scott, involving Holmes posing as a reporter and then shooting Scott at a lonely spot in Cornwall. They also discussed the use of slow-acting poisons.

Scott married on 13 May 1969. His wife became pregnant. Soon afterwards, they started divorce proceedings. A further plot was discussed by Thorpe to kill Scott in Florida. It came to nothing. In May 1971, Scott's claims were investigated by a Liberal Party inquiry, conducted by two MPs – David Steel and Emlyn Hooson. They interviewed Scott, who gave them a detailed, confused and exaggerated account of his affair. Hooson spoke to Bessell who, caught off his guard, confirmed that Scott was telling the truth. Bessell spoke to Thorpe and, between the two of them, they tried to cover up the story with Steel and Hooson by suggesting that Scott was a liar and fantasist. In June, the Liberal peer Lord Byers also interviewed Scott in a formal inquiry, but decided that he was lying. Nothing further was done. Bessell then stayed out of the picture until January 1976, when Holmes went to see him in California, after Newton was arrested, but before his trial. He successfully persuaded Bessell to write a letter to Newton's solicitor Michael Barnes in February accusing Scott of having blackmailed him, not Thorpe. By May, Bessell had told the *Daily Mail* that this claim was untrue. That ended his evidence for the prosecution.

The night before cross-examining Bessell, George stayed up till 3 a.m. drinking wine and talking endlessly with his junior. He would keep the former Bodmin MP in the witness box for two and a half days. In a battle of attrition, he wore him down. Starting with motivation, he suggested that revenge and money were behind his decision to give evidence, which of course Bessell denied. He moved on to character. Bessell agreed that he had told lies, but did not concede that he was a 'hypocrite'. He confirmed that he had been a lay preacher when Thorpe proposed murder:

CARMAN: 'Did that trouble your conscience?'

BESSELL: 'No, sir, it did not.'

CARMAN: 'Did you feel it was your duty to tell the party that its leader was a man intent on murder?'

BESSELL: 'My first loyalty was to Thorpe. I thought it could be prevented. I saw no purpose in seeking to damage his career in that way.'

CARMAN: 'Didn't you think Mr Thorpe must have needed to see a psychiatrist?'

BESSELL: 'Yes, I suppose that's true.'

George moved on to Bessell's 'incredible attitude'.

CARMAN: 'A lot of things you have done are incredible and disgraceful, are they not? Let us pass on to something even more totally incredible. Before Mr Thorpe, on your account of the matter, had in mind sending Mr Scott to his death in 1971, in the United States, you have asserted he proposed the murder of another person to you in 1970?'

BESSELL: 'Yes, sir.'

CARMAN: 'A man called Hetherington.'

BESSELL: 'Yes, sir.'

(Hetherington was a blackmailer who knew about the Scott affair in 1970, and whom Bessell, by his account, paid and frightened off. His name was never introduced into evidence by Taylor and his identity therefore never properly explained to the jury.)

CARMAN: 'If your evidence has a vestige of truth, the leader of the Liberal Party had proposed the death not only of Norman Scott but of another person . . . this time it was not the unfortunate Mr Holmes but you who were to be the assassin?'

BESSELL: 'That is correct.'

CARMAN: 'What steps did you take to acquaint the Liberal Party, police, doctors, Mrs Thorpe, with the fact that the leader of the Liberal Party was insane?'

BESSELL: 'None, sir.'

CARMAN: 'Yet when he got his vote of confidence in 1976 you were delighted?'

BESSELL: 'Yes, sir.'

CARMAN: 'Does this make you a thoroughly amoral person?'

BESSELL: 'I think it does.'

CARMAN: 'If you were publicly preaching Christianity, add hypocrite?'

BESSELL: 'Yes.'

CARMAN: 'Amoral, hypocrite, liar – is that not a scoundrel?'

Bessell did not agree with the last question. The willing victim of character assassination had already seen his credibility seriously damaged. Worse was to follow. George turned to his *Sunday Telegraph* contract under which the newspaper would serialise a book that he planned to write. This was structured on the following basis: £25,000 if Thorpe was acquitted and £50,000 if he was convicted.

CARMAN: 'It's what you might call in popular language a "double your money" contract. Half on acquittal and double on conviction.'

BESSELL: 'I accept that.'

George did much to prove that Bessell was a liar in his business and political life, with the witness making many concessions on the point. He also agreed that he was an opportunist and, as George called him, 'a good Janus, capable of facing both ways ... You can be all things to all men at the same time.' Bessell accepted this. George moved on to ask why Bessell had decided to write about his old friend for a large sum of money.

BESSELL: 'I would not have been here if I had not believed it was my responsibility to give evidence which must inevitably, if it is believed, contribute towards a conviction.'

CARMAN: 'Does it not prick your conscience to have entered into a contract by which you and your family achieve double the money on the conviction of a former true and loyal friend?'

BESSELL: 'Yes, it does.'

CARMAN: 'You are prepared to betray a friend for money, aren't you?'

BESSELL: 'I think that's an overstatement.'

Bessell then agreed that the *Sunday Telegraph* money was important to him and that his status as a witness had made the book more profitable to him. George went on to demonstrate the sensational nature of the book by getting Bessell to agree with some of the names of people mentioned: Harold Wilson, Margaret Thatcher, Sir Frank Soskice, Lord Goodman and so on.

He next turned to Bessell's addiction to the sleeping drug Mandrax, which Bessell claimed had 'muddled' his moral values when he had defrauded the Liberal benefactor Jack Hayward. A letter he wrote to Hayward was examined sentence by sentence. George had worked on this theme many weeks before at home, pursuing the witness with a series of questions: is it the truth, is it false or is it partly true and partly false? He was to use the same tactic with Jonathan Aitken eighteen years later. Bessell agreed to making four false or partly false statements. By now, he was on the ropes:

CARMAN: 'So you deserved to be put behind bars, did you, in 1974?'

BESSELL: 'Yes. What I had done in respect of Mr Hayward was in my view totally unforgivable, inexcusable, and therefore deserving punishment.'

CARMAN: 'Did you use Mr Thorpe as the innocent dupe to your fraud?'

BESSELL: 'No, I did not. It had been agreed between us.'

CARMAN: 'That puts you in the role of a liar but you are back again as a hypocrite?'

BESSELL: 'No, I should have rejected the idea. I should not have allowed Mr Thorpe or myself to have any part in this disgraceful, inexcusable, totally damnable episode.'

CARMAN: 'Mr Bessell, I do not wish to use this as a confessional box, I just want to find out the truth of what you say and the extent to which your evidence can be relied upon.'

BESSELL: 'I am sorry, sir. I was merely expressing the emotion of the moment.'

George neared his conclusion.

CARMAN: 'Would it be fair to say to you that you have demonstrated you are a man capable of consummate deviousness in his business and personal activities?'

BESSELL: 'I have to reply that you have shown undoubtedly that I have been guilty of deviousness, that I have been guilty of quite disgraceful behaviour.'

So came the last question after ten hours of cross-examination:

CARMAN: 'May I suggest that you have reached a stage of being incapable of belief by anyone else?'

Bessell remained completely silent. After a tense thirty seconds or so, Cantley intervened: 'You can't expect him to agree to that. That is a question to put to the jury, not to him.' Bessell then answered: 'If I believed I were no longer capable of being believed, I would not be here at the Old Bailey. I would be in Oceanside, California.'

There was one further episode when Bessell was recalled to give evidence. As George often did, he returned to a point explored earlier, surprising the witness. In this case, he produced a copy of the *Western Morning News*, dated 16 June 1970, brought up by car from Jeremy's mother's house in Devon. This showed a front-page photograph of Bessell campaigning with Thorpe in Cornwall. It proved that Bessell had got his date wrong in evidence when he said that on that day he had spoken to Thorpe in an incriminating long-distance phone call. George said: 'It takes a long time to nail some of your lies, but we have done so at last, have we not?' 'You have a point,' replied Bessell, before giving an ineffectual answer. Thorpe remembers this as 'one of the highlights of George destroying the prosecution case'.

The chief Crown witness had agreed with George that he was a liar and a hypocrite, that he had behaved disgracefully and that he stood to gain financially from a conviction. All of this was done in a witness-box confession, given in the manner of Catholic penance. George was delighted that Bessell had cracked. Now it was Scott's turn.

Despite Thorpe's alleged comment in the early 1960s that Norman Scott was 'simply heaven', the thirty-nine-year-old former male model who arrived at the Old Bailey could not be described as good-looking in any conventional sense. Tall with dark hair combed down and wearing a dark three-piece suit, he appeared uncomfortable and a little weary at having to tell the same story yet again. Overall, he lacked spontaneity at the big moment. In response to Taylor's questions, he spoke softly with a thin, affected upper-middle-class accent. Cantley had to keep asking him to speak up. His evidence can be summarised as follows.

When Thorpe first met Scott in 1960 at the Oxfordshire stables of his friend Van de Vater, the MP told him that if he were ever worried he should get in touch with him. After a nervous breakdown and a stay in a psychiatric clinic, Scott took him up on the offer, visiting Thorpe in the House of Commons in 1961 with his Jack Russell Mrs Tish. Thorpe took him to his mother's house in Surrey, where he seduced him, sitting on his bed and calling him 'Poor Bunny'. He then had anal sex with him or, as Scott called it, 'made love to me'. Scott bit the pillow so as not to wake Thorpe's mother.

Thorpe gave him money to find a flat, which he did at 21 Draycott Place, Chelsea. He visited Scott there most evenings when he was in London. Over Christmas 1961, when staying in North Devon, Scott received the 'bunnies' letter from Thorpe in London. This concluded with: 'Bunnies *can* (and *will*) go to France. Yours affectionately, Jeremy. I miss you.' For the next twelve months, the affair continued. But by the end of 1962 Scott was unhappy and wished to kill himself and Thorpe. He went to the police, making a statement about his relationship and handing over two letters and a postcard.

Scott moved to Ireland, then to Switzerland and then back to Ireland. His suitcase containing Thorpe's letters was mislaid and he wrote to Thorpe's mother to get her to intervene. Bessell met him and the £5 weekly payments started. He changed his name from Josiffe to Scott and was given £75 by Bessell to set himself up as a model. He got married in 1969, had a child and started a divorce, using a solicitor suggested by Bessell. The tale of woe continued with nervous breakdowns, drugs, drink and the Liberal Party inquiries in 1971, culminating eventually in his trip out with Andrew Newton, who called himself Peter Keene, in October 1975. Scott agreed to meet him outside the Delve's Hotel in Combe Martin. Later, on Porlock Moor, Rinka was shot, the gun jammed and Newton left with the words: 'I will get you.'

On the morning of 22 May, George began his cross-examination. He approached Scott in his quiet, reassuring voice, as if he were a doctor at the bedside of a sick, disturbed patient. This was reflected in his first question: 'Are you undergoing medical treatment at the present time?' The answer was negative. George focused on the events of October 1961. This was a month before Scott had visited Thorpe at the House of Commons and, on his account, been taken to Ursula Thorpe's house in Surrey.

CARMAN: 'Do you remember when the police called to the house and you told them that your boyfriend was having an affair with a girlfriend?'

SCOTT: 'I do not . . . I was very drugged at the time and some details may have gone out of my mind.'

CARMAN: 'You don't remember telling them that you knew Jeremy Thorpe?'

SCOTT: 'I still had a bundle of love letters of Jeremy Thorpe that he had written to Van de Vater.'

CARMAN: 'Never mind what you say are love letters between Mr Thorpe and Van de Vater, answer the question.'

CANTLEY (intervening): 'You are not giving a proper answer. That was just a bit of dirt thrown in. Listen to the question and answer, and behave yourself.'

CARMAN: 'You met Thorpe [at Van de Vater's] and talked to him for five minutes or less. He hadn't written you a single letter before you went to the House of Commons, neither had you written a single letter to Mr Thorpe before that. Why did you say Mr Thorpe was a friend of yours when all you had ever done was speak to him for less than five minutes?'

SCOTT: 'Because I had had the therapy at the hospital. I was going through a delusion, and I had these letters. I was using them to say that I had a relationship with him already . . .'

CARMAN: 'You were saying that you had a sexual relationship with Mr Thorpe before you went to the House of Commons?'

SCOTT: 'Yes.'

CARMAN: 'Quite obviously that was not true?'

SCOTT: 'No, it wasn't.'

CARMAN: 'In fairness to you, were you saying it because you were suffering from a delusion?'

SCOTT: 'Yes.'

CARMAN: 'And you had suffered from other delusions, had you not?'

SCOTT: 'Yes, sir.'

George asked Scott if it was a delusion when he said that he was the son of an earl and that his parents had been killed in a plane crash.

SCOTT: 'No, sir, it was a lie . . . I pretended I was the Earl of Eldon.'

CARMAN: 'Do you think that was a wicked thing?'

SCOTT: 'Yes, I do. But I have done so many wicked things in the past . . . but I have not lied since that wretched man tried to kill me because I suddenly realised there was no point in all this lying.'

In leading Scott down the same confessional road as Bessell, George was obtaining an identical response – I was lying then, but I am telling the truth now. He got Scott to concede that he had given different accounts in 1962, at Minehead and in his evidence at the Old Bailey concerning details of homosexual acts by Thorpe. Scott explained that he had been afraid of prosecution for admitting buggery in 1962. The court adjourned for lunch.

That afternoon's cross-examination produced some of the most explosive moments of the trial. During quiet, uncontroversial questioning by George, there was a sudden outburst from Scott.

SCOTT (shouting): 'Jeremy Thorpe lives on a knife edge of danger.'

CARMAN: 'What about you?'

SCOTT: 'I don't at all. I have certainly lived in danger for many years of my life because of your client ... I feel nothing, neither vindictiveness nor anything at all, just great pity. The man has destroyed me totally.'

George moved on to the alleged first night at Thorpe's mother's house.

CARMAN: 'Are you claiming the sexual activity on the first night at the home of Mrs [Ursula] Thorpe was without your consent?'

SCOTT (shouting): 'There was nothing I could do because I was at their house, tired and woozy. I was broken and crying. I did not know what was happening until it was too late. I assure you it happened.'

CARMAN: 'Do not get excited.'

SCOTT (shouting): 'I am not getting excited but it is stupid. Do you think I enjoy saying these terrible things or talking about it? It is most horrendous.'

CANTLEY: 'If you only spoke like that when you began your evidence, we could have heard everything you said. It shows you can speak up.'

Things deteriorated further:

SCOTT: 'Sir, I am in contempt of this court. I will not answer any more questions.'

CANTLEY: 'You may find that an uncomfortable place to be.'

SCOTT: 'I have gone on enough over the years with this story. I will not say any more.'

CANTLEY: 'Do you want to go home now?'

SCOTT: 'I don't mind where I go. I won't have myself destroyed in this way when he knows very well his client is lying. I have had enough.'

CARMAN: 'I am sorry, Mr Scott, but it is my professional duty to ask a considerable number of further questions. Are you going to answer them?'

SCOTT: 'I have nothing to say.'

George was enjoying himself. For years after the case, he would recall Scott's petulance with great amusement, imitating his voice and histrionics. Such behaviour was a gift because it demonstrated Scott to the jury as an hysterical, neurotic figure. Whenever he angered a witness or opposing counsel to this degree, George knew he was winning the argument and, more than likely, the jury. Eventually, after a lecture from Cantley, Scott apologised and continued to answer George's questions. George moved on to the heart of the matter.

CARMAN: 'You knew Thorpe to be a man of homosexual tendencies in 1961?'

SCOTT: 'Yes, sir.'

CARMAN: 'He was the most famous and distinguished person you had met at that time?'

SCOTT: 'Yes, sir. I think so.'

CARMAN: 'You were flattered that for a short time he introduced you into a different social world. I suggest you were upset and annoyed because he did not want to have sexual relationships with you.'

SCOTT: 'Of course that is ridiculous because he did.'

The admission by George on Thorpe's behalf of 'homosexual tendencies' was crucial. It came partly as a result of Peter Taylor disclosing privately to George that the prosecution had significant evidence proving his client's homosexuality. This included a sexually explicit postcard written by Thorpe to a man called Bruno, in San Francisco. Taylor's honourable gesture reflected his strong commitment to fairness and objectivity. Many prosecutors in his position would not have done the same. Some were to comment afterwards that he had been over-cautious in being seen to do the right thing, but George was relieved both on Jeremy's behalf and for the integrity of the Bar that Taylor acted as he did. Thorpe's admission of 'homosexual tendencies' meant that Taylor did not introduce any of the additional evidence of homosexuality in the prosecution case. This was a good deal for Thorpe.

George sat and watched as the next prosecution witness was called. This was the 'hitman' Newton, who was destroyed most effectively by the forensic skill of John Matthew, counsel for Holmes. The evidence of the remaining witnesses focused mostly on the financing of the alleged conspiracy and the trail of £20,000 given by Hayward at Thorpe's instigation to Holmes. Some of this, the prosecution argued, was passed on to Le Mesurier and ultimately to Newton. There was little mileage for George here and his cross-examination work was soon over.

Deakin was the only one of the four accused to give evidence. As Lord Williams told me, his client's case was 'different' and, as is not uncommon in criminal cases, there were many tense arguments between leading counsel over the varying defences. When he had finished, George got to his feet and said: 'My Lord, on behalf of Mr Jeremy Thorpe, I call no evidence.' George had decided very early on in the proceedings that his client should stay silent. The Bruno postcard removed any doubt he might have had on this decision. Thorpe had always assumed that he would give evidence: the natural instinct of the politician wanting to defend himself, with the witness box as the obvious platform. Persuading him to stay silent was not easy, but as in all decisions affecting the conduct of his case, Jeremy ultimately showed complete confidence in the advice of his legal team. This has been called a very brave gamble by George. In fact, he had no other option. To let his client become a willing victim of Peter Taylor's cross-examination would never have been a wise choice. All that remained were the closing speeches and the judge's summing up.

As a setpiece, his closing speech is the last chance an advocate has to address the jury and to convince them of the argument presented by the evidence. Peter Taylor continued in his role of gentleman rather than player. He had avoided going for Thorpe's jugular throughout the case and the closing speech was no exception. Nevertheless, it was at times a masterful display of erudite advocacy, of which the highlight for the press was an eloquent passage, interpreted as being sympathetic to Thorpe: 'The tragedy of this case on any view is that Mr Thorpe has been surrounded and in the end his career blighted by the Scott affair. His story is a tragedy of truly Greek or Shakespearian proportions – the slow but inevitable destruction of a man by the stamp of one defect.'

After a lengthy two days, Taylor sat down. John Matthew and Gareth Williams both delivered excellent performances for Holmes and Deakin, Denis Cowley QC spoke briefly for Le Mesurier, leaving George to close on behalf of Jeremy Thorpe. He had discussed this speech at home as far back as January, with notes, ideas and quotations scattered all over our house in Altrincham. It was now 14 June. His language and the theme of tragedy picked up where Taylor had left off: 'Privately, he is a man with a life that has had more than its fair share of grief and agony. Nature so fashioned him that at the time he had the misfortune to meet Norman Scott he was a man with homosexual tendencies . . . You will recognise from the evidence that a political life and political future are now irrevocably and irreversibly denied to him.' He went on to talk about the private

Thorpe: 'His frailties, his weaknesses have been exposed to the public gaze.' Again echoing Taylor, he described Thorpe's character: 'He is human like us all. We all learn, do we not, that idols sometimes have feet of clay.'

There was praise for Marion Thorpe, 'whose constant presence in this court speaks eloquently for itself'; scorn for Bessell, 'the Judas Iscariot of British politics'; and a final dismissal of Scott: 'sad, mad or bad or a combination of all three, I care not'. On the backdrop issue of homosexuality, George said: 'We live, I hope, in a civilised society, in a tolerant society . . . Homosexual activity of any kind was, of course, contrary to the criminal law of this country until the late 1960s. Times have changed. Parliament reflecting public opinion changed the law.' In assessing the evidence, he told the jury, 'You must not suppose that a not-guilty verdict is some sort of certificate of innocence awarded by the jury. In law, it means that the prosecution has failed to make out the case.'

The conclusion of George's speech had been determined on successive Sunday afternoons of oratory and over-brimming ashtrays: 'You have the right as citizens to vote in elections. But you have a much more important right and a much greater responsibility to vote guilty or not guilty. Mr Thorpe has spent twenty years in British politics and obtained thousands and thousands of votes in his favour. Now the most precious twelve votes of all come from you [he pointed dramatically to each of the jurors]. In accordance with your conscience, I say to you, on behalf of Jeremy Thorpe, this prosecution has not been made out. Let this prosecution fold their tent and silently steal away.' As George sat down with Longfellow's adapted words echoing in the courtroom, he was exhausted. Jeremy passed him a note from the dock. It read: 'Well rowed, Balliol.' He had done all he could. Now it was the turn of Mr Justice Cantley.

Much has been said about the summing up, most of it critical for being pro-Thorpe and therefore pro-acquittal. It became such a talking point afterwards that the satirist Peter Cook delivered his own humorous West End verdict on Cantley, a stage and vinyl parody called *Here Comes the Judge*. Things did not seem quite so funny to George at the time. He welcomed pejorative comments about Bessell, whom the judge called 'odious' and a 'humbug', referring to his 'deplorable contract' with the *Sunday Telegraph*, and about Scott: 'You will remember him well – a hysterical, warped personality, accomplished sponger and very skilful at exciting and exploiting sympathy.' There was more: 'He is a fraud. He is a sponger. He is a whiner. He is a parasite. But of course he could still be telling the truth. It is a question of belief.' Cantley's contempt for these witnesses did not prevent him from fairly detailing the prosecution case. At the end, George was worried that he had put the boot in on the evidence about the money from Hayward and its use by Thorpe, thereby underpinning the conspiracy argument.

After a little over two days' summing up, the jury was sent out on Wednesday morning to consider their verdict. During any criminal trial, the jury's deliberation is a time of high anxiety. For George, it meant an even heavier consumption of cigarettes, while Jeremy remained calm and in good humour, keeping everyone's spirits up. After the jury failed to reach a verdict that day, a night in Brixton prison was not so congenial for him. It was a similar pattern on Thursday as the jury went for a second night to an hotel, near Lord's cricket ground. Again Jeremy went off to prison, lying on the floor of a police van to avoid photographers, handcuffed to George Deakin.

On Friday 22 June, the four defendants had lunch in a private room at the Old Bailey, consuming smoked salmon, beef and Chablis. These were provided by Thorpe's former parliamentary colleague and close friend Clement Freud. Jeremy's jokes flowed as easily as the wine, while they sat round playing cards. Then at 2.30 p.m., fifty-two hours after they had begun their deliberations, the announcement came that the jury was ready. The foreman, Celia Kettle-Williams, rose to give the jury's verdicts: 'Not guilty' on all charges. Thorpe threw several cushions in

the air and turned to Marion with a smile: 'Darling, we've won!'
So had George. He would later describe this moment as being
beyond words. He was delighted for his client, but also for
himself. Fate had given him the chance. He had seized it with
both hands. He had won in style. His career and his life would
never be quite the same again. It was the start of two decades
at the top. Murray was right: his name had become known
throughout the country. It gave him a courtroom reputation to
live up to. In that arena, he was not going to disappoint anyone.

A crowded umbrella stand adorns the hallway of Thorpe's Orme
Square house. Resting inside is a ceremonial Russian sabre. This
was given to Jeremy's grandfather by Nicholas II, the last tsar
of Russia, only months before he was executed. When I was
invited for lunch in May 2001, Marion handed it to me so that
I could examine the Romanov crest on the hilt. George had told
me that during the case Jeremy had pretended to knight him as
a High Court judge, by touching him on each shoulder with
the sword and saying, 'Arise, Sir George.' A grand statement
followed: 'George, if you get me off, I will give you this sword.'

George had not taken the promise too seriously, but he had
expected a letter of thanks for his effort. Facing up to writing
it must have caused some difficulty. It was not until mid-October
that Jeremy's familiar blue-ink scrawl appeared on an envelope
in the morning post. There was gushing praise. He gave George
alpha-plus marks for advocacy, style, effort and speech-making.
Acknowledging his desire to be a High Court judge, he concluded: 'As for the Bench, I am sure that it will only be a matter
of time.' It was signed in jest: 'Yours affectionately, Jeremy'.

In his closing speech, George had said: 'This is not a court
of morals.' Despite his acquittal, many in the world outside
decided that Thorpe should enjoy a Pyrrhic victory. The immor-
ality of past behaviour guaranteed him ruin in public life. At
that lunch in summer 2001, he was a gaunt figure, seventy-two
years old, severely incapacitated by the ravages of advanced

Parkinson's disease. The memory of his ordeal lingered just behind the sunken eyes, dark-blue suit and impeccable courtesy. When people think of Jeremy Thorpe, they remember the trial of the century.

5

The Great Defender

In England Justice is open to all, like the Ritz Hotel.
Sir James Mathew, Lord Justice of Appeal

The impact of victory in Thorpe left George feeling flat. National recognition did not provide the automatic flood of high-profile work he had hoped for. With reluctance, he accepted that it would take time to consolidate his reputation – to be known as the best would require more than one good result. Among solicitors, the Carman name had joined the ranks of top-drawer advocates alongside John Matthew QC and Richard du Cann QC. But some at the London criminal Bar regarded George as a Northern interloper and tried to dismiss the significance of his achievement. Public school snobbery still played its part. 'There was a lot of jealousy that he had cornered Napley, the biggest fish among criminal solicitors,' according to one of his juniors.

Consolation arrived with an enhanced ability to command bigger fees. Ronnie pushed up the prices. Instructed by Kingsley Napley to do a fraud case for William Press, a public company subjected to a dawn raid and prosecution by the Revenue, he suddenly found himself earning nearly £50,000 in six weeks. This was a relative fortune and more than he had ever been paid for doing anything comparable. He maintained a personal injury practice, continuing to do some legal aid work and, for a while, stuck to the 'cab rank' principle of the Bar. This meant that he was for hire – on a 'first come, first served' basis – in any suitable case where a solicitor might choose to instruct him. As the decade progressed, strong demand meant that he could pick and choose between cases on offer. Privately paid criminal work predominated. Legal aid was done only if it was a case of national prominence. Publicity was the main attraction. Large fees ran a close second. The ideal retainer combined both elements.

Commercial fraud is boring. That was George's usual assessment. But the January 1980 committal at Leeds Crown Court involving his client Kagan Textiles fascinated him. Co-defendants Lady Kagan and her son, Michael Kagan, were represented by a different counsel. Also named in some of the charges – but outside the jurisdiction with his lover in Spain – was the Gannex raincoat king Lord Kagan. Harold Wilson's notorious resignation honours of March 1976 had produced a clutch of knighthoods and peerages allegedly dispensed as debt repayment to the Prime Minister's former business friends. Kagan's name was top of the list. His conduct was central to the case. Amusing stories were told of his effective product placement, with Gannex raincoats appearing on the shoulders not only of Harold Wilson, but also of Prince Philip and nearly every other Royal.

The case produced more serious revelations. It emerged that in the 1960s Kagan had had some unusual meetings at his London flat. As a KGB officer went out of one door, Harold Wilson came in through the other. Kagan was also said to have been paying Wilson £5,000 a year as a retained adviser before he became Labour leader – a sum greater than his parliamentary salary. Within eighteen months, Wilson had become Prime Minister, winning the first of four General Elections.

George succeeded in getting the proceedings against the company thrown out at the committal. Following an April arrest in Paris, Kagan was found guilty of theft and false accounting at a separate criminal trial in December 1980. His wife and son were both acquitted. Kagan himself received a ten-month prison sentence. The knighthood and royal warrants were removed, but his peerage remained intact, and after release he sat regularly in the Lords. While inside he negotiated textile contracts for prison uniforms to be supplied by Kagan Textiles.

Before he left Manchester, George's last prominent case was

the coroner's inquest on Jimmy Kelley, a drunken middle-aged labourer. His death on waste ground 'involving police' in Huyton, Liverpool became a politically sensitive *cause célèbre* of its time. George was instructed by the Police Federation on behalf of four police officers. Support came from the local MP, Sir Harold Wilson. The jury returned a unanimous verdict of death by misadventure.

In the summer of 1980, George, Frances and I moved to London, to a flat in Lincoln's Inn. This had been rented since 1978 when George became a Master of the Bench (or bencher) of his Inn – an honorific title given to senior barristers and judges. The move came partly by design (the Thorpe victory being the main trigger) and partly because the house in Altrincham had to be sold quickly to meet a series of post-dated cheques issued to the Manchester Playboy Club. On one of our last mornings in the North, George called me in a panic, asking that I meet him outside his bank, Barclays in Manchester's King Street. He had been out all night. Totally washed out and unshaven, he stumbled out of a taxi and thrust £7,500 into my hands, saying: 'Pay it into my account, it's all we've got.' The bailiffs were avoided by only a matter of days as the house was sold very quickly. Eight months later, George had earned enough to put a deposit on a completely modernised Elizabethan house in Glatton, near Huntingdon, in addition to the rented Lincoln's Inn flat. 'The interior was furnished like a show room from Harrods,' recalls one visiting barrister. That was not so far from the truth.

Shortly after the move to London, George became head of New Court Chambers, following a split with the sister chambers in Manchester now headed by his former colleague Ben Hytner QC. The historic link between the sets, caused by the necessity for Manchester QCs also to have chambers in London, was now broken. At the time, people talked of animosity and personality differences – routine issues throughout the Temple. Today, Hytner tells a different story, showing no hint either of bitterness or of past discord. By contrast, he speaks generously of George's skill in dealing with the 'forceful characters' whom he inherited with the headship. At the time, George saw it as a mixed blessing. The juniors in London had encouraged the split, using his arrival as an opportunity to force it through. There was 'a lot of talent' in that set, according to Hytner, a view which George shared. After some time in the role, the new head decided to manage chambers affairs through committees whenever possible and not get involved in day-to-day problems unless they affected him personally.

His new senior clerk for both sets of chambers, a replacement for the retiring Ronnie Lynch, was Bill Conner, a bright thirty-year-old from Essex. He was to be the most important individual in George's professional life over the next twenty years, forging a very close working relationship with him. Small and stocky with dark hair and equally dark eyes, he wore dark suits and white shirts. Quieter than Ronnie and more restrained, he brought a different set of skills to the job. And for the man who was soon to be the country's best-known barrister, Bill was the perfect foil. His hobby was birdwatching, which seemed to suit his calm, courteous, diligent and diplomatic nature. His head of chambers was demanding, uptight and difficult: all the attributes to be expected from a successful prima donna – actor or advocate. In Bill's view, George was both. He was assisted in all clerking duties by Paul Read, a smart and loyal number two. Together, they would negotiate fees and allocate George's precious time efficiently and effectively, dealing with many of the toughest and shrewdest solicitors in the country.

Bill says of George that he was very hands-off in chambers matters, 'but no one expected him to be anything other than a figurehead. He was interested in other members of chambers who were successful, but not in those who weren't. In meetings, he was a superb head to have as a cannon blasting away. The trouble was, every now and then, someone would swivel him round in the other direction. It wasn't then as pleasant. Overall, he was too self-centred in the position and that's the reason it didn't work very well.'

When solicitors approached, George was extremely hands-on. He wanted to be in charge at all times. According to Bill, 'He was very demanding. He liked to be in control and wanted to know every single detail and had no patience. He would say: "Let me speak to the solicitor." If you dissuaded him from doing it you were very fortunate. He would love to come back with a flourish and say, "Ah well, what you wouldn't have known was . . ." He also enjoyed getting involved in fee negotiation, even if it was not always to his advantage. He had a constant insecurity about work drying up when he was sometimes quiet. He never lost that hunger, no matter how busy he was. He was never satisfied and always wanted more. In terms of communication, he was just as good at chatting to the cleaner as talking to Robert Maxwell. He would treat them both the same. He had a tremendous ability to talk to everyone.'

Bill adds: 'I was not aware of any other barrister who demanded the same amount of attention. I enjoyed it. But considering I had thirty barristers to look after, I was spending up to 75 per cent of my time looking after George Carman. You had to. The man was a star and needed star treatment. A lot of it was chatting. I spent many hours with him discussing his personal problems, which he needed to confide in me. It was part of the man. Because he had no hobbies, there wasn't much that interested him outside work. In quieter moments, there was nothing else for him to turn to.'

Privately, George would moan about the lack of success of some members of chambers. He judged them mostly by their earnings and the class of their degree, not by what they were like as people. The successful few at the top or younger barristers who showed promise to reach those heights were the only ones that mattered. Every so often, Bill would give him a list of each barrister's earnings for the year to date compared with the previous year. He would go through this with me in great detail, explaining why the earnings of X had gone up by £50,000 while Y had remained at a constant £175,000 and so on. Typical one-line comments might be 'He should be earning more,' 'Clever but lazy,' 'She's going a long way,' 'He won't last here' and so on.

He tried to help those whom he regarded as bright, sometimes using them as juniors. Michael Brompton and Tony Clover both supported him in criminal cases during the 1980s. In addition to being led by him, Brompton shared his room in chambers for eight years. He was able to observe him closely: 'People thought George's preparation was meticulous. In fact, he could get away with doing far less than many imagined. One hour of his time was worth ten of other people's. A fantastic intellect enabled him to read through the contents of a Lever Arch file once quickly, absorb and analyse its contents, articulate the material and retain it in his mind. The rest was frenetic energy as he focused on the few points he had isolated. It was incredible to watch.'

His star performer was Hugh Tomlinson, a distinguished Balliol scholar with an academic record and thoroughness that made a deep impression on George. Proud to have someone of his ability in chambers, he pushed him hard, insisting that he become his junior in the two Branson libel cases. With others, whose practice was very different, it was not really feasible. But he maintained a high regard for some, especially Charles Howard QC, who had been his junior in two drugs cases – the successful defences of Thin Lizzy singer Phil Lynott and actress Maria Aitken. After reintroducing him to an old friend, the *Independent* and later *Express* editor Rosie Boycott, with the line 'He's divorced, depressed and very rich,' George became best man at their 1999 wedding. 'I always got on with him very well,' says Howard, a member of George's chambers for twenty-five years, 'but he wasn't very nice to men who he thought were intellectually inferior to him.' Overall, the various factions in chambers depressed George. He dismissed a number of the personalities involved, wishing that they would leave altogether. Eventually, some of them did. His headship of chambers was not a great success.

While George enjoyed the part-time role of recorder, he yearned for higher judicial office. The 1978 drink-driving conviction gave him a black mark in the Lord Chancellor's Department. They banished him to Altrincham County Court the following year to do judgment summonses – the lowest class of judicial work possible. The Thorpe victory now made him a different proposition for the High Court, or so he thought. He swiftly joined the bamboo circuit – doing cases in Hong Kong, Singapore and Malaysia. Strong courtroom performances for the Royal Hong Kong Jockey Club and in a subsequent criminal trial soon made a mark. Local success brought him to the attention of the colony's Chief Justice, Sir Denys Roberts.

In the summer of 1981, the offer came of a High Court judgeship in Hong Kong. George paused for thought, telling Sir Denys that he needed a little time to consider. What he really wanted was the same position in England. He needed to know if it was within his reach. A chat with Lord Denning, the eighty-one-year-old Master of the Rolls and the most distinguished judge in England, was the obvious next step. Believing that George should be an automatic candidate for the bench, Denning volunteered to have a word with Geoffrey Lane, then Lord Chief Justice. As the provider of recommendations to the Lord Chancellor for senior appointments, 'He should know the position.' This was the establishment at work. A few days later, Denning called and asked George to pop in. 'I'm very sorry, but you're not on Geoffrey's list,' was the embarrassed announcement. George deeply resented the rejection.

The next day, he told Sir Denys that he would accept. 'Carman Gets Set for Hong Kong,' ran an *Evening Standard* Londoner's Diary headline in early September, as he announced his plan to go in late November. Another newly bought house was sold, he formally arranged to leave chambers and the flights were booked. Frances tried to sort out the chaos of their financial affairs and packed the bags. While staying in a hotel near Leicester, George had several changes of heart. For weeks, Sir David Napley, Lord Justice Oliver and many others had been telling him that Hong Kong was a waste of his talent, a legal backwater, and that he would go mad with the work there. In essence, it would ruin him. The penny eventually dropped.

It also helped that George had been taking a closer look at the income tax position. Unsure that he could pay what he owed the Revenue plus his outstanding debts to the casino and move to Hong Kong, he realised the sums didn't quite add up. An excuse was needed quickly. Frances's epilepsy seemed like a sensible explanation. So George gave her 'ill-health' as the reason, indicating that the stress of a move to a hot, humid climate might cause problems. It seemed unimpeachable. A number of people knew or suspected otherwise. Ironically, George's replacement in the Hong Kong position, Charles Mantell QC, a fellow Northern circuiteer, not only worked his way up to become a High Court judge in England after his Far East stint, but was even promoted to the Court of Appeal.

As the Hong Kong saga unfolded, there was one other contributory factor to the decision to stay – the Dr Arthur case, which was occupying George's attention at Leicester Crown Court. This eighteen-day trial involved the death of a three-day-old baby, John Pearson, at Derby City Hospital. The man charged with his murder was Dr Leonard Arthur, a caring and conscientious paediatrician and a quiet and gentle man. John Pearson had been born with Down's Syndrome and was rejected at birth by his mother, a thirty-two-year-old grocer's wife, Molly Pearson. Both parents agreed that they did not wish the child to survive. After consulting with them, Arthur prescribed 'nursing care only'. Accordingly, the baby was 'fed' for three days on a mixture of water and a drug known as DF118 or di-hydrocodein, a sedative and appetite suppressant, which affects the respiratory system. The intention was to spare suffering and allow the baby to die peacefully. An anonymous informer had reported Arthur to the organisation LIFE. When LIFE told the police, a prosecution ensued. The case aroused strong emotions and huge publicity. George was retained to defend Arthur. He was immediately sympathetic to his cause and believed passionately that natural justice should prevail. He was determined to win. The evidence was complex, but, as with every criminal trial, it was left for a jury to decide.

George fought very hard against Douglas Draycott QC, prosecuting counsel. They did not get on. One prosecution witness, a nurse called Margaret Slater, gave all the answers that Draycott wanted. She had cuddled and done her best to relieve the distress of the baby John Pearson. George got to his feet and asked simply: 'What do you think of Dr Arthur?' She paused before replying: 'What do I think of Dr Arthur? Well, my daughter would have died if it had not been for Dr Arthur.' It was a moment of pure drama that George had not anticipated. Totally unknown to both sides, she had watched Arthur save her own baby's life when it was touch and go. At least one woman juror was in tears.

On the question of whether Arthur should give evidence, George decided against because of what he termed 'the Ruth Ellis reason'. Ellis had shot her lover and been charged with murder in 1955. Christmas Humphreys QC had asked her in cross-examination: 'When you pulled the trigger what did you intend to do?' To which her answer was: 'To kill him.' One question and one answer hanged her. If Leonard Arthur had been asked, 'When you decided on the way to treat this baby, what did you intend to happen?' Arthur would have replied, 'I intended for it to die.' End of story. He did not go into the witness box. George closed his speech to the jury by asking: 'Are we to condemn him as a criminal because he helped two people at the time of their greatest need? Are we to condemn a doctor because he cared?'

As defined by law, Arthur may technically have been guilty of murder. The jury of six men and six women responded with the right decision on the evidence, reaching a unanimous not-guilty verdict. There were powerful reasons for acquittal on the basis of what they had heard from various experts. George had destroyed the Home Office pathologist (Professor Alan Usher), securing favourable answers on the interpretation of slides detailing the baby's brain tissue. He had presented a mass of medical opinion endorsing Arthur's course of treatment. The judge, Mr Justice Farquarson, had been persuaded that there was a way out when during the trial he reduced the murder charge to attempted murder. But George remained convinced that the unexpected bonus of the nurse had helped to swing the case.

If winning mattered, here was a case really worth winning. As Cherie Booth QC comments: 'George's own high profile raised the profile of the Bar and demonstrated what a good advocate can achieve not just for his client but for justice. The Dr Arthur case surely shows that.' George had made the right decision in staying on to do the job he did best. He regarded the acquittal as a greater triumph than Thorpe. Arthur died of a brain tumour on Christmas Day 1983, only two years after the trial. After George's retirement seventeen years later, a long and thoughtful card from Arthur's daughter took pride of place in his kitchen.

By contrast, the next high-profile client caused him disgust and revulsion in equal measure. Geoffrey Prime was a Russian-speaking civil servant charged with spying. At Cheltenham GCHQ, Britain's secret communications headquarters, he spied on behalf of the KGB for fourteen years, handing over hugely damaging information on the entire NATO security operation in Europe. As if that was not bad enough, he was also a paedophile with detailed card-index files of little girls in the Cheltenham and Gloucester area. Additional charges were brought of indecent assault against three schoolgirls. Perverted sexual activity may have made Prime a target for the Russians. But this is purely conjecture. He was only discovered when his second wife Rhona, a devout Christian, went to the police. He had confessed everything to her when she discovered spying equipment under the bed.

There was no defence to the spying charge or to indecent assault. George was asked to do the plea of guilty, which involved significant access to top-secret information. He got Tony Clover in his chambers as junior. At the November 1982 trial, Lord Chief Justice Lane gave Prime thirty-five years for spying and an additional three years for indecent assault. When George did the appeal against sentence, Lord Justice Lawton said of his client's spying activities: 'In time of war such conduct would have merited the death penalty.' The appeal was dismissed. Prime was released in March 2001 after serving half his sentence. For some years, Rhona remained as his wife, visiting him in prison and writing a book about his struggle. Eventually, she divorced and remarried.

The prominent Italian financier who was next to enter George's professional life was no less remarkable. Gian Roberto Calvi was president of Italy's largest private bank, Banco Ambrosiano, the Vatican bank, and was called (not surprisingly) 'God's banker'. That position made him one of the most powerful men in Europe. But George never met him, because on 18 June 1982 Calvi was found hanging under Blackfriars Bridge in the City of London.

An inquest was held on 23 July, less than five weeks after his death. The solicitor representing the family that day was Sir David Napley. There were unusual circumstances. Calvi was found suspended from scaffolding under the bridge with a rope around his neck, dressed in a suit, with bricks stuffed in his underpants. It was suggested that he climbed on the scaffolding at night, before inserting the bricks and then hanging himself. Dr David Paul, coroner of the City of London, conducted a rushed inquest. The hearing started at 10 a.m. and went on until

10 p.m. Napley protested, but Paul did not listen. Some evidence was omitted and much was left unquestioned as the jury was warned against an open verdict during the coroner's brief summary. There were two remaining options – suicide or murder. Professor Keith Simpson, who carried out the autopsy within twelve hours of death, gave evidence that there were no apparent signs of struggle on the body. This proved conclusive. The jury returned a suicide verdict.

George was brought in to rescue the situation for the Calvi family – the banker's widow Clara and son Carlo. They were convinced that he had been murdered and that everything pointed to a ritual killing with Masonic symbolism and Mafia methods. Again, George found himself up in front of Geoffrey Lane. On 24 March 1983, the Lord Chief Justice, sitting with two other judges, agreed to overturn the verdict and order a fresh inquest. In June that year, the jury this time had two weeks of evidence to consider under a new coroner, Dr Gordon Davies. The new inquest was thorough. George examined expert medical witnesses and raised questions about the time of death, the tide level on the Thames, the saturation of clothing, the water damage to Calvi's two watches (one of which remarkably had not been looked at during the nine months since his death) and a host of other matters not considered properly, or at all, at the original hearing. The information provided for the jury was detailed, precise and comprehensive. Joshua Rozenberg, the BBC legal correspondent who covered the inquest, tells me: 'George was very skilful. He showed apparent courtesy to the coroner but underneath there was carefully disguised contempt. It was very effective.'

The cumulative evidence of the water level, the position of the scaffolding and the state of the body and clothing combined with injury to the neck and the fact that Calvi could not swim made the possibility of such an elaborate suicide look more remote. George highlighted the fact that, even if such a 'bizarre manoeuvre' along the scaffolding had been possible, carrying twelve pounds of bricks could only have added to the difficulty. He put forward a hypothesis that Calvi could have been brought to the scaffolding by boat and tied to it, before being left to hang. He further suggested that a drug or 'curare-like' substance could have been administered, without leaving any trace on the body. The River Police and medical witnesses accepted the feasibility in the respective parts of his hypothesis. He argued cogently that there would also have been easier methods of suicide since twenty-eight different types of drugs were found in Calvi's suitcase at his Chelsea Cloisters apartment.

During the inquest, Bill recalls meeting George one morning at court before the day's hearing began. 'He told me that Frances had received a threatening phone call at home that morning from a man with an Italian accent. He said it was awful. She was really scared and very worried. I said: "Well, have you called the police?" He said: "No, I haven't yet." And the reason he hadn't was that he wanted to announce it at the start of the day's proceedings for full dramatic effect. I'm not sure what effect it had on Frances waiting there. I was shocked. I would not have been capable of doing it. It was an indication of how focused he was on just one aim. Everything else got pushed to one side. He took things to an extreme I've never seen in any other barrister.'

After inconclusive evidence from the people who had accompanied Calvi in his last few days as he fled from Innsbruck to London to escape prison using an altered passport, his widow and son gave powerful testimony that Roberto was a man with a purpose in his last telephone calls to them. Clara threw a little light on the incredible financial background. Calvi had been tried for illegal currency export in Milan in 1981. He had been sentenced to four years in prison but given bail. Clara said that he had hoped to reach a bargain over Banco Ambrosiano with Opus Dei, an elite group of rich right-wing European Catholics. She claimed that the Vatican had reneged on guarantees of $1.4 billion, which had 'gone missing'. This was the root cause of

Banco Ambrosiano's problems since the bank was effectively insolvent. But, she said, Calvi was very happy about doing a deal with Opus Dei. Such detailed financial intrigue may have bemused the jury. However, the overall picture of scandal involving politicians, the Mafia, the Vatican and P2, a secret Masonic sect whose alternative name was the Black Friars, was clear enough. Although the family wanted a verdict of murder, there was insufficient proof. Clara and Carlo were nevertheless pleased when the jury returned an open verdict on 27 June 1983. The exact cause of Roberto Calvi's death remains a mystery.

Three weeks later, George was off to spend five days in Burnley, defending a fifty-three-year-old actor called Peter Adamson, better known as Len Fairclough from *Coronation Street*. He was charged with indecent assault on two eight-year-old girls. Two things determined the prosecution: evidence from the girls and eyewitness accounts from two police officers who had witnessed the alleged assaults. The offences occurred after specific complaints were made to the police about Adamson's conduct during his regular Saturday morning sessions playing with groups of children at Haslingden swimming pool, near Blackburn. Alerted to the possibility of indecent assault, the police set up a viewing position through a port-hole at the side of the swimming pool on the following Saturday, 16 April 1983. On schedule, Adamson visited the pool and played with the children.

The evidence of the girls was unsworn, since they were too young. Both girls talked of Adamson touching them and one referred to his making contact with 'my foo' (genitals) under the water. No advocate can really challenge very young witnesses in cross-examination, particularly in a case involving sexual abuse. Nor can a jury rely on such evidence if uncorroborated by medical or other suitable independent evidence. The danger of mistake or misunderstanding is too great. Everything therefore hinged on the two police officers, Detective Constable O'Neill and Woman Police Constable Musker. As often with police evidence in court, their answers were based on what was written in their notebooks, contemporary to the alleged events. Five distinct extracts from O'Neill's notebook entry made at the time read as follows:

1. I then saw him pull his hands apart in an outwards direction bringing both his hands simultaneously out of the costume.
2. In the same movement Adamson moved his thumbs back *inside* the costume.
3. Again moving them round to her vaginal and rectum areas. He then removed both thumbs out of the costume.
4. Moved both hands further under her bottom after moving down further into the water himself.
5. And with out-stretched hands pushed the girl by *her* bottom out of the water.

Musker's notes were almost verbatim identical, except that 'into' appeared instead of 'inside' and 'the' instead of 'her'. Under George's cross-examination, they separately produced their notebooks and foolishly denied ever conferring with each other in writing them. Musker called it 'just one of those coincidences in life'. George termed their notes 'incestuously identical' since eighty out of eighty-two consecutive words were the same. In detailing ten reasons for acquitting Adamson, he concluded by saying: 'I hope that the day has not yet arrived in our system of justice when juries are asked to convict on evidence from witnesses part of whose evidence is plainly disreputable and plainly discredited.' After thirty-six minutes, the jury of eight men and four women returned a not-guilty verdict. The courtroom burst into applause.

There was a problem. In 1988, Adamson confessed his guilt in a front-page *Sun* exclusive. This gave George no pleasure. It caused him repeated embarrassment when he was asked about it. He gave a formal answer that it was 'naturally disturbing when a client has protested his innocence by way of instructions'. Privately, many jokes were made about confessions emerging from other guilty people he had got off. George brushed these aside with a smile. The result in the Adamson case did however serve to enhance his reputation. As Professor George Steiner remarked in hyperbolic fashion in 1989: 'If I went to him accused of machine-gunning twelve Salvation Army officers on the streets of London, I know that George Carman would get me off.' He would never have claimed it to be the case, but the Adamson verdict crowned his reputation as the Great Defender.

Just as this position in the courtroom was being confirmed, so his personal life again hit the rocks. Frances waited until the conclusion of the Adamson case before announcing in August 1983 that their marriage was over. As much as possible, she had confined herself to living in the Little Missenden country cottage, which they had bought the previous year. George incorrectly suspected her of adultery with a local man. He got drunk and, in controlled anger, insisted on driving me to the man's house. On arrival, he lost that control. There was quite a scene. He shouted at me to restrain the man by putting my arms around him from behind. I did as he asked, and then George attacked from the front. The man who later married Frances received two fractured ribs. George left unharmed and satisfied. In the divorce settlement Frances received a one-off payment of £30,000.

Although married myself, I spent almost every night with him for many months, except when he went off to do a lengthy case in Hong Kong. His despair followed a similar pattern to the split with my mother. Typically, I would meet him in Daly's, before we moved on through London's bars and into the twilight zone. For a while, he became an insomniac, drinking heavily and talking endlessly, sometimes staying up until dawn. We returned to Igls in December, where he struck up a friendship with the woman he had met ten years before. This time, no return trip to London was on offer. After six months or so, his mood slowly began to improve.

He desperately wanted to have a female partner at his side. I listened to him express his thoughts on finding someone. For a while, this seemed to be of greater concern to him than work.

As before, he forged friendships with a number of interesting women in quick succession: Sue Cooke, the BBC *Crimewatch* presenter; Pippa Jessel, the former wife of then Tory MP Toby Jessel; and barrister Frances Heggarty, better known as crime-writer Frances Fyfield. Her first novel was based on George's real-life defence of the contract-killing murderess Katherine Calhaem in 1984. (Later, Baroness (P.D.) James came to watch George in court when researching her 1997 murder thriller *A Certain Justice.*) Above all, he admired Lady Annunziata Asquith, an earl's daughter, Oxford graduate and former Burberry model for Patrick Lichfield. He hoped to marry her. But even George's powers of persuasion did not come close.

Following a 'quickie' divorce in December 1983, George decided to resign as a recorder. The work, he said, had become 'really boring and a waste of my ability'. Intellectually, he thought he should be in the Court of Appeal by that stage – not, as he was, sitting in judgment on petty criminals at Knightsbridge Crown Court. The periodic elevation of a number of his former contemporaries to the High Court and Court of Appeal depressed him. It was easy to laugh off. 'I earn nearly ten times what a High Court judge makes' developed a hollow ring when repeated with each appointment to the bench of a less able or less successful silk. Eventually, he reached the conclusion by 1990 that he really was better off in every respect being a barrister. Once that Rubicon was crossed, all regrets ended.

In a straw poll of forty or so barristers, judges and solicitors taken when interviewing for this book, the overwhelming opinion is that he would not have made a good judge. No one doubts his intellectual capacity or ability, nor his commitment to fairness and justice. But a large number question his judgment, doubting whether he had the patience or temperament to remain suitably anonymous, detached and uninvolved in proceedings. 'God knows what sort of judge he would have made. Impartiality would not have come easily to him,' wrote Anthony Scrivener QC. We will never know, as one senior judge put it to me, whether he would have 'risen to the challenge as superbly as he might . . . since, in the end, his appointment would have been too great a risk'.

Among the many talented barristers at New Court in the 1980s was Cherie Booth QC, better known as Cherie Blair, who remembers that 'George was not always larger than life and could be quite subdued at times, particularly when his personal life was unhappy, but he was kind and helpful to me. I personally felt that he did not get sufficient recognition for his intellectual abilities.' Like George, Cherie got a first in law at university. She had followed in his footsteps of twenty-five years by coming joint top in the Bar finals. Cherie's husband also became George's junior. Tony Blair was then a young working barrister who had recently cut his political teeth as the Labour candidate for the safe Tory seat of Beaconsfield. Instructions came from Sir David Napley on behalf of the theatrical impresario Harold Fielding. Tony remembers 'George's quick grasp of the issues together with an amazing ability to sell a settlement to Harold Fielding which the client really did not want to agree to.' In George's assessment, Tony was a thorough, competent but unremarkable barrister. What stood out was an excellent client manner that made Fielding warm to him. At chambers parties or over a drink, he would tease Tony, making comments such as 'Why bother with politics? The Bar is much more fun' or 'How's the Labour Party?' The young Labour lawyer took the jokes. He was used to the ribbing. At the time, the Labour leader Michael Foot seemed to have consigned his party to a generation in the political wilderness.

In late 1984, George developed a close relationship with a thirty-year-old woman called Belinda (the name is changed to protect her identity). Introduced to him in Manchester by Phyllis, she soon became infatuated. Their ten-month relationship ended with disastrous consequences. After transferring her job to London and moving into his Lincoln's Inn flat, she was surprised when he showed no physical interest in her. She was emotionally volatile and his subsequent humiliation of her and physical violence towards her precipitated a nervous breakdown. George was terrified by anything that suggested mental illness. He asked me to go with him as he registered her as a psychiatric in-patient, before telling her mother to come down and pick up the pieces.

When introduced to the thirty-year-old Karen Shirley Phillipps in 1986, it was George's turn to become besotted. He had met his match. This slim, blonde, well-manicured barrister was to become his biggest challenge. In spite of a difference of twenty-six-years in age and four inches in height, she remained an important part of his life thereafter. Her friends included Julia Morley, who co-ran the Miss World beauty contest, the comedian Russ Abbott and Winnie Forsyth, a former Miss World and the wife of entertainer Bruce Forsyth. The names of well-known people frequently cropped up in her conversation. On the face of it, the two barristers had little in common. Karen detested smoking, drank little, played tennis regularly, enjoyed watching all sports and was physically very active – the total opposite to George. But he regarded her as his perfect woman: young, attractive, always expensively dressed, tough, strong-willed, totally undomesticated and happy to be his glamorous, bejewelled partner for dinner and at social functions with no sexual relationship required. For Karen, he provided status, a superb opportunity to mix with the 'rich and famous', wonderful holidays and a fabulous lifestyle.

Until she gave up legal practice to become a lady who lunches on the charity circuit in the early 1990s, George used to ask solicitors to instruct Karen as his junior in various cases. They acted together for Elton John's wife Renate in her divorce from the singer. Renate had been a co-director of one of Karen's companies, and in this case it was George's turn to be invited by Karen to lead her. In May 1987, he got her involved in an important case concerning his former best man and Oxford law chum Vivian Price QC. Charged with attempting to pervert the course of justice and twice driving while disqualified, Price knew that the outlook was bleak given his position as a senior barrister and deputy High Court judge. But for medical evidence that George secured 'at the eleventh hour' showing that he was suffering from a brain tumour, Price 'would have faced a substantial period of imprisonment', according to Mr Justice Farquarson. In handing down a nine-month suspended sentence at Maidstone Crown Court, the trial judge (familiar to George from the Dr Arthur case) was merciful. Price remains 'eternally grateful for the superb way George handled my case'.

Karen was naturally sociable, popular and could be very good company. Her developed sense of fun sometimes brought out George's lighter side. When things were good, he felt very proud of having a young, blonde, vivacious companion. At any party, she was a role model in winning and influencing. He liked her considerable ability to charm and engage people in conversation. And there were many who liked her. But although crowded with friends and fixtures, her life lacked the substance of real commitment. He bought a £30,000 engagement ring from Graff, which he then had to sell at a significant loss. She refused his several marriage proposals despite the big diamond and another similar bauble purchased some years later. There was no future in becoming the fourth Mrs George Carman. The idea did not suit. Her father's sudden departure to Australia when she was twelve affected her deeply after he re-married and had another family. It dented her trust in men. She also put up with a lot from George, who treated her from time to time just as if she were one of his wives. Realising this, she decided to remain a free spirit, guarding her independence and maintaining their friendship on her terms.

From 1980 to 1993, Karen also shared a life with David Green, a wealthy, married businessman, seventeen years her senior, whose main home was in Northamptonshire with his wife and children. He bought her a BMW convertible and a flat in Belsize Park which they jointly owned, where she lived most of the time, while he stayed there a few times each month when in

London. George and I would sit in his red Jaguar sports car outside Karen's front door in the early hours, waiting for her to return, and he would ask me the same questions over and over again: Where is she? What is she doing? We met Green once, by chance, in Le Rififi club. He remembers it well. As we sat down, George was amazed to see Karen's head visible through the tropical fish tank, a prominent feature of the intimate Mayfair night spot. Sitting next to her was Green. Apart from the hostesses, she was the only woman to be seen. George introduced himself to his rival as if they were fellow guests at a smart cocktail party. The six foot four Green was fully aware of his friendship with Karen, but, being married himself, was in no position to complain. They would speak often in the years to come.

Karen's life and whereabouts became George's passion. He moaned endlessly. Yet a kiss would make him forgive her completely – until the next time. United by the common purpose of splitting her from Green, he forged an alliance with Green's wife Rosemary, whom he had traced through good detective work. Over six years, they spoke regularly on the phone, sometimes dining together or meeting for a drink to review events. But Karen and David were to remain an item until his business went into liquidation. She then kept the flat and the BMW.

Day-to-day dramas were discussed at great length in Daly's with a fellow barrister in her King's Bench Walk chambers, George Papageorgis, and with former Kingsley Napley solicitor Judith Preston-Rouse. Both showed infinite patience. George became paranoid that Preston-Rouse was keeping a secret diary on him after they did a three-week case together in the Bahamas. The whole thing had been a joke, but he failed to see the humour. By the mid-1990s, she agreed with Papageorgis that KP was off limits for discussion. George would always ignore comments, as his clerk Bill recalls: 'I don't think he liked what I said to him. Nor did he like what Sir David Napley said. But he only ever listened to what he wanted to hear. It did not help his stability. He became very unhappy. Eventually, the people he normally spoke to disagreed with him or had a different view of the relationship, and he stopped talking about it.'

Karen would embarrass him publicly. Adrienne Page QC remembers: 'She used to talk at the top of her voice everywhere about how they had no sexual relationship.' Karen herself told the *Sunday Telegraph* in September 2000: 'I've known George for fifteen years but I've never had a relationship with him – we've only ever been friends.' But, for George, a platonic friendship was not enough. Despite an inability to satisfy her physical needs, he wanted to keep her for himself. He bought a flat in Chelsea, in the hope that she would live with him. The offer was declined despite repeated requests over many years.

In trying to possess Karen, he spared no expense. He and David both responded to her Christmas requests by buying the same present: an eighteen-carat gold Rolex with diamonds. Two men, two identical watches. She remained elusive. That was the attraction. Away from public gaze, mind games kept things going. Karen told me that she was the sort of 'strong woman' whom he needed and that all his wives had been 'too weak'. Their relationship became a battle of wills. In a game played to perfection, their unusual pairing puzzled many observers.

The latter half of the 1980s saw George in regular action overseas, defending wealthy tycoons and business people in Hong Kong, Singapore, Malaysia and Bermuda. He also went to advise clients in Jersey, Italy, Switzerland, Taipei, Washington and even in a New York prison, where he had to be searched thoroughly for drugs, which is standard practice, especially for lawyers. Lonely, depressed and in need of company, he asked me to go with him on a couple of trips, to Singapore and New York. I also went on holiday with him to Rio at Christmas 1988 when his taste for unusual clubs became even more apparent. Six months later, he asked me to spend a few weeks with him during a trial in the North. It was the only time that I was able to watch George in action for a sustained period. Neither of us knew it at the time, but Ken Dodd's fight against the taxman was to be one of the last big criminal cases for the Great Defender.

6

The Squire of Knotty Ash

We should all pay our tax bills with a smile. I tried – but they
wanted cash.

Anon

A monument to Victorian provincial pride and commercial success, Manchester's Midland Hotel is famed as the place where
Rolls first met Royce and together they decided to build cars.
Tucked away at the side of the hotel is a casino, which George
knew well. In the mid-1970s, he had applied for the continuation
of a gaming licence to operate there on behalf of Cyril Stein, then
chairman of Ladbrokes. In front of a panel of nine magistrates,
Maurice Drake QC, who was to become trial judge in many of
George's prominent libel cases, fiercely opposed the application
on behalf of Manchester's existing casinos. To Stein's delight,
George won. Drake recalls with a chuckle that Stein 'liked
lawyers who were as ruthless as he was'.

The casino was subsequently sold in the early 1980s to Leonard Steinberg, chairman of Stanley Leisure. And it was to the
eponymous Stanley casino that George took me on a hot Sunday
afternoon in June 1989. The staff all knew 'Mr Carman' very
well, greeting him as an old friend with cheerful Northern smiles.
In the salon privé, I sat to watch him play two boxes of blackjack, a game in which skill plays a part. The allure of the green
baize remained as powerful. The cards, however, were definitely
not falling his way. Resisting requests to leave and wrapped in
cigarette smoke, George winced slightly as the dealer seemed to
win almost every hand. Such bad luck was uncommon. When
I had seen him play at Aspinalls, it was more through the effects
of excessive champagne that disastrous losses would occur. That

afternoon, he was just unlucky. Trying to beat the house always gave George a thrill. He could ill afford to lose. His gambling-inspired overdraft had prompted regular communications from the bank. Yet he could still manage to laugh at the situation. When Leonard Steinberg told him that he had invited 500 guests to a lavish Park Lane wedding reception for his daughter, George joked to me that he had paid not only for the champagne reception, but also for the dress, the honeymoon and all the extras.

By the time we emerged into the Manchester sunshine, he had lost £35,000 in a little over two hours – more than the entire brief fee for the five-week Ken Dodd trial which had started in Liverpool a fortnight earlier. As we walked slowly towards Albert Square, he turned to me and said: 'Well, I'd better go and win the case now.' While winning in the casino against the odds was exciting, losing there unquestionably provided some extra stimulus to succeed in court – a forum where he could exercise real influence over the odds. When Dodd later remarked to me during the trial, 'Your father wants to win this more than I do,' he was totally unaware of how much George really needed to win, professionally, personally and financially.

For the duration of the trial, George stayed in a Manchester flat, arranged by Phyllis. In need of support, he asked me to spend the crucial weeks of the defence case watching him on his feet. Most nights he partied, revisiting some of his old haunts, buying vintage champagne for girls at the bar and dropping two fifty-pound notes into an eighteenth-birthday card for one of them. Everyone was asking him about Dodd. He was in his element. As we drove to and from Liverpool each day, discussing how things were shaping up in court, George realised that this could be another new peak in his career if he got a good result. But it was a big if.

Fleet Street regarded Ken Dodd's tax case as excellent copy, guaranteed to provide entertainment from first to last. Dodd himself was not so tickled by the prospect. Facing seven charges (later reduced to four) of cheating the Inland Revenue from 1973 to 1986 and four of false accounting between 1982 and 1988, he was looking at a prison sentence should the jury find him guilty. (Sir Ronald Waterhouse, the trial judge, has told me in interview that, if convicted, he would have given him between two and three years.) The 1987 example of Lester Piggott, who had been sent to prison for a similarly large tax fraud, loomed large in Dodd's mind. Piggott had pleaded guilty. He was certainly not going to do that.

After seeing several London QCs in late 1988, he told his solicitor: 'I want to see George Carman, I must see George Carman.' He did, and George was retained the following day. Dodd remembers: 'I found him to be welcoming in his quiet, caring and concerned manner. From the very start he inspired confidence that we could win. That was a great comfort to us at a very difficult time. From the moment I began talking to him and giving him a vast amount of information on various matters, he had this extraordinary ability to cut through all the verbosity and at the end of a meeting he could perfectly précis the whole thing in a few sentences.'

Ken Dodd, then aged sixty-one, was a national institution. He had been a successful comic and singer since the 1950s, with roots firmly in the music-hall tradition. His enormous talent and fertile imagination drew audiences into a fantastic world of diddymen, jam-butty mines and tickling sticks. The trademark teeth, hair and eyes enhanced the total eccentric persona that captivated those who watched him on television and especially in the theatre. For it was live on stage that Dodd – who had an entry in *The Guinness Book of Records* for telling 2,000 jokes in three hours and seven minutes – really came alive. Characterised by gentle double-entendres, phallic humour, silliness and a rich seam of Northern caricature, Dodd's stage monologue became a stream of consciousness – effortless, engaging and seemingly without end. He reached out to his audience directly. 'Yes, Missus,' prefaced a thousand one-liners that kept his many fans laughing for hours. By the late 1980s, his popular peak

– regular television shows and Royal Variety performances – belonged to earlier decades.

Charmed by his personality and strength of character, George warmed to Dodd from the outset. Underneath the Liverpool comedian with little formal education, a ramshackle lifestyle and an endless fund of good jokes, he saw a highly intelligent, shrewd operator with a strong appreciation of comedy and its history, a deep interest in human frailty and its humorous consequences and a heightened awareness of his own predicament. Dodd has said to me: 'Your father liked people with awkward, sticky-out personalities . . . like me.' A very fair assessment.

George certainly understood his client's problems very well from first-hand experience. His own father had been investigated by the Revenue in similar circumstances. From the cash takings of their Blackpool dress business before the war and then in the late 1940s and early 1950s, Alf and Evelyn made regular deposits in a Dublin bank. In 1969, Alf decided to repatriate the money without consulting his barrister son or accountant son-in-law John Blane. As large sums were suddenly transferred to his bank in Blackpool, the Revenue demanded to know where they had come from. Eventually, a settlement was reached, involving nearly £100,000 to be paid in back-tax and penalties, leaving Alf in much reduced circumstances for the last fifteen years of his life. Just before seeing Ken Dodd in 1988, George's father died. 'He [George] was the most unsentimental person I have ever known. The clerks almost had to force him to go to the funeral,' according to his chambers colleague Hugh Tomlinson.

For the Inland Revenue, Liverpool Crown Court seemed a bad away fixture. The prosecuting counsel, Brian Leveson QC, had chosen to fight the case on his home ground. George regarded him as 'a bright chap', and was amazed to learn that he had rejected the opportunity to have the case tried elsewhere; George believed that this was a strategic mistake. Not that a Liverpool jury would necessarily win him the match, but it could do no harm, he thought.

At the first hearing on 6 June, George opened with a bomb-shell, revealing that Dodd had a potentially fatal heart condition, ventricular tachycardia, which involves rapid pulsating of the lower heart chambers and ventricles. 'We are extremely anxious that there is no suggestion that his condition is other than grave,' he dramatically told the court, before adding, 'It may be highly improbable that Mr Dodd will ever be fit to stand his trial or appear in live performances again. He does not seek any favours from the court and he does not seek your sympathy.' George was trying to get the case stopped altogether. Mr Justice Water-house was infuriated by this late application. He demanded to know why George had sent his client for a check only two weeks before when the trial date had been fixed seven months previously. George explained that the solicitors had wanted the medical report to be as up to date as possible. Waterhouse retorted, 'It is inexcusable and inexplicable,' and went on to refer to 'lamentable administration for not revealing his state of health sooner'.

On examining Dodd, consultant physician Rhys Williams, from Manchester Royal Infirmary, had found 'a grossly irregular pulse'. Electrocardiograph tests showed his heart gave extra beats after every two normal beats, or up to 20,000 extra beats a day. 'It could be life-threatening,' said the consultant, and 'he should avoid situations of emotional or physical stress which might have unfortunate consequences'. The judge seemed cynical.

WATERHOUSE: 'Do you envisage from a medical point of view that this man should never stand trial?'
RHYS WILLIAMS: 'Most certainly.'
WATERHOUSE: 'I suspect this report could have been written about an awful lot of people in their sixties.'

Waterhouse remembers that, immediately before the case began, 'I was warned to watch George.' It was suggested to him that 'He would produce cards out of his hand at the last moment.' He had apparently developed a reputation for this among some barristers and judges. Although 'he did love his surprises', the judge thought that George behaved 'entirely professionally' throughout. Tracing the origin of these rumours is beyond the scope of this book. They seem to date from the mid-1970s in Manchester, further assisted by enemies George had made at the London criminal Bar in the 1980s. One case involving many defence counsel – the corporate manslaughter charges against P & O and others over the 1987 *Herald of Free Enterprise* disaster at Zeebrugge – caused particular problems. He was aware of it, but thought it the product of jealousy and no more than the inevitable price of success.

Proceedings in the Dodd case were postponed for two weeks. The adjournment for tests provoked a front-page *Sun* headline 'Tax Trial Could Kill Off Doddy' and a cartoon which caught the public attitude to an unpopular prosecution. This showed Dodd in a mobile hospital bed next to a barrister addressing the judge, with the strap-line: 'The Revenue feel the show must go on.' After further tests had been conducted, Professor John Cramm, a leading expert in Dodd's medical condition, pronounced the comedian fit to stand trial. The prosecution case opened in Court 5-1 on Monday 19 June.

Fairly new in silk and just about to celebrate his fortieth birthday, Brian Leveson QC was twenty years younger than George. Like the accused, he was a local boy, educated at Liverpool College before going on to Merton College, Oxford. Yet in style and personality he was the antithesis of Dodd. Short, dark, stocky and serious, the balding, bespectacled figure whose manner and method epitomised the industrious accountant was an ideal choice to open the Revenue prosecution. In the clinical setting of a modern court building, equipped with bright lights, green fitted carpets and clean white walls, Leveson set about the forensic task of conducting a complex post-mortem on a large body of financial information. First, he set the scene: 'There is no doubt that Mr Kenneth Dodd is one of the greatest entertainers of our generation. He is a character and an institution not merely here in Liverpool, but also nationally.' He continued: 'One of the consequences of his ability and fame has been fabulous earnings – more fees in a month than most in work earn in a year. It is therefore a particular tragedy that there is another side that during the course of this trial you will have to consider: that for years and years, his dealings with the Inland Revenue, to which everyone pays tax, have been characterised by dishonesty. When Mr Dodd was given a chance to come clean and tell the truth he became devious and deceitful.'

Leveson went on to describe how the Revenue first began investigating Dodd's affairs in 1984 when his former accountant, Reginald Hunter, was prosecuted for false accounting. (Hunter had been fined £6,000 at Mold Crown Court after pleading guilty to charges of false accounting relating to other clients.) There was no suggestion that Dodd was in any way involved. Leveson turned to the relevant detail. In June 1984, two tax inspectors had met Dodd. One of them read the Hansard Extract to him. 'Under Hansard', as it is known, is a non-statutory concession that derives from a parliamentary answer recorded in Hansard under which a tax-evader may avoid prosecution by paying all taxes outstanding and making a full declaration. Dodd had made a list of his assets. 'But it was not worth the paper it was written on,' said Leveson. 'Mr Dodd fed his accountants with absolute garbage. Not once did he lie, but many, many times. It was a tax fraud, not just a few pounds but on a grand scale.'

In October 1986, Dodd had provided a list of bank accounts to the Inland Revenue. 'He did not mention a single account in Jersey or the Isle of Man although he had twenty such accounts. At that time, he had different accounts in which he had accumulated £700,000, but stated to the Revenue that he had only two accounts, one with NatWest and one with Barclays. He kept silent, not only to the Inland Revenue but also to his own accountants trying to put things right.' Leveson said of the twenty accounts: 'They were secretly funded using money which had been kept in secret. There is only one question. Where did all this money come from? Doubtless it was earned, but how much was ever declared?'

Dodd, he said, had asked his accountants Thornton Baker (later Grant Thornton) to manage his affairs, but did not disclose the accounts to them. 'If the accountants were to help him, all that was required was honesty; in the same way you don't keep symptoms from your doctor. So if your own accountant is to help you, you tell him the truth.' When he told Thornton Baker there were no other accounts, this 'was totally untrue because at this time he had over £500,000 in the Isle of Man and Jersey bank accounts. This lie was repeated again and again as the accountants tried to make sure they had missed nothing.' The money had been deposited in Jersey and the Isle of Man in a series of 'cash and carry' flights with £298,000 deposited offshore in sixteen weeks in 1980. 'For years he had been reporting that his profits were far less than in truth they have been. He has been receiving cash and putting the cash in his back pocket.' Leveson explained that he would often get two fees for a performance, one with VAT that went through the books, one for cash that did not. He cited recent examples: 'Some of these happened during the very period when the Inland Revenue was conducting enquiries. He then put the cash in banks in Jersey and the Isle of Man, earning thousands of pounds of interest none of which he has declared.'

A lighter note was introduced in the opening speech when three letters were read out. These had been sent to the Revenue attached to a note prepared on Dodd's behalf by accountants Arthur Young. They were from Harold Wilson, Edward Heath and Margaret Thatcher. Wilson's letter had been written when Prime Minister, thanking Dodd for a wonderful evening. Dodd had sent a trademark tickling stick to Heath made of blue feathers. Heath wrote back: 'I was very much thrilled by the blue feather duster.' Finally, Thatcher had written to thank him for an enjoyable show and to say she 'was only sorry that Denis could not be there'.

On the second day, Dodd's cash came under the microscope. Leveson revealed that Dodd had kept £336,000 hidden at his three Liverpool homes in shoeboxes, under the bed and in wardrobes. The comedian's purpose, Leveson claimed, was to conceal it from the taxman. He also highlighted Dodd's meanness: the comedian spent a modest £470 a year on clothes and only £26 a week on food. Eventually, he explained, Dodd was cautioned by two Revenue inspectors at the start of an interview in October 1987, when he was accompanied by two accountants and two solicitors. Dodd had said that he did not understand accountancy and had believed that interest from offshore bank accounts was tax free. To all other questions, he had answered that he could not remember.

The first two days of Leveson's opening produced good copy for the headline writers with a variety of puns: 'King of the Diddle Men', 'Diddled Men of Knotty Ash', 'Knotty Cash' and, probably the best, 'Doddy's Knotty Stash'. But the Ken Dodd Laughter Show was absent from the court building as the comedian contemplated the weight of evidence and the scale of the problem facing him. He made an effort to look smart for his daily appearance, arriving in a slightly ill-fitting shiny grey suit, alternating with a darker version of the same. His ties seemed far too short, as if borrowed at the last moment from one of the diddymen. Outside, he would smile for the small band of well-wishers who turned up every morning to support him in his fight, often managing a quick one-line gag for their benefit.

Once in the dock, he would lean forward, his eyes darting between Leveson and the jury, taking copious notes to be passed on to George. His facial expressions, capable of such extraordinary versatility on stage, ranged from furrowed brow and glaring incredulity to blank numbness. There were few smiles. Anxiously watching every day of the case was his forty-four-year-old companion Anne Jones. Dodd knew that he was fortunate to have such an outstanding partner, and had entrusted the organisation of his life and work – no easy task – to her capable hands.

Lawrie Bellew, his loyal and dedicated agent, also turned up on most days to lend support. Between them, Anne and Lawrie ensured that Ken's morale remained strong.

Reinforced by the superb skill of accountant Robin Thomas, George got to work on the grey ranks of tax inspectors as they gave evidence. To one who said of Dodd, 'I would not say he was displaying a particularly happy nature during our interview,' George responded, 'People don't normally dance with glee when you interview them, do they?'

The prosecution evidence as summarised by Leveson was formally presented in great detail with a variety of supporting witnesses. This was very different from the Thorpe case. There was no room to challenge the integrity or honesty of the prosecution as an army of accountants and Revenue officials marched through the witness box to give extensive, often technical evidence. Much of this involved Leveson trying to produce a complicated reconstruction of Dodd's income and expenditure over many years as proof that a significant element of his earnings was undeclared for tax. The allegation of dishonesty was based on inference since there was insufficient concrete evidence to determine Dodd's exact income going back over twenty years.

In cross-examination, George got witnesses to agree that his client was extremely disorganised, unsophisticated, naive and uninterested in finance. The picture of domestic chaos was unchallenged. Stories emerged of Dodd's deliveries to his accountant – receipts bundled into plastic bags or black binliners with no explanation of their origin. Critically, he also got concessions on the part-cash, part-cheque payments for one-night performances, or gigs. Two prosecution witnesses agreed that some of the money received in cash was paid there and then to the band and to the supporting cast of diddymen and others. This was an important step in undermining the edifice of the prosecution case, since several of the charges focused on these cash payments as evidence of tax evasion.

In one interview, Dodd had told two tax inspectors: 'I like

having a lot of cash. They were my savings from my taxed income.' He moved on to tell them about the Winter of Discontent in 1979: 'I would have been taxed at 98p in the pound. Banks were collapsing and the pound was collapsing. I thought we were nearly up to civil war in this country. The whole economy was going wrong.' In another, he complained that two tax men were subjecting him to 'Gestapo tactics' by making repeated requests to visit his home.

At just short of three weeks and with nearly thirty witnesses, the presentation of the prosecution had been too long. Leveson had not kept the message short and simple. That was George's view. More importantly, he believed that the jury probably thought the same. He guessed that while they might not be totally enamoured of Dodd, Leveson had not succeeded in carrying them completely over to the Revenue's side. These were still early days. Dodd had yet to undergo the critical ordeal of giving evidence. Ultimately, everything would depend upon how he performed in the witness box, how he answered the difficult questions and whether he could convince the jury of his innocence.

George got up to open the defence: 'To the allegations that Mr Dodd has lived in a world of fantasy, a world on occasion of folly and a world of insecurity, we say yes. To the allegation that this man is devious, this man is deceitful, this man is dishonest, we say no, and we shall continue to say no. His conduct, so obviously eccentric, was to be explained not by dishonesty but by the close-knit family upbringing of which he was so much a part for most of his adult life. It was an upbringing which stamped on him for the rest of his life the values almost of another age: thrift, relentless hard work, close family loyalty and great charity for others. Money is not the beginning and end of Ken Dodd, far from it.' He added: 'It came as a complete and devastating shock to learn that Mr Hunter [Dodd's former accountant] had been prosecuted for dishonesty.'

At last the Squire of Knotty Ash stood and took the oath in

a deep voice. The double act of Carman and Dodd was about to get under way. The jury listened to every word.

DODD: 'My grandmother was the first lady magistrate in Liverpool and also chairman of the Old Swan Labour Party.'
CARMAN: 'And she had sixteen children?'
DODD: 'She knew all about labour, yes.'

As Dodd began to talk about his early life and his move into show business, he told the jury that his elder brother Billy was still in charge of the Knotty Ash coal business which their father had founded in 1919. He had been to infant and junior school in Knotty Ash and then to the Holpe School. He was twelve when war broke out and he missed some school because of evacuation, finally leaving without any formal qualifications.

DODD: 'I started work in my father's coal business at fourteen. My father had chronic bronchitis and emphysema, and I helped my brother. I did about six years in that business until I was about twenty.'
CARMAN: 'Was that essentially manual work?'
DODD: 'Yes. We would go down the railway yard, load the coal in hundredweight sacks, stack it in the lorry and take it to places around Knotty Ash and west Derby. I think I started off on about £2 10s a week when I was fourteen. I think I probably got to about £5 a week, something like that. But I enjoyed it. I worked with Billy and we had a great time.'

On the second day of Dodd's evidence, the court was shown a six-minute video taken inside and outside his home. George and I had been invited there for tea two weeks beforehand – the video was produced following that visit. The thousands of joke books, scripts and costumes that confront visitors to Knotty Ash reveal the phantasmagoria of Dodd's mind: a Gustave Doré illustration brought to life. Powerful though he is as a communicator, it was evident that visual evidence was the best way to bring home to the jury the delightful, creative anarchy of the comedian's home environment. It also provided more immediate intimacy between the accused and the jury than a thousand tax returns or balance sheets ever could, as Dodd took them on a guided tour of the house where he had lived since the age of five. The camera panned across the neglect and decay of his 1782 home to reveal not Georgian elegance, but jumbled disorder: a garden full of weeds, crumbling outbuildings, defective brickwork and a garage full to the brim with long-forgotten props, diddymen outfits, tapes and scripts. It had been described in an accountant's letter as 'an Aladdin's Cave', a phrase which had first alerted the Revenue to investigate further. This was not a superstar's house, likely to grace the pages of *Hello!* or *OK!* magazines – another very good reason for George to get it in front of the jury.

The film ended. Dodd and his diddyman QC were back in action, discussing the long-forgotten world where Dodd's father delivered coal, while his mother went to knock on doors every Friday night and from 8 a.m. until 11 p.m. on Saturday collecting payment in cash. No one in their part of Liverpool used a bank account. As Dodd explained: 'My father didn't trust banks. I don't know whether he thought they were a bit posh. Instead, they always kept their cash in the house where it was readily available.'

CARMAN: 'Please, Mr Dodd, describe your childhood.'
DODD (in sombre tone): 'I can remember my mother and father being very poor, working hard, very hard, but giving a very, very happy childhood.'
CARMAN: 'Did the bailiffs ever come?'
DODD: 'Unfortunately yes, once or twice we had the bailiffs at the door.'

His father bet heavily on horses. Dodd began to talk about his career: 'It is a gift, not an acquired skill. I take no credit for it. It's a blessing, which should never be taken for granted.' George took him through his early years in performance, starting at the age of thirteen, when he found that he had an ability to make people laugh. He went on to do an evening's work in the working men's club, where he was paid with 'damp pound notes'. In the course of his evidence he revealed that diddy was a scouse term for anything small, loving and whimsical. Dodd also described his distrust of accountants, saying he was told to produce receipts for everything: 'It was no tickee, no laundry.' Once the laughter had died down, the judge told him to respect the court.

George invited him to address the allegations of dishonesty repeated at such length by the prosecution.

DODD (with indignation): 'I don't have to be [dishonest]. I'm a successful entertainer.'

CARMAN: 'What is your attitude to money?'

DODD: 'Money was not important to me just as a measure of success. It was my nest egg. It is important only because I have nothing else. I had no children, I'm sorry to say. I didn't want a Rolls-Royce. How can you go and collect fish and chips in a Rolls-Royce? I had no villa in Spain – I've never been to Spain in my life. I just wanted to live like I always had. I didn't want the swimming pool or fast car. Remember today's star can be tomorrow's flop. It is a strange thing that happens to you when you get paid a lot of money. Some people go crazy and go in for all sorts of things. But most entertainers suffer from the basic fear of stage fright when you wonder what the audience will be like and whether they will like you, and from the big fear that maybe next week or next year there will be no more bookings. Show business is littered with people who have gone bankrupt. I know hundreds of people who have earned very big wages. I wanted to save my money. I had this nest egg. This money was mine and I knew it was there. It was security and reassurance that I had made it. It made me feel very proud that I had generated this kind of cash and I know that my father and mother were proud of me.'

He answered George's questions on the growth of his career and earnings. During the late 1950s, he had been earning £750 a week. In 1963, the Beatles were guests on his radio show. By 1965, when he fulfilled his ambition of playing the London Palladium, his weekly earnings reached £3,000. In that year, his number-one hit, 'Tears', outsold all the Beatles singles. He had a string of other hits, including 'Happiness' and 'Love Is Like a Violin'. The Diddymen were created, broadening his appeal to children. There was tragedy in 1977, when Anita Boutin, a nurse who had been his manageress, fiancée and companion for twenty-two years, died of a brain tumour. At that point, Dodd decided to end his career. He changed his mind when invited to help save the Palace Theatre in Manchester. After that, he helped to save lots of other theatres.

He explained that the decision to open bank accounts in the offshore centres of Jersey and the Isle of Man had been made in the belief that the interest paid was free of UK tax. 'I was paying 83 per cent tax, the top rate of tax, plus 15 per cent on top of that. I would get £2 out of every £100 I earned in interest.' He talked about saving money. In 1954, after working for his father for six years and a further six years spent as a chandler, he had savings of £4,000, hidden in a shoebox in the bedroom he shared with his brother. He remarked that 'The old white five-pound note was very nice, like a document.' He was twenty-six and had just turned professional, earning £75 a week as 'Professor Chucklebutty, operatic tenor and sausage nut'. The cash hoarded at home had increased to £30,000 by 1960, £100,000 by 1970 and £336,000 by 1980, when he decided to open accounts in Jersey and the Isle of Man: the first time he had ever had a bank account. The initial reason for moving the money was because the house needed repairs. He denied opening the accounts in secret since he walked up to the cashier in each case and used his proper name. Some visits developed a party atmosphere when he was introduced by the manager to various members of staff. There would be photographs and he would sign autographs. He admitted that he had taken £181,000 in cash to the Isle of Man, but said: 'I'm not abnormal, just a bit eccentric.' Referring to the wads of banknotes, Waterhouse asked: 'What does it look like?' Dodd replied: 'It's not as much as you would think. It all fitted into a briefcase.'

The issue of bank deposits was further examined:

CARMAN: 'Why did you not use British banks?'

DODD: 'I had read these advertisements that said interest in the Isle of Man and Jersey was tax-free.'

CARMAN: 'Did you realise that the actual law of this country was that if you lived in England but invested money abroad, you still had to pay tax on the interest earned?'

DODD: 'That isn't what the advert says. I didn't realise that.'

CARMAN: 'Now that you know the true position, do you think you were misled by the advertisements you looked at?'

DODD: 'Yes, I was misled. As soon as I found out I had made a mistake I told the Inland Revenue about every one of the bank accounts.'

He said that when he signed a mandate allowing Revenue inspectors access to the records of his Isle of Man bank accounts, he had been 'puzzled by the exchange of gleeful grins'. He telephoned the bank manager, who told him: 'You're in a bit of bother, Ken. You've got the wrong end of the stick,' and Dodd learned for the first time that the accounts were not free of UK tax. The following day, he took advice from another accountant and made an immediate disclosure of all overseas bank accounts to the Revenue.

Before Leveson got stuck into his client, George got Dodd to explain that he had not read crucial records – statements of assets and certificates of disclosure – at Grant Thornton because he had been 'shattered' that morning. This had followed an eight-hour drive from Norwich after two shows there. He explained that he and Anne were under great stress because they had been trying to have a child and, to maximise her chances of becoming pregnant, she had had to have a course of injections. Intercourse had to take place within thirty hours of each injection. Finally, George asked whether he had taken the Revenue investigation seriously or not. Putting a hand to his forehead, Dodd replied, his voice trembling with emotion: 'I have had five years during which I have not had one happy day.' The last eighteen months had been 'torture', he concluded.

Dodd stood up vigorously to Leveson. He met each accusation with calm indignation and consistent denial. Humility and sincerity were offered without affectation. When things heated up, his responses were as quick as his jokes:

DODD (on the Revenue): 'I thought they were being nosy.'
LEVESON: 'Why not say, "What's it got to do with you?"'
DODD: 'You don't talk to tax inspectors like that.'

This was followed by:

LEVESON: 'When you realised that the Inland Revenue was on to these accounts, you did not know what they would be told, so you had better tell them everything just in case.'
DODD: 'Rubbish. I earned every penny in those accounts perfectly legitimately in my own name. I told them if I had made a mistake then everything must be disclosed.'

Leveson said the reason for so many cash deposits was that Dodd had never paid tax on the money.

DODD: 'Untrue, Mr Leveson. That is completely untrue. I am an honest man and I realised I had made a mistake. I had done nothing dishonest; mistaken maybe, but not dishonest.'

The judge intervened to ask Dodd if he understood why the Revenue wanted to know about his money.

WATERHOUSE: 'If you see a man driving around in a Rolls-Royce and see him in a big house and the Inland Revenue know he has been declaring £10,000 a year, do you understand they will want to know where it came from and how he managed to pay for that house?'

DODD: 'I don't want to be facetious, but I don't have a Rolls-Royce and I don't have a big house. As far as I was concerned, I was trying to be honest and had nothing to hide.'

Although Doddy had given a virtuoso performance, for the first time in his career no one clapped. Widespread praise soon followed. Comedians Roy Hudd and Eric Sykes gave character evidence, eulogising his talent, his charitable work and his contribution to comedy. They also confirmed his eccentricity, not that this was ever in real doubt. Michael Billington of the *Guardian* paid eloquent tribute to his 'comic genius', saying that 'He often goes on stage to get a rest,' while John Fisher, head of variety at Thames Television, called him 'the greatest stand-up comedian of all time'. Among several tributes to his considerable work for charity, Sheila Murray, secretary of Clatterbridge Hospital cancer research trust, told how Dodd had helped to raise £10 million under his patronage. This was the hospital where his former fiancée had died. Giving evidence, Ken's loyal partner Anne Jones made an excellent witness. Modest, natural and eminently likeable, her moving confirmation of the unsuccessful attempts to conceive and the strain it placed on both of them went down well with the jury.

Leveson's closing speech was as precise and thorough as his presentation of the case: 'If this trial was about Mr Dodd's rating as a comedian and entertainer it would not have lasted very long . . . If this trial had been about the extent of his charitable activities, it would not have lasted very long . . . What you are concerned with are not these issues but whether Mr Dodd had a very different attitude towards a very different institution which affects every one of us, the Inland Revenue.'

George decided to keep his speech much shorter than Leveson's, believing that that would have a greater impact. He delivered it with barely a note in front of him, looking directly at the jury. He focused on Dodd's total naivety with money, his charitable nature and all that had been said on his behalf. There was a sting in the tail as he launched an attack on the prosecution for failing to call Reg Hunter, Dodd's accountant for ten years from 1972 to 1982, because 'he might risk a prosecution where the stakes are high'. He reminded the jury of Hunter's conviction for false accounting and of the 'disgraceful way he kept accounts which was the reason Mr Dodd was now in a mess'. That, of course, was why the prosecution did not call him. He concluded: 'One thing we have learned from this trial is that comedians are not chartered accountants, but sometimes chartered accountants are comedians.'

During a five-week trial, the jury of seven men and five women had listened to evidence from forty-four different witnesses. They had heard little from the judge, who maintained a light touch in proceedings. He had however intervened to stop George on occasion leading his witnesses, which was to be expected. The former leader of the Wales and Chester Circuit was born within a few miles of Dodd's birthplace. Urbane and clever, Waterhouse was of similar vintage to George, having been president of the Cambridge Union in 1950, when Jeremy Thorpe was campaigning to be president of the Oxford Union. He knew his counterpart as a fellow Liberal, but had declined an invitation to give evidence to the Oxford inquiry concerning Thorpe's alleged sabotage of electoral procedure during the Union presidential campaign. Waterhouse had joined the Garrick Club in 1964, the same year as his very good friend Sir Robin Day. It is indeed a small world.

The summing up was subtle and scrupulously fair. After detailing the prosecution case, Waterhouse gave full credit to Dodd for being a hard-working and dedicated performer and a charitable man. He invited the jury to give 'appropriate weight' to the strong criticism made of the prosecution for failing to call Hunter to give evidence. He did not say so in interview, but I do not think that Waterhouse would have taken any pleasure at all in sending Dodd to prison had he been convicted. On the morning of Thursday 20 July, he sent the jury out to consider their verdict. It took nine hours and fifty minutes of deliberation before they returned the following afternoon. 'Not guilty' was the answer to all eight charges facing the accused, Kenneth Arthur Dodd. Exhausted, elated and relieved, he was able to leave a free man.

Departing from Liverpool Crown Court with George at his side, the stage performer took over. He sculpted his hair into a point and pulled a face for the army of television cameras and photographers. A large number of fans and reporters barred their exit. Dodd stood and told the crowd: 'Thank you all. Thank God it's over. Thanks for all the thousands of people in Liverpool and Merseyside who have said their prayers for me. God bless you all.' He added: 'Anyone know where I can get a gig tonight?'

The maxim that there's no such thing as bad publicity could have been coined for Ken Dodd. His career received a considerable fillip. Income tax troubles provided rich pickings on stage and a new diddyman called George was added to the line-up. Several months later, George and I went to see him perform his new routine on stage. Even the Revenue prospered from the case, far beyond the £825,000 paid by Dodd in back tax and penalties. The publicity created by such a well-publicised prosecution produced an avalanche of extra money from accountants up and down the country, anxious to be making full declarations for their clients.

Ken Dodd remained an icon. Widely championed as the King of Comedy, this living legend continued to appear in successful one-man television specials and to undertake a punishing schedule of performances around the country. One mystery remains: his age, which I have not ventured to ask. At the time of his trial in July 1989, he was universally reported to be sixty-one years old. Indeed this was in evidence. With a birthday of 8 November, that would make his year of birth 1927. But his

Who's Who entry has always read '*b* 8 Nov. 1931' – a difference of four years. Perhaps this minor inconsistency proves, beyond any reasonable doubt, that Mr Dodd was never very good at doing his sums.

For George, this victory confirmed his reputation as the Great Defender, almost exactly a decade after Thorpe. He enjoyed the publicity and liked watching himself on television next to Dodd. 'Lots of people will see that,' he said, confident that this would ensure a good supply of quality work to come. Everyone wanted to know how he had done it. From the limited and sometimes misleading reports in the press, this had been presented as an impossible case to win. At times, he was lost for an answer, preferring instead to quote his favourite line of Dodd's evidence on the subject of money: 'A lady always knows her way to a gentleman's inside pocket.' In the late 1990s, James Price QC recalls discussing the case with George: 'I said to him tongue-in-cheek, "Getting Ken Dodd off must be the greatest achievement of the twentieth century." To which he replied in all seriousness: "Oh do you think so? I am pleased."'

Several weeks after the trial, George and I were walking down Chancery Lane near his chambers. A man pointed at him from the other side of the street and a couple of complete strangers nodded as they passed. 'Why do you think they're looking at me?' he asked rhetorically. As his sixtieth birthday approached, the lure of real fame was beginning to take hold as a substitute for personal happiness.

7
King of Libel

It is out of bad temper and ignorance that most libel actions
are born.

Sir Patrick Hastings KC

The year was 1275. Marco Polo had just reached the court
of Khubilai Khan in Beijing. Edward I was contemplating the
conquest of Wales and the statute of Scandalum Magnatum first
came into effect in England, forming the genesis of a body of
law called defamation. Defamers were punished severely: ampu-
tation of the hand for libel (written defamation) or the ear
for slander (spoken defamation). Other punishments included
mutilation and whipping. The evolution of libel as a criminal
offence became a means by which the Crown controlled a critical
press. Parliament followed suit. In 1792, Charles James Fox – a
hard-drinking gambler and Whig politician – introduced a libel
act, allowing juries to fix damages and moving trials from the
criminal to the civil courts.

The development of law since then and the protection
afforded to an individual's reputation in England and Wales
have combined to make London the libel capital of the world.
The First Amendment to the Constitution and the 1964 *Sullivan*
v *New York Times* decision made defamation cases difficult to
establish in US courts. This is why some American publications
with international circulation find themselves facing defamation
actions in London. When it comes to forum shopping, libel
plaintiffs know where the best goodies are on offer. England
wins hands down.

During the first half of the last century, great advocates fought
in many arenas. From Sir Edward Carson, the destroyer of Oscar

Wilde in his full-distance fight against the Marquess of Queensberry, through to Sir Patrick Hastings, who verbally bludgeoned victims in cross-examination during the inter-war years, libel had been part of their battleground. Hastings retired in 1948. Forty years on, the Bar had become more specialised, with two sets of chambers dominating the field: 1 Brick Court and 5 Raymond Buildings. These were filled with skilled libel technicians, highly competent advocates, but not in the Hastings mould. Yet very few stars at the criminal Bar, the natural home of jury advocates, were able to challenge the duopoly successfully. One notable exception was the polymath commercial silk, Robert Alexander QC, dubbed by *Private Eye* as 'the best legal brains that money can buy'. He flourished in several libel cases, most notably for Jeffrey Archer against the *Star* in 1987, before tiring of the law and moving on to the City, becoming NatWest chairman in 1989. Twelve years later, he returned to the Bar.

George yearned to be in the libel spotlight, where the work was high profile, glamorous and exciting. Dealing in people's reputations was fun. It also presented the perfect opportunity for a synthesis of his skills as a civil lawyer and as a criminal advocate. In contemplating the jump from crime, he calculated that the Ken Dodd victory would at last facilitate such a move. Among those who promoted his cause were solicitor Brian Hepworth and barrister Jonathan Crystal. George had since my childhood recalled memorable exchanges from great libel cases of the past. Among these, the wit of Oscar Wilde in his ill-fated libel action of 1895 was his favourite.

By the late 1980s, damages had reached the stratosphere. Newspapers were very unpopular with juries. The climate of the times seemed to create a collective frenzy in which ever larger awards were made against organs of the Fourth Estate. Jeffrey Archer had won £500,000 in his 1987 battle with the *Star*. In December 1988, the *Sun* agreed to pay Elton John £1 million over false rent-boy allegations. Sonia Sutcliffe, wife of the Yorkshire Ripper, received an infamous £600,000 award against *Private Eye* in May 1989, provoking the editor Ian Hislop to comment: 'If that's justice, then I'm a banana.' The amount was later reduced to £60,000 by agreement. For George, the timing was good. In the next decade, he would become involved with each of the three award-winning litigants and represent all of the defendants.

The break came when Mirror Group in-house lawyer and old-hand libel solicitor Oscar Beuselinck decided that George's jury skills might help stem the tide. In October 1989, George was doing a big criminal case – one of his last. He successfully represented Carole Richardson, one of the Guildford Four, in her appeal against a murder conviction, following a 1975 IRA terrorist bomb. While preparing for this, Oscar retained him to defend an action brought by the Olympic athlete Tessa Sanderson. The case hit the courts in February 1990. George never looked back. His last decade became dominated by events in the Strand. The Victorian Gothic splendour of Courts 13 and 14 at the Royal Courts of Justice became the venue for most of his major libel battles.

So what is libel? If they are to do their job properly, every journalist and publisher in Britain should know the answer to this question. Ignorance is no defence. In theory, it starts with the noble idea of protecting priceless reputations. In practice, it is a complex and highly developed area of law with many arcane and unusual features. A full examination is outside the scope of this book. The *Oxford English Dictionary* definition is 'a published false statement damaging to a person's reputation'. This may offend some lawyers as inadequate, misleading or plain wrong, but as a starting point it is probably enough to enable the non-lawyer to comprehend the core issue. If a person decides to take legal action over defamatory words – whether written or spoken (slander is treated almost identically in law) – the legal remedy may be a form of apology, damages (an award of money to compensate) or usually both. Fortunately, few libel actions ever reach a courtroom. Most are settled between the parties or by their solicitors before reaching that stage.

Nearly every libel case that does go all the way is tried by a jury, except where the detail or volume of evidence is judged too complicated, as in Jonathan Aitken's case against the *Guardian*. It is the most notable area of civil law where a jury is used. The burden of proof in libel (as in all civil actions) is lower, based on the balance of probability, compared to a criminal case, where a jury must find beyond reasonable doubt. Almost always tried by a High Court judge, libel trials are invariably slow, expensive and time-consuming. This deters many litigants since the barriers to entry are high. Accordingly, libel is often called a rich man's game. As Sir Patrick Hastings wrote in 1949: 'Very few people have ever embarked on a libel action without bitterly regretting their adventure before the case comes on for trial. Tempers have died down, bitterness has evaporated and the delay caused by the necessary legal preliminaries seems interminable. All that remains to whip up enthusiasm, already nearly dead, is the prospect of ever-increasing liability for costs.'

In the context of lawyers' fees, much has been said and written about George's earnings. He enjoyed playing the game with those who asked by saying that it was 'between me and the Revenue'. The numbers were high. His total annual income exceeded £500,000 by the late 1980s. That figure would twice pass the £1 million mark during the 1990s. More typically, it was between £800,000 and £850,000: a very large sum, but not as high as some speculative estimates. Like that of many high earners, his disposable net income dramatically increased after Nigel Lawson's March 1988 budget. This reduced the top rate of income tax from 60 per cent to 40. George was fond of saying that newspapers do not pay that well compared to clients in general commercial work. Without doubt, his annual income would not normally have placed him in the top twenty earners at the Bar, despite his regular appearance in such league tables, based on guesstimates. Fame does not always deliver the highest financial rewards. Nowhere is that more true than the law. Compared with libel, the payback from less newsworthy practice areas – banking, shipping, planning and tax – can be much greater. No one outside the commercial field can name partners in Britain's best law firms: Slaughter and May, Linklaters & Alliance, Freshfields or Allen & Overy. Yet in each of these and other City firms there are dozens of solicitors earning more than George did at his peak. Except to the readership of *Legal Business* magazine, their blessed obscurity remains intact.

Money was important to George. It was proof of success to others as much as himself. And he liked to spend conspicuously. In addition to his expensive companion, he also had an expensive lifestyle. This included regular breaks at the Cipriani in Venice. By chance, Desmond Browne QC was there with his family at the same time on one holiday: 'We arrived to find George sitting at the bar, drinking bellinis with an open telephone line to Bill, his clerk. It surprised me that he didn't seem to leave the hotel at all to see the wonderful churches or galleries of Venice, preferring to sit by the pool.' In London, George partied on Dom Pérignon in Mayfair and dined in the smartest venues the city could offer. Home cooking was never an option. He ate out many nights each week, with Chinese or Indian takeaways in between. A desire to be seen in chic restaurants – the Ivy, Le Caprice and the Ritz – was not complemented by an interest in food. His culinary choices were uncomplicated, as Clement Freud discovered in interview. Small portions of plain, simple fare were his favourite. Beef was ordered well done. If it arrived looking anything less, he would send it back to the chef with the comment: 'Tell him I want it burnt.'

Virtually penniless apart from his pension fund (for which I provided endless valuations and spreadsheets), George eventually stopped his gambling after repeated warnings from the bank in the face of a swelling six-figure overdraft. His financial knowledge and acumen were limited. He began to accumulate money only in the last seven years of his life, mostly through the purchase of a substantial London property that more than doubled in value. Since he had started playing at illegal tables during the late 1950s, he had lost about £3 million when adjusted for inflation. Of course, had he invested that money instead he would have acquired capital of a much higher figure. Like his drinking, gambling was an addiction that was to some degree controlled, but was always denied. Both had far-reaching consequences. Both were forms of escape. Both were self-destructive. Yet both were strangely beneficial in making him a better advocate in the courtroom. If success came at a high cost, he was happy to pay.

In 1993, to prove his success, he took a sizeable mortgage to buy a large, new detached house in Marryat Road, adjacent to Wimbledon Village. It had six bedrooms and five bathrooms. He lived there alone. Karen stayed at weekends, playing tennis at Queen's Club or the Vanderbilt every Sunday and sometimes Saturdays too. In the week, she resided mostly at her newly acquired three-bedroom Belgravia flat, then valued at £500,000. George was puzzled at how she could afford to buy this and maintain a smart lifestyle – *de rigueur* in London's most expensive district.

During his six years in residence, 8 Marryat Road retained its original show-house function. A peep through the window revealed a sterile soul. There was little trace of character or personality. The ambience was that of a modern luxury hotel suite: comfortable, anonymous and bland. New silk rugs lay on top of soft white carpets next to heavy silk curtains. Mostly modern furniture mixed with a few elaborate antiques. Reproduction gilt Louis XVI sofas and chairs – prized possessions – were offset by nineteenth-century French gilt mirrors and several unremarkable oils in newly gilded frames. Modern paintings of Venice matched a collection of new Venetian glass ornaments. A Bang & Olufsen television/stereo with four large conical speakers dominated the sitting room.

Leather-bound books decorated the shelves. Bought by the yard in 1987, they remained largely unread in neat little rows. The new Bosendorfer baby grand – from Harrods – remained largely unplayed under bright spotlights. The gleaming new Jaguar remained largely unused in the garage. The gleaming new kitchen remained largely untouched by cooking. Uneaten food from M & S that filled the fridge was bought and then disposed of each week. Soft toys rested next to carefully piled back copies of *Hello!* and *OK!* magazines, which adorned various parts of the house. These were purchased by Karen and read occasionally by George. Most of the bedrooms retained their showroom hollowness. The central feature of George's bedroom, an alarming multi-coloured Versace bedspread, was reflected in the many mirror-fronted built-in wardrobes. These were filled with Italian suits and shirts and several hundred Hermès ties. Outside, the small manicured garden was regularly groomed to perfection by a visiting gardener. The designed effect was clean, clinical and shiny – just the safe and impersonal impression he wanted.

The study had a lived-in look. It was the one room with signs of real activity. George worked increasingly from home when preparing cases, using chambers mostly for consultations with clients and solicitors. His method of working remained the same. Papers would be scattered around with bundles of files towering towards the ceiling or in dozens of boxes. The fax machine was permanently broken or out of paper – George had several models installed. He could master none of them. Practicality was a virtue he despised. There was no computer. He could not use one. Assorted ashtrays were piled up with fag ends. Cartons of Silk Cut, later Marlboro Lights, lay scattered about.

Reading instructions or papers at great speed, he made few notes. As time went on, he focused only on what he thought were the important documents. Much of it was kept in his head. 'I used to worry to death that he never read the papers and just wanted to talk about the case,' comments Adrienne Page QC. The view is endorsed by Victoria Sharp QC: 'Someone described being led by George as "a white knuckle ride" because you were never sure if it would all come together. Somehow it always did.'

For reading up on the law, he came increasingly to rely on an excellent spread of juniors. In addition to Adrienne Page and Victoria Sharp, these included Andrew Caldecott, James Price, Heather Rogers and Hugh Tomlinson. Between them, these six provided outstanding support in more than 90 per cent of his libel work. They were all excellent lawyers who admired and respected their leader's ability. With such high-quality juniors, George learned to delegate effectively, allowing him to concentrate on the key issues, mulling these over in his mind while developing the right strategy and tactics. It was his preferred method always to look at the totality of a case, isolate only the detail that mattered and then proceed unswervingly along the shortest route to winning.

In reading the narrative of his libel trials, it is worth remembering that one week George might appear for a newspaper, robustly defending its cause and journalistic integrity against a hostile plaintiff whose frailties would be examined with remorseless Jesuitical scrutiny. The next week he could be acting for another plaintiff suing the same newspaper, which would then be pilloried and vilified for its disgraceful conduct and underhand methods in terms of outrage, horror and disbelief. To the jury, hearing it for the first time, either argument would seem to be delivered with absolute conviction and sincerity. Across all areas of legal practice, only defamation requires such well-managed schizophrenia from the advocate.

By way of example, George appeared against the *Sun* twice, winning damages in separate cases for the two actors, Jason Connery and Stefanie Powers, while defending the paper against Gillian Taylforth and Bruce Grobbelaar. He won Elton John's case against the Mirror Group yet defended them against Graeme Souness, Mona Bauwens and Tessa Sanderson among others. He saw off challenges from Jani Allan and Inspector Gladding for Channel 4 and won damages from them for Chris Brasher. For the Express Group, he lost the case brought by Peter Bottomley MP, while winning against them for Tom Cruise and

Nicole Kidman. Finally, less than a year after Aitken's defeat against the *Guardian* and Granada Television, he represented Marks & Spencer in their £50,000 damages victory against Granada over child-labour allegations.

The next five chapters examine many of his more celebrated encounters in the libel courts. That is what the public knew him for in the 1990s. But it should not be forgotten that he continued to practise in other areas. There were shipping cases for Ince & Co. and a copyright tribunal case for Denton Hall on behalf of all the national newspapers in a dispute over television listings payments. For a few years, criminal clients still came and licensing work for casinos continued through the decade. Ironically, the lesser-known cases often paid the best money – one good reason why George enjoyed doing them.

During all the moments of drama, tension and surprise in libel, he never deviated from the principal task for which he was employed: advocating his client's case whatever its inadequacies. The client was always right, and he never forgot that inside or outside the courtroom. In classic tradition, he believed the role of the advocate was to represent fearlessly and with passionate conviction whomever his client happened to be and to put their case across to the best of his ability, while upholding the highest standards of the Bar. The rights and wrongs of the argument were for others to decide. There was only one certainty when he went into court, as Ian Katz wrote in May 1994 for the *Washington Post*: 'In the land of libel, George Carman is king.'

8
Damaged Reputations

Reputation, reputation, reputation! O! I have lost my reputation. I have lost the immortal part of myself, and what
remains is bestial.

Shakespeare, *Othello*

'Any woman facing George Carman in court does so at her peril.
She must prepare herself for the bloodless abattoir and thence,
almost inevitably, the bone yard of damaged reputations.' So
warned Jani Allan, the South African journalist, eighteen months
after facing George in her action against Channel 4. Mona
Bauwens and Tessa Sanderson endorsed her sentiments in print.
A common theme among women who faced George in court is
that they felt, as Gillian Taylforth put it, that 'The whole thing
was a big drama in George Carman's hands and the evidence
just got lost.'

Women made George's reputation in libel. In a series of cases
brought by female litigants during a four-year period from February 1990 to January 1994, he achieved several outstanding victories. Even when defeated, damages were often modest. From
that period, six of the most prominent trials are examined in this
chapter. Each of these featured a sexual element or sexual matters.
Where it was not a part of the original libel, George introduced
the theme to the courtroom, encouraging widespread coverage in
both broadsheet and tabloid newspapers. Dramatic consequences
were guaranteed. His methods and language aroused considerable
controversy as he conducted himself with a style that was fearless
and devastating. As Victoria Sharp explains: 'He understood
women very well. He tested women in exactly the same way as
men. Perhaps some women are not used to it.'

The first woman to experience George's distinctive approach to the libel courts was Tessa Sanderson, the thirty-three-year-old javelin thrower and 1984 Olympic gold-medal winner. She had sued the *Sunday Mirror* and the *People* over articles which suggested that she had stolen Derrick Evans (a.k.a. ITV's 'Mr Motivator') from his wife Jewel, thereby destroying their nine-year marriage. George represented both newspapers. At the heart of the libel was whether Tessa and Derrick had sex in 1988 when they shared a hotel bed in Jamaica and later during a training weekend, at a time when he was still living at home with Jewel. George told the jury, 'It is straining your belief that a virile young man who has met an attractive young woman like Tessa Sanderson shares a double bed by choice and with deliberation, without any sexual contact whatsoever.'

Tessa remained cool under pressure from George, sticking to the story that the affair began as a business relationship and that no sex took place before Derrick Evans left his wife in 1989. He pushed as hard as he could on the detail, but made only limited progress. Derrick then confessed under cross-examination to lying about the affair, when he admitted having sex with Tessa two weeks before he had denied that they were lovers in a solicitor's letter. George was making headway. The storm then reached its height when Evans's estranged wife Jewel gave evidence. 'Tessa Sanderson was so butch, she looks like a man. I can't imagine him being with her. I was laughing at them. From the time I have known my husband he has abhorred homosexuality.' From the privilege of the witness box, her attack continued as she branded Tessa 'brazen', 'trash' and 'a bitch' and said that 'her skin was on fire for a man' when she had met Derrick. She claimed that the state of their marriage had been good and that they had continued to have a sexual relationship after Derrick met Tessa. Jewel gave further evidence that he saw Tessa as an opportunity to boost business at his north London gym.

The language in George's closing speech was touched by religious metaphor. He told the jury that Tessa 'had sought to put herself on a high moral pedestal and fallen from it in the oldest drama of human life – the eternal human triangle. If you put yourself on a high moral pedestal you have only yourself to blame if your conduct knocks you from it. If a young lady chooses to get into bed with a married man, she can't expect to be treated with the reverence given to a Mother Superior of a convent.' He added that 'The cast of characters included the jilted and perhaps embittered wife, the opportunist husband and the other woman. Miss Sanderson's case seemed to be "It is true that I was an adulteress but not a marriage breaker, or if I did, it was only a little bit of harm; it's true I've damaged my own reputation by my adultery but you [the newspapers] have added to the damage." Members of the jury, forbidden fruit may be sweeter to eat. But it was not right to suggest that one got compensation for the consequences of eating it.'

George was concerned that Jewel had overplayed her bitterness and alienated the jury. He was right. They preferred Tessa's account, awarding her £30,000. 'It has been an awful experience, but worth the hell I've been through after feeling cheap and dirty,' she told reporters. Mirror Group was not entirely displeased. A modest award compared with the recent trend meant their gamble had nearly paid off. They had already paid £20,000 into court (an offer of damages made before trial). Had the jury awarded any less than that sum, Tessa would have had to pay all her own legal costs, which were more than £100,000. 'He lost it very well,' according to his junior, Adrienne Page. Defamation solicitors and newspaper in-house lawyers began to take a closer look at George. They talked of him as someone whose combative style might just move the pendulum of damages awards back a little in newspapers' direction. His next big libel case more than confirmed their optimism.

Sonia Sutcliffe, a former Bradford schoolteacher, was the wife of Peter Sutcliffe, the Yorkshire Ripper, a serial killer who in April 1981 had been convicted of murdering thirteen women.

After his imprisonment in Broadmoor, she had seemed to carry all before her in litigation, winning a string of separate libel and copyright actions over a seven-year period. Most had been settled out of court until *Private Eye* chose to do battle in May 1989. This was a brave decision because of the potential exposure on costs and damages – significant for a publication without substantial resources. To their surprise, the jury found in her favour, awarding an astonishing £600,000, although this was later reduced to £60,000 by settlement between the parties before the Court of Appeal. Sonia had now picked up a total of £334,000 in net damages from nine different cases. She seemed invincible and probably believed as much.

The *News of the World* was added to the list of defendants on 4 December 1988 as two articles headlined 'Sonia Loves a Ripper Double' and 'Killer's Wife in Sexy Fling' prompted an automatic writ. The stories claimed that in May 1988 while holidaying in Greece with *Mail on Sunday* journalist Barbara Jones, Sonia had a love affair with George Papoustis, a Greek travel agent. He was, according to the newspaper, the 'spitting image' of her husband. The articles claimed that she had concealed her identity from Papoustis. He was quoted as saying that when he found out, 'I felt sick. I have been kissing and caressing the wife of a monster.' Sonia's complaint, however, rested not on the account of her alleged relationship, but instead on a false accusation of her deceiving Mr Papoustis and of stealing, by charging a hotel bill to him.

It was plainly defamatory. News Group, publishers of the *News of the World*, paid £50,000 into court. But Sonia was getting greedy. She refused to take the money, which she could have done without incurring a penny in costs. The newspaper dug its heels in. There would be no better offer. News Group lawyer Tom Crone chose George to take her on in front of a jury. In December 1990, for fifteen days, the strange and chilling world of Sonia Sutcliffe came under the spotlight in Court 13 at the Royal Courts of Justice.

Barbara Jones had taken Sonia on holiday with the intention that they collaborate on a book about Peter. She was named as a co-defendant or third party in the libel action by the *News of the World*, to whom she had sold the story on a freelance basis. This meant that, if Sonia won, the newspaper would in theory have been able to claim indemnity damages and costs from Jones. The prospect of financial ruin created 'total hostility' between her and News Group. She was surprised and grateful for George's quiet support and encouragement as she undertook her own defence in court. The journalist had crucial documentary evidence: two receipts signed by Sonia and her mother for £10,000 and £15,000 which she said were proof of cash payments for her co-operation in the book.

George believed that a jury would instinctively latch on to any justifiable opportunity not to award her damages. He started the newspaper's defence by examining the damages hoard of £334,000, pointing out that 'Not one penny had gone to the families of her husband's victims.' He listed each award slowly and deliberately. Wearing dark glasses throughout, Sonia stood stiffly upright to give evidence. Her slight five-foot frame was motionless. Staring straight ahead at the jury, she responded in a lifeless monotone, even when angry. It was a precise, educated voice with barely a trace of emotion: 'I have not sought to profit from the crimes. I accept that I should not profit directly – but indirectly if wrong aspersions are being cast on me. I think I should have a right to put those matters right.' George moved on to the two payments.

CARMAN (referring to her evidence in the *Private Eye* libel case): 'Your position in the witness box was that you would never wish to profit directly or indirectly out of your husband's crimes.'

SUTCLIFFE: 'I made a qualification then as I do now, that is directly I would not wish to profit.'

CARMAN: 'Would you accept now that the money [the £25,000 paid by Jones] was in connection with a potential book?'

She disagreed, giving a long rambling answer when shown the two receipts.

CARMAN: 'Mrs Sutcliffe, these two sums total £25,000. Whether they be loan, advance or payment, they are in connection with a book, are they not?'
SUTCLIFFE: 'Not to my understanding they are not.'

During the *Private Eye* case, she had made no mention of the receipts. George swooped: 'You took a conscious decision to lie on oath to the *Private Eye* jury about the £25,000.' Sonia denied it, but agreed that she was 'making fine distinctions'. She was shown to have misled Bradford Council in a housing benefit form about the money she had received. Her answers were evasive and contradictory. George moved on to ask her about Papoustis, whom she described as 'not a polished sort of person'. 'And Peter Sutcliffe?' George ventured. Sonia replied: 'I thought he was an uncut diamond . . . I always found Peter gregarious.' She denied any affair with Papoustis, pointing out that she had made a pact with her husband that for ten years 'I would continue to see him.' There was a further agreement to remain sexually faithful and not to seek a divorce because of his strong Catholic beliefs.

Barbara Jones recalls George telling her: 'Don't let Sonia rile you, you must rile her. Stay calm.' The time Jones had spent with her proved invaluable in unlocking her mind in the witness box: 'Sonia, tell us how you feel about your husband's nickname,' was one question. The response was a fifteen-minute soliloquy, delivered without interruption: 'I think not "the Ripper" because my husband believed he killed them humanely in that when he took a hammer to the back of their heads they died instantly and he did not torture them when they were alive.' She talked of 'Pete's mission' to clear prostitutes from the streets and of her visits to him in Broadmoor. She launched into a long explanation of the murder of prostitute Helen Rytka: 'They were there in the car driving along. She was in the process of arousing him against his wishes . . . He had taken a hammer, either from the dashboard or in his coat pocket . . . He struck her on the head – only a soft blow – it didn't stun her or end her life. She said: "Oh you don't have to hit me" . . . He put his hand around her mouth so she couldn't scream and he sort of landed on top of her . . . then she squirmed, she ran away, and he knocked her on the head and then she did die.' As she spoke, two jurors bowed their heads in pain. The air in the courtroom was cold. When she had finished, there was a full twenty seconds of total silence as the full impact of her words sank in.

In addressing the jury, George concluded: 'She has lied on oath and conspired to conceal the truth. Oh what a tangled web we weave when Sonia Sutcliffe practises to deceive . . . Maybe she has come to regard libel as a fruitful source of income beyond that of a Bradford schoolteacher . . . Financially she has been untruthfully evasive, showing enormous self-pity . . . She was no shrinking violet.' Presentation of the defence case had centred on her perjury in the previous *Private Eye* case. In cross-examining Sonia, George had treated the substance of the article and the sting of the libel as peripheral to the issues of her truthfulness and willingness 'to commit perjury'. From first to last, he concentrated on her lack of honesty. That was where he wanted the jury to look.

If they were thinking about damages, George offered two alternatives in his closing speech: 'the smallest coin in the realm' or 'the price of a one-way ticket to Bradford'. He placed Sonia side by side with Peter in the jury's mind: 'There's a little bit more than money at stake in this case. By her own evidence in this court she was lying in the *Private Eye* hearing. She's also used, unnecessarily, the occasional giving of evidence to mount a spirited defence of her husband and seeking to dance on the graves of his victims. She is a clever, confident, cold, calculating woman. She has sought to excite sympathy at every available opportunity in the witness box. The truth and Sonia do not make good bedfellows.' Mr Justice Drake gave an impeccable summing up before sending the jury of nine men and three women out to consider their verdict. Six hours later, they returned with a unanimous decision in favour of the newspaper. 'I was not allowed to applaud from the bench but I was glad that a just result had come about,' recalls Drake, now retired from the bench.

George congratulated Barbara Jones. He thought she had performed very well. Tom Crone addressed reporters on behalf of News Group: 'Sonia Sutcliffe came to this court hoping to pick up massive damages. Instead she is leaving with a bill for a quarter of a million pounds. She has only her own greed to blame. We trust that her gravy train has finally hit the buffers.' There was a wider message. His judgment spoke for all newspapers involved in libel cases. The victory against Sutcliffe was championed with one voice by a press which had a common interest in stemming the tide of libel awards. They had a new hero, the man who had made it possible, George Carman QC. Praised and congratulated from all sides, he was propelled by the Sutcliffe victory to new heights. He was now firmly established as a front-line libel advocate. He was there to stay. Even at *Private Eye*, Sir George Carphone QC (as the magazine called him) got star treatment. They published a one-off victory special, *Ripping Yarns*, and at Lord Gnome's party George ended up playing the piano with vocal accompaniment from Messrs Hislop, Cook and Ingrams.

The next prominent libel challenge started with a throwaway comment by the actress Charlotte Rampling and ended with a former Tory minister satirised across the tabloids in cartoons of her wearing sexy underwear. In interview, Rampling had described Clara Paige, her character in the David Hare thriller *Paris by Night*, as 'an Edwina Currie-type figure'. Minty Clinch wrote an article in May 1989 incorporating the quote for the *Observer* magazine. No harm done. But in the film Paige was a thrusting politician who takes a younger lover, resorts to murder when blackmailed, neglects her family and drives her husband to drink. The result was a libel writ for the *Observer* from Messrs Carter Ruck, representing the former Conservative Health Minister. On reflection, her QC Richard Hartley recalls that the article 'was scarcely defamatory'. Edwina thought otherwise. The case reached court in May 1991.

Demurely stepping into the witness box in a black and white check suit, she told the judge and jury: 'I was really upset about it and still am. I couldn't just let it lie.' The character in the film was 'directly antagonistic and opposite' to the way she lived her own life. George began to cross-examine on her nicknames. How did she feel about being called Cruella De Vil? 'She does evil things to dogs. I don't like dogs very much so I don't mind that.' And Vindaloo? She thought that complimentary because it 'was hot and fresh and spicy'. She said that she would never contemplate murder, 'even under cross-examination from Mr Carman'.

When shown a copy of a recent interview she had given to *Punch* magazine, Edwina called it 'outrageous'. Her comment was inspired by a cartoon accompanying the interview that caricatured her wearing sexy silk underwear. The judge Sir Maurice Drake recalls: 'She looked at George and she carefully undid her coat and said: "Do you want me to strip and show you everything, Mr Carman?" That got the jury on her side.' Edwina said that she had not realised the *Punch* article would be a parody of *Cosmopolitan*'s column 'Are you a good flirt?' Although she had given answers about her underwear, she was extremely surprised by the content. 'For instance, I did not say that my earliest sexual activities took place under the influence of drink. I said I could not remember.' George asked if she recalled being asked about her clothes. She replied, 'I can remember him asking about various items, like suspenders and a short skirt. The answers are accurate. The fact that I have suspenders in my wardrobe should not lead anyone to assume that I wear suspenders. I do not intend to tell this court, or anybody else, what I wear for underwear.' She denied that she had made obvious reference to sex: 'I can make my point without recourse to sex or anything irrelevant.'

In addressing the jury, George suggested that calling somebody an 'Edwina Currie-type figure' was a figure of speech. He continued: 'Would any sensible person say that Mrs Currie has murder in her heart? It's rubbish, isn't it, absolute rubbish.' He said the *Observer* article carried no more than 'a casual reference in a respectable newspaper by a respectable journalist about a respectable film'. His speech went further: 'The case is so far removed from the reality of a proper libel case as to be laughable were it not involving a waste of public time and money. It is wildly extravagant and unreal to suggest that the single line might damage her chances at the General Election [one of Edwina's claims in evidence]. Have you ever heard such a flight from reality as that proposition? The idea that a film review in 1989 is going to affect the vote one way or another is one of the most far-fetched claims you may think you have ever heard. Is she a lady who is shy of publicity or is she glad to be back in the limelight? It's a trivial claim.' Before George finished, he managed to refer to Edwina as 'no shrinking violet', a favoured epithet for women in Court 13.

Richard Hartley QC was a very experienced libel specialist. He chose to mount a strong personal attack on George's methods: 'It was one of the most eloquent, but I would say nasty, hatchet jobs of character assassination ever heard in this court.' Following the 'disgraceful and scurrilous article' came George's efforts to 'humiliate her in a nasty, spiteful attempt to embarrass her in the eye of the jury'. Of *Punch*, he said, 'You may well wonder why that article was put to you.' He said that Mrs Currie had been questioned 'about her sex life, her underclothes and when she first made love. One moment the defence are playing to the gallery for cheap laughs and the next minute – God, don't they love it – they go in and put the knife in.' After forty-five minutes' deliberation, the jury's award was a modest £5,000, allowing Edwina to claim victory. Years later she told me over a leisurely lunch how much she had enjoyed the experience of meeting George in court, terming it 'quite fun'. She was proud to have come off as the winner. After the case, they met each other socially a few times and got on very well. Such fierce battles in the law courts, as in the House of Commons, have little personal significance once the dust has settled. Although aggrieved by the result, the *Observer* and its editor Donald Trelford walked away feeling that a 'trivial' libel had been met with an award not much better than trivial. George was disappointed. Yet the damages were only 1 per cent of those awarded to Jeffrey Archer four years earlier. The pendulum was still swinging.

By the time the forty-year-old journalist Jani Allan took on Channel 4, she had won £35,000 in two separate libel actions against the *Evening Standard* and *Options* magazine. She was suing over an April 1991 programme, *The Leader, His Driver and His Driver's Wife*. This repeated allegations made in the two articles, namely that she had had an affair with Eugene Terre Blanche, the leader of the South African neo-Nazi AWB party. At the opening of the case, on 20 July 1992, Allan gave evidence that she had interviewed Terre Blanche several times in 1988, but had 'thought he looked rather like a pig in a safari suit' and had 'always found him repulsive'. She described how he had pestered her and become obsessed, often phoning her at night when drunk and turning up unannounced at her flat. She denied the programme's suggestion that there had been three alleged incidents of sex, cuddling in a car or talk of marriage plans. Her complaint centred on the portrayal of her as 'a lady of easy virtue', prepared to have sex with a married man.

What happened next was the cause of much discussion. On the second day of the case, a brown-paper package arrived by courier at the court addressed to George. His junior, Adrienne Page, recalls the 'pass the parcel' episode: 'I tapped George on the shoulder in court. He said: "I don't want that." I thought, I don't want to be the one blown up by this. So I then handed it to Susan Aslan [D. J. Freeman] and Jan Tomalin [Channel 4], whose eyes lit up and they shot outside with it. They realised what it was.' The brown paper was removed to reveal a notebook which Allan had used as a diary in 1984–5. It proved to be a bombshell for her. The existence of a diary had been known before trial, but it was not known if it would ever materialise or exactly what it would contain. Its arrival at 12.30 p.m. – just after she had denied adultery on oath – was most unfortunate timing for the plaintiff. Her counsel Charles Gray QC was highly suspicious and remains so. He protested in the strongest terms about its admissibility, but the judge, Mr Justice Potts, let it in as evidence relating to credit. Charles Gray told Jani privately over lunch: 'This is Christmas for George Carman.' Over two and a half days, she would be questioned closely on the contents.

The diary detailed Allan's explicit affairs with two Italians, a married pilot called Ricardo and a gun smuggler called Maro, while she herself was still married. George read an entry to her: 'I remember us laughing about the freckles on our backs. I remember it hurting when he was in me. I remember the silk of his skin and the way he kissed my ****.'

ALLAN: 'It was untrue. It didn't happen.'

CARMAN (reading another entry): 'Went to the flat. It was heaven ... On the way home he cried. I stayed the night and it was heaven. We were stoned. We made love twice. It was freaky.'

ALLAN (after denying it): 'This notebook is deeply embarrassing. I wrote it when I was under psychiatric care.'

CARMAN: 'I am suggesting this is a detailed sexual account by you in a private notebook of a passionate affair with a married man and, because you were caught out in perjury this morning, you have come up with this story about it being a fantasy.'

ALLAN: 'I understand ... It is easy for your purpose to destroy me in this way. I am at your mercy.'

CARMAN: 'We are both at the mercy of the truth, Miss Allan. That is what we are pursuing at the moment.'

He turned to the money she had already made from libel claims, rather in the way he had approached Sonia Sutcliffe: 'If you win this and win the other two [outstanding claims against the *Daily Mail* and *Daily Telegraph*], libel is going to prove a very fruitful source of income for you.' She denied this. He then turned to her truthfulness, which provoked the quote of the case from Allan. The best advertising brains could not have conjured a better line in promotional copy for her tormentor's skills.

CARMAN: 'You have lied about your sexual relationship because it is easy to lie – because you think that way is the way to obtain more damages from the jury.'

ALLAN: 'Whatever award is given for libel, being cross-examined by you would not make it enough money.'

The following day, George turned to Terre Blanche. Allan reiterated her antipathy towards him and accepted that he had been obsessed by her because she was different from the *Hausfrau* Afrikaner women. George read a passage from her newspaper column.

CARMAN: '"He speaks with a rich earth-brown voice. Sometimes it has the loamy texture of a newly ploughed mealie field ... I'm impaled on the blue flames of his blowtorch eyes." What do you mean by that?'

ALLAN: 'His eyes bore into me much the way your eyes are boring into me.'

He returned to the diary. In dismissing the entries as fantasy, she had said she had 'problems in dealing with the reality of sexual experience'.

CARMAN: 'What do you mean? You are a woman who has had sexual intercourse with your husband? [She agreed.] And with other men?'

ALLAN: 'No . . . it's true to say I have had sexual foreplay, as it were.'

CARMAN: 'It may well be you have had sexual foreplay. But are you saying you have not had sexual intercourse with any other man except your husband in the whole of your life?'

ALLAN: 'I certainly can't remember.'

CARMAN: 'You can't remember? What do you mean?'

ALLAN: 'I find it very stressful being here.'

CARMAN: 'I'm sure. There are so many other people here and they are not claiming damages. It's your decision to claim damages. Nothing is compelling you to be here.'

ALLAN: 'I am compelled by a desire to rid myself of the taint of something I didn't do.'

On the third day of being questioned, Allan said: 'You have milked this diary so much it is mooing.' George continued undeterred, recycling another favourite, the 'court of morals' phrase used in the Thorpe trial among others.

CARMAN: 'This is not a court of morals, but it is a court looking after the truth. You said you would never commit adultery with a married man because it would be against your moral principles?'

ALLAN: 'Yes, I have said so.'

CARMAN: 'But you would commit sexual foreplay with a married man?'

ALLAN: 'I'm not sure whether you would accept it if I say people are organic creatures that grow and evolve . . . [a long speech followed]'

MR JUSTICE POTTS (intervening): . . . Did you have an affair with him [Ricardo]?'

ALLAN: 'I suppose if sexual foreplay is considered as an affair then yes. There wasn't absolute sexual intercourse.'

Allan was asked to read a passage which referred to her hope of marrying Ricardo.

CARMAN (handing Allan the notebook): 'Can you read that sentence?'

ALLAN: 'It says his wife has a weak . . . I can't read that word. I think it says heart.'

CARMAN: 'Are you sure it begins with an H?'

ALLAN: 'It's not the word you think it is.'

POTTS: 'What word is it Mr Carman is thinking of?'

ALLAN: 'A word beginning with the letter C.'

POTTS: 'Well, what word is Mr Carman thinking of?'

CARMAN: 'A word referring to a woman's private parts, my Lord.'

ALLAN: 'I didn't know they could be weak in that area. So I don't think it could be that word.'

George moved relentlessly on to the close.

CARMAN: 'Not only do I suggest you are a liar but you are a hypocrite because you tried to portray yourself as a woman who would not have a sexual affair with a married man.'

ALLAN: 'I understand. I am a lot different now to how I was then.'

On Terre Blanche, he concluded:

CARMAN: 'From first to last, you have lied in the witness box about your relationship with Terre Blanche, in order to persuade this jury to award you money?'

ALLAN: 'That's not true.'

A variety of witnesses was called to substantiate Channel 4's account of her affair, including a number flown over from South Africa. The most important of these was Linda Shaw, her former flatmate who testified directly about Jani's affair with Terre Blanche. In a memorable exchange, George asked her what she saw through the keyhole of Jani's locked bedroom door.

SHAW: 'I saw Jani's feet and her knees were up and I saw this huge white bottom on the floor, and I saw the toes of a couple of pairs of shoes.'

CARMAN: 'You saw Jani's feet. Were the feet in a position where her legs were horizontal or vertical?'

SHAW: 'Her feet were flat, indicating . . . that her knees were up.'

After Shaw had told the court of seeing 'green underpants with holes in', George moved on to the bottom.

CARMAN: 'You said you saw what you called a bottom – colour?'
SHAW: 'White.'
CARMAN: 'Are you able to identify the sex or the shape?'
SHAW: 'I didn't see the genitals. It was a large white bottom. It was on top of Jani, rising up and down. I assumed they were having sex.'
CARMAN: 'Where was the bottom in relation to the knees?'
SHAW: 'It was between her two knees.'
CARMAN: 'There was movement up and down?'
SHAW: 'Yes.'
CARMAN: 'Was it movement in any way indicative of sexual activity?'
SHAW: 'Yes.'

Shaw confirmed that she had witnessed fumbling, kissing and embracing on other occasions. George closed his client's case by branding Allan 'a dangerous and accomplished liar'. Mr Justice Potts thought Jani had made eyes at him during the case. It did not affect the impartiality of his summing up. There was an audible gasp in Court 14 when after a thirteen-day trial and four and a half hours' deliberation the foreman of the jury of six men and six women stood up to say they had found unanimously against the plaintiff. The front pages of 6 August 1992 showed a stunned Allan being supported *en route* to her taxi after an estimated £300,000 defeat. George received acres of copy. The whole affair had suitably entertained the public in what was silly season for the press.

During the ups and downs of Allan's case, David Mellor had been having a sticky summer, competing with Jani for the headlines. This followed his fling with an actress called Antonia de Sanchez. John Major's Heritage Secretary struggled to keep his Cabinet seat. The publicist Max Clifford had embellished the relationship story with the false detail that Mellor had worn his

Chelsea strip while in bed with de Sanchez. Mellor was still just about holding on to office. A decade later, Clifford was unapologetic: 'I didn't rush around looking to bring out a scandal on David Mellor,' he says in his Bond Street office. 'Clifford is a scumbag,' Mellor told me thoughtfully, after a good lunch at Langan's. 'If newspapers wish to run an alternative criminal justice system, then everyone worthy of being put on trial should be put on trial.'

His problems were certainly not at an end by September 1992. Two years earlier, he had gone on holiday to Marbella with Mona Bauwens, the daughter of Jaweed Al Ghussein, chairman of the Palestinian National Fund. He took his family and stayed for a month in a six-bedroom, six-bathroom villa owned by a Belgian count. It was rented at a cost of $20,000. The timing was unfortunate. The day after the holiday began, Iraq invaded Kuwait. At the time, Mellor was Chief Secretary to the Treasury under Margaret Thatcher. The *People* newspaper launched an attack under the headline 'Top Tory and the PLO Paymaster' and supported by an editorial written personally by the proprietor, Robert Maxwell. Bauwens issued a writ for libel claiming that the article made her 'a social outcast' and that it had picked on her as an Arab.

The case reached court five weeks after Allan's had finished. The thirty-three-year-old Bauwens was pretty, blonde and photogenic, unlike the bespectacled Mellor, ten years her senior. Acting on Mona's behalf was the familiar, white-haired, country-parson figure of Richard Hartley QC (or 'Sir Hartley Redface' as the *Eye* calls him). George introduced a sexual theme to the case on day one. After Bauwens had told the court that she shunned publicity, he produced photographs of her in cross-examination.

CARMAN: 'I want you to look at these photographs of yourself, taken at the Bishops Avenue mansion in Hampstead. You are posing on the dining-room table.'
BAUWENS: 'Yes.'

CARMAN: 'Are you wearing – well, I suppose it is some kind of body stocking and tights and high-heeled shoes.'

BAUWENS: 'It is a leotard.'

CARMAN: 'Here you are with a rocking horse – with your legs astride. Then there are other photographs of you on a bed. Is that your bed?'

BAUWENS: 'No, it is my mother's bed.'

CARMAN: 'Another photograph of you with your legs astride the rocking horse. Is that a leotard with those lacy bits?'

BAUWENS: 'Yes.'

On day two, revealing photographs of Mona monopolised the tabloid spreads. The judge, Sir Maurice Drake, told me: 'Introducing the pictures which had a nuance that there was something going on was done to test her credit. But it rebounded against the newspaper because some of the jury accepted this had nothing to do with the case whatsoever.' As the jury digested the images of Mona on the rocking horse, she arrived at court arm in arm with the minister's wife Judith, who looked every inch a loyal Tory lady in sensible shoes, skirt and long-sleeved sweater. The noticeable contrast in their appearance only served to highlight Mona's heavy make-up, stylish blonde curls, short skirt and designer apparel. This was a crude stage-managed setpiece. 'It was against my advice. I thought it was dreadful,' comments her barrister Richard Hartley. Like the photograph of Mellor family unity taken only weeks before at his father-in-law's garden gate when the de Sanchez story broke, it smacked of a crisis – badly managed. Bauwens said in the witness box that she had 'nothing, absolutely nothing, to be ashamed of in my friendship with the Mellors'. George had not finished. He pushed further.

CARMAN: 'Is it right that Mr Mellor visited you on a social basis at that time, and not with his wife?'

BAUWENS: 'Oh yes. He would drop by.'

CARMAN: 'Did he call at your Chesterfield House apartment?'

BAUWENS: 'He used to come and have a cup of tea.'

The most deadly question was about the holiday. It was short and simple.

CARMAN: 'Who paid?'
BAUWENS: 'I did.'

The focus of the jury and the press was straying from the hurt feelings of Mona Bauwens, the argument about the PLO and her father's role, the Gulf War and the acceptability or otherwise of adverse comment by the newspaper. All thoughts were on the invisible Mellor and his free holiday – just where George wanted them to be. He held a subpoena threat over the minister that he might be called to give evidence, without any real intention of ever doing so. It added to the suspense and guaranteed press interest. The photographs got a second day's outing under headlines such as 'Mona Teaser'.

After only five days, George was on to his closing speech, producing one of his most famous *bons mots*: 'Marbella has sand, sea, sunshine, and if a politician goes there and, in the honest view of some, behaves like an ostrich and puts his head in the sand, thereby exposing his thinking parts, it may be that a newspaper is entitled to say so.' Like many of his best lines, it was not original. But it was very effective. George had first heard the joke in 1950, delivered in a speech to the Oxford Union by another Balliol man, Sir David Maxwell Fyfe, who (as Lord Kilmuir) became Lord Chancellor under Harold Macmillan. The jibe against Mellor had some personal animosity behind it, as George explained to Jeremy Paxman in a December 2000 interview: 'I had been involved in a debate in the Cambridge Union [in the late 1980s] leading two undergraduate speakers. Mellor was on the other side. As an ex-president of the Cambridge Union, I thought he behaved in a deeply unpleasant way to my speakers. So I used the opportunity of the case to say, "Here's just a little bit back, David."'

Hartley's closing speech picked up with the same sort of personal attack on George as in the Currie case. Reminding jurors they were 'in a court not a theatre', he added: 'I did not think Mr Carman would be doing a music-hall turn as a stand-up comic.' The pace quickened: 'Mr Carman – the stage manager, producer and leading actor – was cruel because at no time did he spare her feelings. No stick was too small to beat her with. It was cowardly, because he was prepared to wound but afraid to strike. Innuendoes were left hanging in the air, insinuating many things. Mr Carman is past master of the wink-wink nudge-nudge, but he never puts a specific allegation. It's a classic smear tactic. She suffered a verbal mugging as the defendants decided to put the boot in and go for broke. You are entitled to take that into account when assessing damages.' Pope's line 'willing to wound but afraid to strike' was one George used himself in several cases, including *Branson* v *G-Tech*. Hartley insisted that his personal criticism of George was 'all posturing for the jury. It meant nothing.'

There was a split in the jury room, straight down the middle – six–six. 'Mona had not been confident at the beginning when she saw six women on the jury,' recalls Hartley. An exact tie is most unusual. As the judge Sir Maurice Drake explains: 'Richard Hartley said that he was content for me to decide the case, which is perfectly allowable practice provided both sides agree. He thought that I was sympathetic. George said no. That was a mistake. I would have given judgment for the newspaper. My sympathy was with Mona, but I would have said it was fair comment on a matter of public interest. When a high-ranking politician accepts hospitality from someone who is so closely connected to terrorism, it doesn't look right.' The case ended with Mona talking of a retrial. It never happened.

Mellor hung on in office for forty-eight hours. But his 'last chance saloon' remark, when he threatened the press a few months earlier with protection-of-privacy legislation, came back to haunt him. On 24 September, he resigned. 'From Toe Job to No Job' ran the *Sun* headline. David and Judith Mellor separated soon after the case ended and later divorced. This was the start of a wave of sleaze and scandal that was to engulf the Major government over the next five years, concluding with Jonathan Aitken and Neil Hamilton. Both of these men were to meet George face to face in the courtroom. Mellor escaped that fate, embarking on a successful new career as broadcaster, journalist and consultant. He would later joke to George that 'You did me a huge favour in the Bauwens case. I have not looked back since.' And neither did George. Two big victories in two months – the hung jury was 'a victory as near as damn it', he said – meant that he was now in demand for nearly every libel case going. His name started to be used liberally by solicitors to frighten off litigants. George got wise to this and responded by charging a £3,000 'retainer' fee simply for the use of his name in correspondence. Many were prepared to pay it.

Gillian Taylforth was not, however, one of those people deterred from litigation merely by the mention of George's name. During the same hot summer of 1992 that Jani Allan, Mona Bauwens and David Mellor had been grabbing the headlines, Gillian, better known as *EastEnders* character Kathy Beale, was at Ascot with her boyfriend Geoff Knights. After a champagne-filled day at the races, she decided to drive Geoff home in their Range Rover. They stopped on a slip road off the A1 where they were seen by PC Talbot. 'I saw what you were doing. You were committing an act of gross indecency,' he told them, believing he had seen Gillian performing oral sex on Geoff. They both protested, saying that Geoff had had an attack of pancreatitis and Gillian was merely loosening his trousers to ease the discomfort.

Knights was arrested, cautioned and released. An unidentified policeman sold the story to the *Sun*. Published under the headline 'TV Kathy's Sex Romp Fury', the article on 19 June 1992 focused on her anger at Geoff's arrest while hinting strongly that oral sex had in fact taken place. She sued for libel. The *Sun* claimed it was true or, if not, that the police had been the source of the story. George was retained to defend the *Sun*. The trial began on 11 January 1994.

In the familiar surroundings of Court 13, Gillian's counsel was Michael Beloff QC, Eton and Magdalen scholar and an extremely able academic lawyer. Although a most eloquent and witty speaker, he was not a regular in the libel courts, preferring to address the more cerebral points of law in the House of Lords. He remembers that 'It was enormous fun to appear against George and I was very much looking forward to it.' Opening the case to the jury, he said that the 'dogged PC had put two and two together and made five', before moving on to *Macbeth* to describe the incapacity of the inebriated Knights: 'Drink provokes the desire but takes away the performance.'

A more earthy analysis was given by Gillian in the witness box: 'If I was going to do something like that, I wouldn't do it on the bleeding A1.' She wept when explaining her hurt at the taunts which she had received when the article was published. Next stop for judge, counsel, jury and the press corps was the car park of the Royal Courts of Justice. They gathered to watch a simulated reenactment of the blow-job incident. Two *Sun* journalists (fully clothed) tested the possibilities in a Range Rover. 'I would have to have had a neck like a giraffe in the position I was in, or he would have had to have been really well endowed,' was Gillian's reaction. 'Yes You Can Do It in a Range Rover' ran the *Sun*'s headline the next day. One of them was wrong.

In cross-examination, George adopted a novel approach. He reminded Gillian of the *EastEnders* episode when she had played the part of a rape victim in court.

CARMAN: 'When you were playing that role, when you were dramatically giving evidence, you described how you felt outraged and cheapened and disgusted and humiliated . . . I mention it because I'm going to suggest to you that your performance this morning in the witness box, when you were telling the jury you were outraged and distressed and felt unclean and ashamed, was very similar to what you had to say when you were playing the part of a rape victim.'

TAYLFORTH: 'No, Mr Carman, that was Kathy Beale. I am Gillian Taylforth.'

CARMAN: 'Did you rehearse what you had to say this morning?'

TAYLFORTH: 'No, I didn't. I was asked how I felt. That is how I felt.'

Next it was the turn of Geoff Knights, giving evidence on behalf of Gillian. Described to me by Michael Beloff in interview as 'a person not unfamiliar with the courts of law', Knights said that he had been too drunk to realise that he was signing a caution in the police station. George asked him to list his criminal convictions. 'What, all of them?' he replied. George read out the eight separate convictions for criminal damage, assault, breaking a man's jaw and burglary. The next day's *Sun* methodically catalogued each conviction and year of offence from 1969 to 1986. It did not create the impression of a man in love with the police. Throughout six hours of cross-examination, Knights completely avoided making eye contact with his questioner.

CARMAN (referring to Knight's detention at Borehamwood police station after the alleged incident): 'Did you challenge these two police officers to "take off their uniforms and come outside for a fucking fight"?'

KNIGHTS: 'I was still very angry at the time. Yes, I did ask them to fight.'

Dr Iain Murray Lyon, a specialist in pancreatitis, then gave evidence. He agreed with George's suggestion that Knights could have faked an attack by falsely describing symptoms. Week one of the case had ended.

The following day, Saturday, George got a call from News International (publishers of the *Sun*) in Wapping. A video had been delivered – for a fee – by two men. He went to see it. His junior Andrew Caldecott recalls George asking him: 'Andrew, what do the words "give good head" mean?' Excited by the video's content, George called me to say that I should watch the legal argument on Monday as he tried to get it admitted. Mr Justice Drake was obviously unimpressed by Taylforth's screen performance. He did not need much persuasion. 'Drake has a very English sense of fair play,' comments Caldecott. 'He thought she was gilding the lily.' In interview, Drake nodded approvingly at this suggestion. By the time the jury saw it, the thirty-five-minute amateur film from April 1988 had already been played and discussed at length by the defence team. Caught on camera were the events at a drunken party, celebrating the twentieth anniversary of the Anna Scher Children's Theatre in Islington, north London.

Taylforth was shown being creative with a bottle and a sausage. Filmed in the street with a wine bottle between her legs, simulating masturbation, after earlier simulating fellatio with the same bottle, she was heard to say: 'I'll sell my services along the road and we'll get around £2.50.' Then with a German sausage next to her mouth, she said: 'I'd like to state, I give good head. I give very good head.' Then, holding the sausage up, she added: 'Has anybody got a battery for this knob?' The video ended, leaving the viewer in suspense as Gillian unbuttoned her blouse. As evidence, it was marginal. As prejudice, it was compelling. Christmas had come again for George as Gillian went back into the witness box for round two.

CARMAN: 'First of all, you let the jury believe you were not in any way an exhibitionist, particularly with anything to do with sex. Looking at this video, is it not right to say you are prepared to be something of a coarse exhibitionist, when in drink, over sexual matters?'

TAYLFORTH: 'Not at all, no.'

This answer was a little hard to swallow. He focused on the detail, starting with the 'good head' remark.

CARMAN: 'Did that phrase have a sexual connotation?'

TAYLFORTH: 'I was very, very drunk and we were all in high spirits. I just moved away and the sausage was there.'

CARMAN: 'What was the significance of asking for the battery?'

TAYLFORTH: 'It was just a joke. I was just mucking about pretending it was a vibrator, that's all.'

CARMAN: 'What did you mean by "give good head"?'

TAYLFORTH: 'I imagine it means holding a man's penis and doing what I was supposed to be doing on the A1. I think they are words that everyone uses in this day and age.'

He moved on to the £2.50 reference.

CARMAN: 'Obviously that was a jokey reference to giving prostitution services?'

TAYLFORTH: 'Of course it was a joke. I didn't intend to go out and sell myself.'

CARMAN: 'You were implying oral sex, weren't you?'

TAYLFORTH: 'I don't think I was. I blew on the bottle to make a sound.'

Finally George pointed out that the episode with the wine bottle in the street took place in public, in daylight and opposite a children's playground.

CARMAN: 'Do you think it is indecent for a woman of thirty-two [her age in 1988], in your position with a regular part in national television, to stand in the street in daylight and simulate masturbation with a bottle next to your vagina?'

TAYLFORTH: 'Had there been people there I wouldn't have done it. It was just a joke between friends. I was very drunk.'

George had been watching the jury closely. He noted a middle-aged Hindu woman looking particularly disgusted at this exchange. Gillian was sunk. There was one last bash on the video: 'The whole impression of your evidence, the language you selected and the expression of outrage and disgust you have given the jury, I suggest all this has been a great show misleading the jury, and the true Gillian Taylforth, when you are in drink, emerges in this video.' When confronted by the undignified spectacle of his client on film, the bearded Beloff (later Master of Trinity College, Oxford) revealed his intellectual pedigree, identifying it as 'Rabelaisian humour'. A belief that the average juror has ever read *Gargantua* or similarly esoteric works is not the hallmark of a jury advocate. The reference flew way over their heads. PC Talbot then confirmed that he saw what he saw and it was on to the closing speeches.

In summing up Gillian's case, George concluded that it was 'riven with improbability heaped on improbability ... Miss Taylforth was behaving in a way one hopes the majority of young women in this country would never behave. And she was doing that because in drink she can be given to a certain coarseness in sexual matters. Of course that doesn't prove having oral sex in a car. But it gives you an insight into a facet of her behaviour. It may be, members of the jury, that the unfortunate words of Gillian Taylforth, uttered, no doubt in jest, on a film which she never thought would see the light of day – "I give good head" – may summarise what happened that night. It may be her epitaph.' Privately, George was not in fact convinced that Taylforth had been lying.

Beloff invoked the words of John McEnroe – 'You cannot be serious' – to summarise the likelihood of the whole episode. He dismissed George's performance as 'a vintage episode of *Rumpole of the Bailey* or the magician's tricks of *Perry Mason*'. He called George 'the Torville and Dean of advocacy rolled into one but with this important difference – straight sixes for style, straight zeroes for content'. It had taken eleven days to examine a fairly simple matter – did she or didn't she? The jury was not unanimous, returning a majority decision of 10–2 in favour of the *Sun*. Beloff remains of the view that 'She would have won that case if it had not been for the video.' But Court 13 had proved unlucky for another litigant.

Taylforth knew how to steal the show, adding her own histrionic conclusion to proceedings. As George made the application for costs, a small wail was heard. It turned to sobbing. Geoff helped Gillian out to the corridor, where she collapsed. An ambulance was called. She was carried from the building by paramedics, strapped to a bed. Dramatic photos stole the next day's front pages. Whatever her other talents, Gillian Taylforth certainly gave good copy. On the court steps, Tom Crone was thrilled to deliver another message for all would-be libel plaintiffs: 'The first lesson of libel is, if you don't like losing, don't play the game.' There was only one consistent winner. And he had already gone off to celebrate his latest performance with champagne in El Vino's. George was at the top of his game, seemingly able to move the pendulum at will.

9
Celebrity Status

Fame, fame, fatal fame, it can play hideous tricks on the brain
But still I'd rather be famous than righteous or holy any day.
Morrissey, 'Frankly Mr Shankly'

There was no single defining moment. But at some point in the early 1990s George graduated from being a barrister whose name people recognised to becoming a celebrity lawyer in his own right. This resulted from the cumulative effect of continued prominence in a string of high-profile cases, reinforced by consistent exposure in the wider media. He worked hard to cultivate interest.

In 1988, he appeared in *Death on the Rock*, *This Week*'s award-winning documentary on the Gibraltar SAS shootings of three IRA suspects. His interview with Julian Manyon, calling for Foreign Secretary Geoffrey Howe to investigate the deaths further, ended the filmed report. In 1989, following the Dodd victory and in the run-up to doing the Guildford Four appeal, there were several glossy-magazine profiles of 'Britain's best-known QC', including one by Victoria Glendinning in *Harpers & Queen*. In 1990, he became the first practising barrister to be Sue Lawley's castaway on *Desert Island Discs*. A licensing victory for Tony Wilson and Manchester's Hacienda Club in the same year came after an ecstasy-related death. It made him an unlikely hero of the club scene. His 1992 appearance for Kevin Maxwell before a parliamentary select committee showed George performing live to a television audience of millions. Further magazine and newspaper interviews followed.

Nineteen-ninety-three was a landmark year. His name started to make headlines by itself. In the media age, some may see that as a definition of celebrity. It began with 'Carman QC May Cross-Examine Major', a front-page *Observer* splash in January when the Prime Minister launched a libel action against the *New Statesman*. The *Sun* ran with 'King Carman Wins Again' in July, following a victory for 'an errant peer'. In October, he was a prickly and slightly pompous panellist on BBC's *Question Time* special on the law alongside a smooth Lord Chief Justice, Lord Taylor, his former Thorpe trial opponent. The chairman, Peter Sissons, seemed very relieved after sixty minutes was up. In November, Mr Justice Drake jokingly suggested in open court to George, who was representing Elton John, that his name would be added to next year's A-list of celebrity guests invited to a Hollywood party. 'I was angling for that,' came the quick reply.

Successful representation of newspapers in libel cases guaranteed him two things: lots of favourable copy and immunity from too much personal criticism. 'The media had almost a reverence for him,' according to Victoria Sharp. Newspaper editors and proprietors never knew when they might need help from Killer Carman. 'Did you ever think of becoming Lord Chancellor?' Conrad Black asked him playfully in the back of his chauffeured car. The Hollinger chairman, owner since 1985 of the *Telegraph* and *Sunday Telegraph*, had become a strong admirer. George was also lunched and loved by the red-top editors – Piers Morgan in particular – and for the *Guardian* he could do no wrong. Such relationships had the added benefit of affording a veil of protection against much adverse copy ever seeing the light of day.

There were a few close shaves. The journalist Charles Nevin had interviewed George for the *Observer* and *Esquire* magazines. He kept his activities under review in the *Independent*'s Captain Moonlight column. The *Evening Standard* Londoner's Diary spotted him around town, as did Nigel Dempster and Ephraim Hardcastle. There was forewarning of a *Daily Mail* interview with Ursula about her exclusion as his first wife from the *Who's*

Who listing. He leaned heavily on the paper's editor Sir David English to get the more damaging copy removed from the article. At George's instigation, English had been fined £1,000 in January 1982 for being in contempt of court during the Dr Arthur case by publishing a prejudicial article written by Malcolm Muggeridge. But he bore no grudge. When George picked up the *Mail* at Victoria just after midnight, there was a look of relief on his face that English had bowed to pressure by getting the journalist Geoffrey Levy to water down the story. This was published two days after the Jani Allan verdict in August 1992.

George's love affair with the media centred on an obsession with seeing his name in print. He found the oxygen of publicity addictive, and it became an important feature of his life. In the words of James Price QC, 'There was simply no amount of flattery that he wouldn't lap up. He adored it.' Drinking and chatting with journalists had been part of an approach to practice since the 1960s. As his career developed, he became more media savvy, alerting court reporters in advance to speeches or cross-examinations that he thought would make good copy. He even predicted that a female juror would cry at his speech in the Dr Arthur case, betting with one of the resident hacks that it would take less than twenty minutes. Legend has it that it took less than ten. 'He loved talking to the press. He kept them very much in his pocket during big trials,' comments James Price, his junior in libel battles against Aitken and Hamilton.

At the Bar, this attitude made him something of an exception. 'Most barristers avoid journalists like the plague,' according to Desmond Browne QC. Yet George never tired of the attention. It endeared him to many, including *Private Eye*, where he was carefully indiscreet over lunch to Messrs Hislop, Ingrams and Foot. He admired their moral approach. They valued his confidence and thought him 'delightfully unstuffy', according to Ingrams. He gave many feature interviews and did a fair amount of television: *Panorama*, *Newsnight* and a variety of documentaries. Before Fleet Street moved eastwards, George would often rush to get newspapers hot off the press to see how many column inches he had got in the reporting of a case and whether his tabloid-friendly phrases had hit the headlines. By the 1990s, the venue for first editions changed to Victoria Station, where he would wait for the newsstand delivery between 11 p.m. and midnight. He also purchased quite a number of courtroom cartoons drawn by Priscilla Coleman, the courtroom artist, and by JAK, the late *Evening Standard* cartoonist. But he never hung them on the walls, preferring to keep them in a pile in the study.

In *A Fish Called Wanda*, the Jamie Lee Curtis character adopts the unlikely role of courtroom groupie in order to gain the confidence of barrister John Cleese. It works. George attracted his own dedicated follower – more mature than Lee Curtis but undoubtedly genuine. A smartly dressed, dark-haired woman with brown eyes and a pleasing smile became a Court 13 regular, sitting two or three rows behind him. Elizabeth was a retired secretary living alone in Surrey. During prominent trials, she got up very early to guarantee her place in the queue for the public gallery if there was no room in the court. This interest flattered George, although he did not acknowledge her presence. When talking passionately about his cases to an assembled group of visitors outside the public gallery, she proved to be very well informed. Without revealing my identity, I once asked her why she thought he was so good. 'He can do such amazing things with words,' was her automatic response.

George considered that the impact of a carefully crafted phrase was significantly enhanced in a jury's thinking if repeated as a newspaper headline the following morning. During well-publicised cases, he would produce several alternatives in advance with that specific purpose in mind. Working on these *bons mots* was fun, but it should be stressed that a number of George's best one-liners were entirely spontaneous. The cut and thrust of cross-examination produced some of the most devastating. In August 1997, by giving advance warning to the editors, he persuaded *The Times* and the *Guardian* to send reporters to

Singapore to cover his cross-examination of the Prime Minister, Goh Chok Tong. George was acting on behalf of an elderly and impecunious opposition politician, Benjamin Jeya. They were not disappointed.

His attack on the authoritarian regime and one-party system of government established by Lee Kuan Yew was dramatic. For many, it was the most aggressive ever witnessed in a court during the thirty-five-year history of the Lion City's independence. Prime Minister Goh (who had tea served to him in a china cup whilst in the witness box) told him that if 'you repeat your comments outside the courtroom, I will sue you for libel'. Critical foreign-newspaper coverage inspired by George's conduct of the case became a major issue. Goh's counsel, Geoffrey Shaw QC, highlighted it as a factor which should significantly increase the level of damages. Using the media had succeeded in raising both the stakes and the tempo. Although George lost the case, the award was only 10 per cent of the damages claimed. Goh was humiliated.

There was another reason for George's love of publicity: insecurity. What had been a driving factor on the way up never levelled off once at the top. Complacency was not one of his sins. He needed to keep on winning, and for everyone to see it. After a big victory was prominently reported by the newspapers, he would often say: 'Plenty of solicitors will see that.' Even as late as 1996, he was relieved to get a good day's press in securing £70,000 damages for the American actress Stefanie Powers. This was settled against the *Sun* over untrue allegations that she was an alcoholic who had sexually harassed a male assistant. George had recently lost several cases in a row and was increasingly fearful of being considered past his best. He phoned me up in Hong Kong and told me to look at *The Times* report. 'A good win,' he said with satisfaction at the settlement, reflecting his strongly held view – and the view he believed of many solicitors – that you're only as good as your last result or two.

The Powers case exemplifies one type of client that helped

make George a celebrity – those who were themselves celebrities. As Kate Muir put it: 'In the way that the rich must have Gucci luggage and stay in the Beverly Hills Hotel, they must also have Mr Carman.' His clerk Bill remembers 'the look of enjoyment on his face whenever you told him there was another high-profile client queuing up. He liked to mix with celebrity clients. They often thought he was the best thing since sliced bread and let him know it. And he loved that. He went the extra mile because of it. The publicity he then got was a measure of his success to other men.'

The first A-list client had arrived back in 1986 when he represented Joan Collins in a fight with Brent Walker over two films in which she had starred, *The Bitch* and *The Stud*. As his instructing solicitor Roger Lane-Smith recalls: 'It was a dispute about undeclared royalties. The main witness on the other side was George Walker. About a week before the trial, I phoned up to let the other side know that George Carman was very much looking forward to cross-examining Mr Walker. Absolute panic broke out in the Walker camp. They settled on very good terms. George had been on to me throughout saying: "I think we really need a conference with Joan and Jackie Collins." I said: "Why, George? They live in LA." He'd only said it because he wanted to meet them.' When advising Liz Hurley in a 1996 libel action, George spoke with her several times on the phone and expressed a similar desire to meet her. But she was busy filming in Hollywood, explained her solicitor, Keith Schilling. To his dismay, the matter was settled with an apology and undisclosed damages.

When there was a fight, the client had to be in court. The first libel celebrity to sit in front of George in full flow was a twenty-nine-year-old Gordonstoun-educated actor. In January 1992, Jason Connery, son of Scotland's most famous export, Sean, sued the *Sun* over an article based on an interview with freelance journalist Lesley-Ann Jones. This accused him of being 'scared to death' at the thought of being conscripted to fight in the Gulf War. George hit Jones hard in cross-examination by raising the issue of her illegitimate child. His opponent Desmond Browne QC believes: 'It was definitely not how I would have done it.' George had told the court that the interview was 'twisted, distorted, added to and invented; and it attributed cowardice at the very moment the Gulf War was about to break out. How low can a journalist get?' He paused. 'I call Jason Connery.' The jury liked what they heard, taking thirty-five minutes to award £35,000 to the former television star of *Robin Hood*.

The eighteenth-century wit Lady Mary Montagu said of the 4th Marquess of Bristol that 'In the beginning, God created three different species: men, women and Herveys.' The 7th Marquess, Frederick William John Augustus Hervey – family motto 'I Shall Never Forget' – did not spring from any conventional celebrity mould. But Lord Bristol – John Jermyn to his friends – did his best to ensure that he would not easily be forgotten. His family certainly had a distinguished notoriety. The 3rd Marquess was an admiral and a well-known philanderer who reputedly seduced a dozen Portuguese nuns. John Jermyn's father, the 6th Marquess, had served three years in prison for his involvement in a Mayfair jewellery robbery.

Rather like fellow Old Harrovian the Marquess of Blandford, Bristol's drug-taking lifestyle and brushes with the law had brought continued notoriety to the family name over many painful years. Decadent tales of blasting fridge doors open with a shotgun to get champagne and of cocaine lined up along the elegant Georgian mantelpieces in the east wing of his Suffolk stately home were entertaining to some. Leaving his wife suspended on a cliff face in a Bentley, deportation from Australia and nine months spent in a Jersey jail in 1988 after cocaine was found in his helicopter did not prove as amusing. In July 1993, George was retained by solicitor Ian Burton to defend Bristol on three charges of supplying cocaine and heroin and two charges of possession.

Burton recalls that 'George lived the case completely, as he always did when I used him. If you'd been out for a good dinner till one o'clock in the morning, he'd still be talking about the case. I would barely be capable of putting one foot in front of the other and George would say: "What do you think about this point, what?" I would say: "George, give me a break, it's time to go to bed." And the following morning, he'd written the whole thing out, very late on his own. Nine o'clock in the morning, there he was. George – absolutely immaculate, striding down the corridor, on the button. Meanwhile Burton is there – puffy face, red eyes, dying. It was amazing. He had a fantastic constitution.'

The jury trial at Snaresbrook Crown Court centred on the evidence of Bruce Smith, Bristol's former business associate. After a disagreement, Smith had tipped off police that the Marquess kept drugs in a false-bottomed canister of Pledge and in a green leather pouch. Bristol's magnificent ancestral home, Ickworth House, was raided in October 1991. Both cocaine and heroin were found. Bristol pleaded guilty to possession but not guilty to supplying. In cross-examination, George got Smith to admit that he had threatened Bristol that he would tell the police about his drugs if the Marquess went ahead with a £134,000 civil action against him. Smith claimed that he had tipped off the police 'out of a sense of public duty'. In the witness box, he frequently changed his story about how many times he had seen the leather pouch containing the drugs.

Judge Owen Stable labelled Smith's attitude in contacting the police 'nauseating hypocrisy' and agreed with George that 'his evidence was riddled with contradictions'. The supplying charges were thrown out on the fifth day. As to possession, George emphasised that Bristol was 'a sad, emotionally deprived figure' who had been receiving in-patient treatment for ten weeks at the Charter Clinic in Chelsea. Deferring sentence until 6 December, Stable gave the Marquess five months to clean up his act: 'If you have relapsed, you will be facing an immediate sentence of ten months' imprisonment.' Bristol told reporters: 'I am extremely relieved and I now just want to get on with fighting this terrible addiction.' George had seen the effects of drugs on his client very vividly before the trial as Bristol disappeared intermittently from conferences to take a few lines of coke. Even during the trial, Bristol was snowballing (taking heroin and coke together) from a cigar pouch in the gents' lavatory. There seemed to be little hope of reform.

In November, Bristol discharged himself from the clinic and went to the South of France where he took drugs in earnest. Before sentence was passed in December, George put in a plea of mitigation. Sensitivity could be an important part of his armoury. In consultation, calling his client simply John, he had listened sympathetically, bringing a lot out from him in calm, patient conversation. It was used to present a melancholy picture: 'Lord Bristol was a man born to privilege but, despite his riches, he was emotionally deprived as a child. Until the age of thirteen, he was not allowed to dine with his parents at all and was compelled to wear on a daily basis long white gloves. It gives some idea of the lack of love he suffered from in childhood. He has spent something like £7 million in the last ten years and the remaining estate is worth £2 million. There have been tax problems and he is unemployable. You are dealing with a man of thirty-nine who has for the whole of his adult life been subject to the tragedy of persistent drug addiction. He has a personality that is inadequate and fragile. He has wrecked his life and inheritance. The damage done to himself is incalculable.'

Judge Stable was distinctly unimpressed. He told Bristol: 'You had a chance in July and you have thrown it away.' As promised, he was sentenced to ten months in prison. A little over five years later, on 10 January 1999, John Harvey, the 7th Marquess of Bristol, died of an Aids-related illness after a life dedicated to extravagant and dissolute self-destruction. He was forty-four. The 8th Marquess, John's twenty-one-year-old half-brother Lord Frederick Hervey, has found it difficult to accept that

Ickworth had to be sold completely to the National Trust by his immediate predecessor. 'It's hard to have such a grand title without the house,' he said in August 2001.

George's next client came from a more modest background. After suffering from similar addictive problems, he had overcome them. Elton John, not yet knighted for his services to music, took the *Sunday Mirror* to court over a December 1992 article headed: 'Elton's Diet of Death. Secret of Elton's Spitting Image'. The *Mirror* had obviously not learned from their rivals at the *Sun*. In December 1988, the *Sun* had paid Elton £1 million in damages and published a front-page apology, 'Sorry Elton', for false allegations about the singer and rent boys. In November 1993, Elton retained George to take on his friends at Mirror Group, whom he had represented or advised in nearly ten different cases over the previous three and a half years. Retaining him did not however force them to settle.

The focus of the 'unforgivably wounding article' was, as George told the jury, a Los Angeles party thrown by John Reid, the singer's manager. Guests in attendance included Jackie Collins and Billy Connolly. One person definitely not there was Elton John. He was at home, 2,000 miles away in Atlanta, Georgia. Tony Brenna, the *Sunday Mirror*'s LA reporter, had co-written the article with Paul Scott, the newspaper's show business editor. They had used a story supplied by a woman who gatecrashed the party. On her account, she saw Elton there chewing snacks and spitting them out into a napkin. Brenna and Scott relied on what she said. The article continued with a warning from a medical expert saying that the diet was potentially fatal. The implication, George said, was that the singer was killing himself with a diet that made him behave in 'a disgusting and shocking' way. By implying that he had lost his sixteen-year battle against bulimia nervosa, they were accusing him of being 'a hypocrite, a liar, a sham, a failure, an addict and on the road to death'.

In claiming exemplary damages on behalf of his client, George continued: 'It is said she somehow mistook somebody else for Elton John. It is a wicked invention for money which should have been checked out by Mr Brenna and Mirror Group Newspapers. And that is the extraordinarily flimsy basis on which the *Sunday Mirror* decided in a World Exclusive to assassinate Elton John's reputation.' Mirror Group accepted that the article was untrue, but denied it was defamatory.

Elton did not need George's costume instructions ('dress as soberly as you can') about how he should appear in court. He was an old pro at this game. From an extensive wardrobe, the brightest of his Versace ties added colour to the darkest of his Versace charcoal suits chosen to grace the witness box of Court 13. The only concession to superstar status were the black cowboy boots. Speaking of 'the most important thing I have done in my life', namely conquering his addiction to food, alcohol and drugs, Elton explained that, had he not had hospital treatment for his condition, he would probably be dead. 'My recovery means more to me than anything else because the time since I've been sober, clean and abstinent has been the best three years of my life,' he confessed to Mr Justice Drake and the jury. He also told them of his anger and dismay when his mother read the article to him over the phone.

George asked him about his addictions and membership of Alcoholics Anonymous, Narcotics Anonymous and Overeaters Anonymous. Elton explained that he had taken a year off work and attended 1,350 meetings of the three organisations with fellow sufferers to cure himself of his addictive conditions. In his closing speech, George employed a story that he had waited forty years to use. He had first read of it in a libel action fought before he came to the Bar and had talked about using it many times. It perfectly suited a claim for exemplary damages. He asked the jury to imagine a board meeting at Mirror Group Newspapers (MGN). 'The chairman says: "How much did libel cost us last year?" And the accountant gives the precise figure from the balance sheet. A look of gloom passes across the faces of the board of directors. Then the chairman says: "But by how much did our circulation and advertising revenue increase last year?" And the figure is duly trotted out by the accountant. A smile spreads across the board's faces. When you come to award exemplary damages, to punish the newspaper, you are entitled to wipe the smile off the board of directors of Mirror Group Newspapers.'

Elton was unduly nervous waiting for the result. His manager John Reid, wearing more mascara than any woman in court, sensed this and did his best to keep his spirits up. (Seven years later, the two men would be back in the same court building, fighting each other in a protracted battle over the split in the singer's multi-million-pound earnings.) Elton chatted about football in the corridor while George puffed away endlessly on Marlboro Lights. There was no need to worry. The jury had embraced the image of the board of directors. They found in his favour by a majority of 10–2, awarding the singer £75,000 in damages with a further £275,000 in exemplary damages for the newspaper's conduct. He announced that the money would go to an Aids charity. A case of champagne arrived at George's chambers with a note: 'Thanks, Love Elton'.

The case made legal history. In 1995, the Court of Appeal reduced the compensatory damages to £25,000 and the exemplary damages to £50,000. They also laid out recommendations for judges on future damages awards, giving them much greater powers to guide juries by specifying a range of possible awards. That decision effectively brought to an end the capacity of juries unreasonably to punish newspapers. The pendulum had swung back for good. One other by-product was the settlement of an outstanding libel action by the singer Michael Jackson against Mirror Group. George had been retained to cross-examine the Peter Pan of Pop about the extent of his plastic surgery. The Elton result encouraged MGN to settle and the much awaited prospect of George's blowtorch words melting Jackson's wax-like image never happened.

With celebrity status came celebrity parties. When hugged by Elton at one showbiz bash, George liked the smiles he got from those watching. The mantelpiece of his room in chambers came to groan with invitations from the great and the good – not to be removed for many months after the event. They proved his popularity. Now an automatic fixture on the guest list of newspapers, solicitors and *Private Eye* lunches, George's name also found its way on to many of the more exclusive soirées in the London social calendar. He became a regular at grand dinners with Conrad Black and Barbara Amiel and at the summer parties of Sir David Frost (also a client). Six months into Tony Blair's premiership, he was on his guest list at a Downing Street reception. George chatted with Tony and Richard Branson only weeks before acting for the Virgin King in the G-Tech lottery libel case. 'Great choice of lawyer. Couldn't do better!' joked Tony to Richard. George was thrilled at the endorsement and quipped that his real claim to fame was leading the Prime Minister when he was a junior barrister.

Another man who drew him into his social world was the cigar-chomping Hong Kong entrepreneur and socialite extraordinaire David Tang. He was a great friend of Diana and Fergie, introducing the Duchess of York to George when she needed legal advice. She consulted him on several matters. One was quite trivial. It involved the *Daily Mail* and the unfortunate Sir David English. A *Mail* journalist had followed Fergie on a trip to buy some videos. After rushing in to the shop to see if she had bought anything at all risqué, he left disappointed at her choice of action and adventure titles. She was furious at the harassment and called George. He spoke to English, asking him to keep his hounds at bay or face legal action. The editor duly obliged. Another call for help was somewhat more important. On a fine spring morning, he went to meet Fergie in a friend's house in Walton Street, Chelsea. The problem was money.

When her Coutts overdraft had reached telephone-number proportions and the pressure was on, Fergie thought the Queen might help. She wanted her Majesty's assistance in paying off debts, but was afraid to put the question. She asked George if he would go to Balmoral that summer to argue her case in person to the Queen and Prince Philip. George could not believe she was serious. 'She must be off her head,' he said incredulously. He had advised Prince Michael of Kent over reports of Coutts overdraft difficulties, but nothing like this. At Fergie's request, George contacted a nervous Prince Andrew, who gave qualified support to the idea. His desire to help was obvious. So too was his concern about parental reaction. The anxiety was well placed. When it was suggested through the usual channels that George go as Fergie's advocate to speak in front of the Queen, there was a swift and dusty answer. She was not amused. A trip to Scotland was out. As is customary in these circumstances, there was no fee for any of this advisory work.

Karen made herself available for social functions with George but rarely reciprocated with her invitations. Since she had long since given up legal practice, there was lots of free time for the retired barrister. Parties became the highlight of her life. New designer outfits and sparkling new jewellery changed with the season. She worked hard to get on with important people, establishing connections wherever possible, using her considerable charm and conversational skills. In July 1995, she 'lent her Belgravia flat to Fergie until neighbours complained that it was being used as an office'. Karen was 'given fourteen days to cease using the flat [as an office] or face eviction'. According to press reports, neighbours said she had 'never lived there' in the previous eleven months. She made friends with many of George's clients, including Norman Lamont, Richard Branson, Aidan Barclay and Marco Pierre White. There was frequent mention of the well-known names she was playing tennis with, having to dinner or involving in her charity ventures. Some of the attitudes rubbed off on George.

Following the publication of a league table in 1998 listing the top earners at the Bar, *The Times* headlined with 'Carman Slips

Out of the Million a Year Club'. They reported that in the previous year Chambers & Partners, a legal publisher, had listed barristers earning more than a million pounds annually. In 1997, this had included George. In 1998, his name was absent. George did not like the implication that he was on the way down. He phoned me up to ask what I thought he should do. Then he phoned up Clare Dyer, the *Guardian* legal correspondent, whom he knew quite well, to get her opinion. Finally he spoke to Frances Gibb, the *Times* legal editor, to make sure that any false impression was corrected. She was briefed on his recent victories and retainers. George asked me to supplement this with an anonymous letter to Gibb, detailing his latest triumphs, so I popped a brief catalogue in the post. He did not want solicitors getting the wrong impression. Gibb later told me that she was 'a little taken aback [by George's phone call], but very anxious to avoid any conflict'. She put the matter right with a quarter-page article the following week. Headed, 'Cruise Hires Bar's Top Gun', this detailed George's 1997/8 victories and forthcoming cases.

For many, celebrity still means Hollywood. And in the 1990s no couple was higher on the A-list than Tom Cruise and Nicole Kidman. When the *Sunday Express* magazine decided to recycle stories from the further reaches of American mainstream media under the headline 'Cruising for a Bruising', they were playing with fire. The article published on 5 October 1997 falsely alleged that the marriage of Hollywood's golden couple was a sham and a hypocritical cover for their homosexuality. It further suggested that Cruise was sterile and impotent. Once retained to act for both Tom and Nicole, George was delighted to have real stars for clients. 'He loved being involved with celebrities and was star-struck in a childlike and charming way,' reports Adrienne Page, his junior in the Cruise–Kidman case.

Lawyers and clients had several meetings in the months leading up to the trial, which was fixed for October 1998. These were attended by the couple's American lawyer Bert Fields. They met at a Regents Park flat and talked strategy at their house near the film set at Pinewood Studios between shoots on Kubrick's swansong *Eyes Wide Shut*. Tom and Nicole were the leading co-stars in this tale of jealousy and sexual obsession. George had to ask both of them many detailed, intimate questions. He was more than satisfied with their honesty. He particularly liked Tom, whom he thought natural, charming and good-humoured, while he found Nicole a little more diffident, although he was invited as her guest to watch *The Blue Room* in London's Donmar Warehouse. It was also apparent to George that they were genuinely very upset about the allegations. Nicole was particularly concerned about the prospect of going public with her medical history, relating to the couple's attempts to conceive and their decision to adopt two children, five-year-old Isabella and three-year-old Conor.

At the end of a meeting in December 1997, Tom brought out the couple's two children to meet George next to the Christmas tree. 'He was as sweet as grandpa,' recalls Adrienne Page, who watched him joke with them. After months of correspondence, compelling medical evidence was presented to the Express Group. Without any evidence to support the allegations, a complete climbdown was made at the eleventh hour. The Express Group agreed to apologise and pay damages. The agreed statement was as follows:

'In summary it was alleged that their marriage was a hypocritical sham, entered into as a mere business arrangement or on the orders of the Church of Scientology, or as a cover-up for the homosexuality of one or both of them and that Tom Cruise was impotent and sterile and that his public denial of this was untrue. The article further alleged that they had adopted two poor children, following some dictate of fashion in uptown Los Angeles. They married solely because they loved each other and their marriage is a close and happy one; they both love and are very devoted to their two young adopted children. They have brought proceedings to put an end once and for all to these highly offensive rumours which have been so hurtful to their married life together and to their role as parents.'

George's address to the court on 29 October 1998 confirmed the settlement with damages of £100,000 plus costs. The money was given to charity. Listening to him attentively, with shoulder-length swept-back hair, suntan and healthy stubble, was a diminutive, soberly suited Tom Cruise. Before the announcement, he had joked with those who came to court early as he did, saying: 'Which side do I stand on?' The press had not yet arrived to witness the unprecedented display as he signed autographs in Court 13 for what seemed like every black-gowned court usher in the building. News of his arrival at the Royal Courts of Justice had sent a clutch of these middle-aged ladies clattering along the marble-floored corridors to form a queue.

But there was no Nicole. George had pleaded with her to attend the brief hearing. So had Tom and Bert Fields. To no avail. Pressure of work with *The Blue Room*'s imminent run in New York was given as the public reason. Privately, she said she could not face the cameras. Her absence did not attract press comment at the time. George was astonished that she had passed up the opportunity for a public show of unity on the courtroom steps. The whole thing would have taken only an hour out of her schedule. Tom smiled for the cameras and issued a short thanks to the throng of reporters before disappearing into a silver Mercedes.

He sent a case of 1979 Château Pétrus to say thank you. Although a great consumer of wine, George was no connoisseur. He asked a couple of his chambers colleagues what it was like. The smiles said it all. He phoned up dealers to find out how much the wine cost. Several hundred pounds a bottle they told him. George gave me one. The rest of Cruise's Pétrus would remain unopened in the garage alongside Karen's discarded golf clubs and another unused gift from Charles Purle QC, given to George for defending his son William in May 1995. (Purle had thoughtfully sent him vintage claret from 1929, 1953 and 1971 – the years of his birth, call to the Bar and appointment as silk.)

George continued to advise Tom, who called him up on several matters. But within two years Cruise and Kidman had divorced. Another Hollywood fairy tale was shattered.

Drink and drugs came back to Court 13 in April 2000 when Marco Pierre White, the 'celebrity chef', sued two American newspapers over false allegations published in May 1998. The journalist Florence Fabricant had claimed that 'beneath Mr White's rock star veneer, including a well-publicised bout with drugs and alcohol, lies a very savvy and rich businessman'. George was retained to take on the *New York Times* and *International Herald Tribune*. He told the jury that Marco had been harassed after the articles were published in London as the newspapers had tried to 'dig up stories' about his lifestyle of 'sex, drugs and rock 'n' roll'. The newspapers, he said, had amended their defence shortly before trial, abandoning their assertion that the articles were true and instead taking the unusual line that they had caused no damage and had even 'enhanced' his reputation. 'He has suffered two years of anxiety, upset, irritation and no doubt secret anger at the high-handed, somewhat arrogant way he has been treated by them,' George concluded.

He admired Marco's tremendous achievement from humble beginnings. He thought the jury would think likewise. George talked of his 'glittering career' and said: 'He is probably the most outstanding and distinguished restaurateur and chef this country has produced in the last thirty-five years.' The chef talked eloquently in a cultured voice. He was a confident witness. When questioned, he spoke passionately, telling the jury that his Italian mother had died when he was six, and that thereafter he had been brought up by an alcoholic father on a Leeds council estate: 'I saw the destruction it [alcohol] caused in the family.' For that reason he 'rarely drank', confining himself to the occasional social glass of wine. As to drugs, 'My reputation might have been as a bad boy, but not as a drug-taker or an alcoholic. I have never taken drugs in my life. I object to drugs. It is something I don't approve of. I think it's very destructive.'

George took him through his career. As a dyslexic school drop-out, he had arrived in London at nineteen with £7.36 to his name and worked up to eighteen hours a day, sometimes seven days a week. He was trained by Albert Roux at Le Gavroche. Within ten years, he had won a Michelin star for the creations at Harvey's, his first restaurant in Wandsworth. He was now the only Englishman to hold three Michelin stars. In business, his success in a joint venture with Granada Group embraced part ownership of a string of restaurants including the Oak Room, Titanic, the Café Royal and the Mirabelle. In cross-examination, there was not very much that Geoffrey Robertson QC could say on behalf of the newspapers.

It did not take the jury long to return with a verdict in Marco's favour. They awarded him £75,000. He smiled and nodded to all twelve in appreciation. With cigarette in hand, Marco beamed for the cameras, standing on the courtroom steps in overcoat and trademark Homburg and made a brief statement: 'I am very happy at the outcome. Thank you very much. Have a nice day.' He strode off down the Strand with his Spanish fiancée Matilde Conejero at his side. They married the next day. It was Marco's third wedding. Michael Winner was the best man and George an honoured guest.

Dinner conversation was not George's thing. But he liked playing host at parties. In the 1990s, there were two of note. The first of these was quite a big bash in Lincoln's Inn in the summer of 1993. There were crowds of judges, barristers and solicitors. The Lord Chief Justice was there. Sue Lawley came. So did Ian Hislop. And Norman Lamont. 'Why was he there? Was he a client?' asked a guest. The questions came from Sir David English, by now chairman of Associated Newspapers, the majority shareholder of Euromoney Publications and therefore my ultimate boss. For a good hour, he engaged me in conversation, mostly about my father. I gave glib answers. George was gregarious, jumping from group to group with nervous smiles and quick introductions. He was in his element.

A more intimate affair was held at the Ritz. The hotel's Marie-Antoinette suite is, as it sounds, like an anteroom at Versailles – heavily gilded, wall-to-wall mirrors, high ceilings and crystal chandeliers. It was 7 p.m. on 31 July 1998. The timing was not good. Many people were away. 'Warmest thanks for inviting us to your glittering gathering of the great and the very great at the Ritz . . . unfortunately . . . Floreat Domus. Yours ever, Tom [Bingham]' – the Lord Chief was unable to make it. Frost could not come. Nor could Branson or Hislop. Imran and Jemima were busy and so was Elton. Mo Mowlam was invited and Jeffrey Archer too. They had to decline. George got worried about numbers.

But over champagne and canapés, an eclectic mix of familiar faces chattered away: various editors including Dominic Lawson, a genuflecting Sir Robin Day, Sue Cooke, Baroness (P. D.) James, Freddie Forsyth, Lord Alexander, Lord Williams, Lord Grabiner, Aidan Barclay and the usual host of judges and distinguished lawyers. On their way to Tuscany, Tony and Cherie popped in, looking smart but casual in lightweight suits. They worked the room in style. Within forty minutes, they were on their way to the airport. Conrad Black arrived too late. The expansive Canadian had wanted to lecture Blair on the euro. The party ended. George was delighted. Chatting with Robin and Freddie at Le Caprice finished the evening. Being a celebrity was fun.

In May 1999, George moved again. He wanted something clean and fresh. Another brand-new Wimbledon house was bought. Built by the same developers, it was of similar size to Marryat Road, with five bedrooms and five bathrooms. The atmosphere and décor were identically immaculate and impersonal with the addition of fitted speakers in most rooms. He disposed of some of his own antiques and kept all the new show-house furniture and ornaments instead. It was here that he gave a drinks party on Boxing Day 1999, five days after winning the Al-Fayed case against Hamilton. Unless it was related to work or he had been out drinking with them, George rarely invited anyone to his home. People in the house made him feel uncomfortable. It was too intimate and too intrusive. Boxing Day drinks became an exception.

Rachel and I went over with our three children. George wanted the children kept away from the guests in a separate room. Apart from a few of Karen's friends and family, these included one or two neighbours and Tom Crone, the News Group lawyer who lived near by. Anxious to prevent the breaking of any delicate glass ornaments on the tables or the marking of the white silk sofas, we stayed with the children. Some of the guests left. Seven of us sat down for a formal lunch: George, Karen, Rachel and myself, Karen's mother Audrey, Dr Veronica Verney and Martin Landau (both friends of Karen). Our two boys, five-year-old Charlie and three-year-old Tristan, stayed in the kitchen with the housekeeper. Baby Isobel went to sleep.

George's patience wore thin. He was abrupt with Karen – quite restrained, but I could tell that others were uncomfortable. She was used to it. Martin Landau left. Then the children got into trouble. They had been shut away for several hours by now and were frustrated. One of their Christmas presents was a painting set. The carpets were white; the result predictable. We cleaned up and left as soon as we could. Being a child in George's home was not much fun.

10

Sporting Heroes

Never read print, it spoils one's eye for the ball.

W. G. Grace

The solemn anonymity of wigs and gowns makes it hard to remember that barristers and judges are also human beings. For when leading sportsmen become involved in the legal process, their lawyers can become just as excited as anyone else. George, however, was never interested in sport as an adult, devoting no time to it either as player or as spectator. He would recognise the names of David Beckham or Mike Tyson, but most lesser sporting personalities would probably be unknown to him. When Jimmy Floyd Hasselbaink, the Chelsea striker, became his next-door neighbour in June 2000, George had no idea who he was.

Yet he enjoyed being involved with a number of distinguished sports stars. As celebrities in a different field, they delivered guaranteed publicity. Ignorance of a sport was never a handicap. Indeed, in at least one case, he used it to his advantage by placing himself directly on a par with non-sporting jurors. During a five-year period, between 1994 and 1999, George became involved in a number of libel cases and disciplinary hearings with sporting figures. Invariably, these brought out the cameras and photographers. It was good for business.

A telephone message left on a hot summer afternoon came from the London office of a small Italian law firm. George was curious. The call concerned Benetton Ford and their star Formula One driver Michael Schumacher, then leading the drivers' championship by twenty-one points over Damon Hill. They wanted help with two matters. The first concerned the Belgian

Grand Prix of 28 August 1994 and in particular Schumacher's disqualification. After the race, a skid-block under his car was found to be too thin, having worn down to 7.4mm. The minimum permitted was 9mm. After he had beaten Damon Hill to win the race, the stewards decided that he should be disqualified from the forty-ninth grand prix of his career. Schumacher wanted to appeal against the decision. The second even more serious issue concerned the German Grand Prix at Hockenheim. This had taken place on 31 July. Benetton faced a charge that they had intentionally and illegally interfered with the refuelling equipment on Schumacher's car before the race. A second Benetton car had been engulfed in flames.

Flavio Briatore, the Benetton chairman, hired George to defend the company and the driver. He was to fight the two charges before a hearing of the World Motor Sports Council of the International Automobile Federation (FIA) in Paris. The stakes were high. If convicted of the Hockenheim offence, Benetton faced the ultimate sanction of expulsion from that year's championship. And Schumacher would have been deprived of his first title.

The hearing was due to take place on Wednesday, 7 September 1994. The night before, George had met with the FIA president Max Mosley, son of the 1930s British Union of Fascists leader Sir Oswald Mosley and Diana Guinness (née Mitford). Also present was Bernie Ecclestone, son of a Suffolk trawler skipper and now the billionaire owner of Formula One. They discussed the charges over drinks at the Crillon, next to the FIA headquarters. The interplay between the two key players in Formula One was intriguing. George was especially impressed by Ecclestone's command and control of events. Next morning, Schumacher sat at his lawyer's side as he began to contest the charges. For two and a half hours, he fought to get the German driver's disqualification from the Belgian Grand Prix overturned. He failed. But he succeeded in getting the more important charge against Benetton dropped. The FIA accepted the three reasons put forward by George: (1) a junior employee had removed the filter without the knowledge of senior management; (2) the team had made no attempt to disguise the removal of the filter; (3) a rival team (Larousse) had received a document which appeared to give consent for the removal of their filter.

Mosley declared: 'Benetton were in error but they were honest. This was an honest mistake. Faced with the decision of whether there was any deliberate attempt to cheat, the World Council decided there was too much doubt, confusion and uncertainty.' The young German was delighted and thanked George warmly for his efforts. That year, he went on to win his first driver's championship.

Chris Brasher is not so much of a household name. But since 1981 the London Marathon, which the former Olympic gold medal winner founded and organised, has become an established event in the sporting calendar. In July 1990, Duncan Campbell, writing in the *New Statesman*, made a series of allegations of fraud and dishonesty against Brasher and his colleague John Disley, vice-chairman of the Sports Council. These were added to by a Channel 4 *Dispatches* programme broadcast in March 1991. Campbell again was the presenter. A report from the producers of the programme was sent to the Inland Revenue, the Fraud Squad and the Charities Commission. Four years later, they had found no evidence of any financial wrongdoing. George stepped in for Brasher and Disley. He settled the case on 23 May 1995 with £380,000 paid in damages. Total costs on both sides, paid by Channel 4, were estimated at nearly £2 million. Brasher and Disley toasted their victory with champagne. Believing that Channel 4 had settled under pressure from Lloyd's brokers so as to minimise costs, Campbell remarked sourly: 'The libel insurers should be drinking vinegar.'

Two weeks later, George was back in Court 13 for Mirror Group Newspapers, defending a libel action brought by Graeme Souness. As the former Scottish international and Liverpool star had proved on the field, he was a very tough opponent. The libel concerned a May 1993 article in the *People* newspaper which made false allegations about Souness's treatment of his first wife Danielle and in particular about the finances of their divorce settlement. In cross-examination, these were scrutinised in great detail, provoking some bitter clashes.

SOUNESS: 'The lawyers' letters I sent to my wife were to focus her mind.'

CARMAN: 'But torture can focus the mind, Mr Souness. If I punch you in the face, it might focus your mind . . .'

SOUNESS: 'Will you listen, please? You have a terrible habit of interrupting. The whole purpose was to focus her mind on the tenancy agreement.'

And some amusing one-liners:

CARMAN: 'Did you try to dominate and control your ex-wife?'

SOUNESS: 'A Bengal tiger could not do that to my ex-wife.'

Mr Justice Morland had to intervene on several occasions, reprimanding the two combatants for 'degenerating into argument'. George tried to get prejudicial evidence admitted about 'bungs' which Souness had allegedly received. Morland would not play ball. Meanwhile, Danielle was said to have received more than £1 million in cash and land. Her story of having to sell jewellery 'to make ends meet' did not cut much ice with the jury. Lord Williams QC, counsel for Souness, said that the *People* had demonstrated 'all the courage of a dead chicken and less decency than an elderly skunk' by not checking the facts with his client. Morland gave a clear direction to the jury about damages being 'fair and reasonable'. He was ignored. Souness was awarded £750,000. The photographs of Graeme kissing his second wife Karen in celebration filled the front pages. The damages were later reduced on appeal to £100,000. Souness had enjoyed the encounter and admired Mirror Group's counsel. Two years later, he even stopped his car in Fleet Street as George was walking along. He wanted to give him his best wishes for the Aitken case.

At the time, the result was the worst defeat in George's career in libel. He was 'looking much less sure-footed in front of goal', wrote one journalist. There were similar comments elsewhere. A year earlier, to the fury of Mr Justice Michael Davies, George had won an extraordinary award of £1.485 million in damages for John and Jean Walker against *Yachting World*. This concerned a defamatory article about their catamaran design. The case had been distinguished by caustic confrontation between judge and advocate. George's argument with Davies has since achieved legendary status at the libel Bar. The Walkers' award in July 1994 had been a high point. The Souness verdict came in the middle of a bad run defending newspapers. George lost several trials in succession. These included:

- Defending *Private Eye*, the *Independent* and HTV against Superintendent Gordon Angelsea over false allegations that he sexually assaulted boys in the Bryn Estyn children's home. Award – £375,000.
- The defence of the *Mail on Sunday* over similar false allegations of sexual abuse involving Indian boys by a former charity head, Joe Homan. Award – a more modest £30,000.
- Defending the *Sunday Express* against Peter Bottomley, who sued over an article headlined 'The Final Betrayal'. This concerned the former Tory minister sharing a platform with IRA leader Martin McGuinness. Award – £40,000.
- The defence of Mirror Group over three articles criticising Dr Anthony Percy, who was dubbed 'Dr Dolittle' over his alleged failure to attend a seriously injured patient. Award – £625,000.

In a little under two years, George had lost five big trials in a row. He hated losing and especially being seen to lose by the public at large. 'There was glee in our clerk's room, where he was regarded as a major rival,' comments James Price QC. Perhaps he was less 'sure-footed'. If self-doubt had started to creep into his thinking, it didn't show.

The summer of 1996 provided a first-class opportunity to put himself back on the winner's podium. A high-profile case arrived that was all about cricket, at least on the face of it. No fewer than three sporting heroes were involved: Ian Botham, Allan Lamb and Imran Khan. For thirteen days in Court 13, this was the libel trial that had everything: star quality, class, race, drugs, sex, humour, anger and a squad of expert witnesses that could easily make up a world-class test eleven. George was acting for Imran Khan, Jemima's husband and the son-in-law of Sir James Goldsmith. This former captain of Pakistan, who was now a politician and a fund-raiser for a Lahore cancer hospital, had been one of the best all-rounders the game had ever seen. He was being sued by England's greatest ever all-rounder and one-time captain Ian Botham and his successful England team mate Allan Lamb. Their counsel was George's familiar sparring partner, Charles Gray QC.

The claim was based on comments made by Imran in two interviews. The first was to *India Today* in June 1994, in which he alleged that the two England players had made racist criticisms of the Pakistani team tampering with the ball as an aid to reverse-swing bowling. He commented on their absence of an Oxbridge education: 'Class and upbringing make a difference.' Separately, he accused Botham of 'being proved a cheat' by picking the seam of a ball with his thumbnail. The second interview was given to the *Sun*, in which Imran claimed that he had copied ball-tampering methods from the England players: 'I started to copy them because it was seen as accepted practice. The biggest names in English cricket have all done it. And when I say big names, I mean as big as you can get.'

Monday, 15 July 1996. Immediately before the case opened, George went up to his opponent in the corridor. Gray recalls: 'He never really wanted to settle cases but he would often approach you at the start and put on his frightfully serious expression and say in a very grave tone: "Sad thing this, isn't it?" He'd say that in any case. You knew he was thinking – Brilliant, I'm looking forward to it. Then he'd say: "Charles, I wonder if we could have a word about this case, on a leading counsel to leading counsel basis." This was done in a theatrical way so that as many people as possible would hear him say it. What on earth did that mean? He said it in order to give this huge gravity to the conversation which usually involved his exploring what weaknesses you felt your case had. It was done for tactical reasons.'

Botham began his evidence. Answering questions from Gray, he told the jury that he 'was neither a racist nor a cheat'. He pointed out that the former West Indian captain Viv Richards was godfather to his elder son Liam and added: 'I didn't think class came into sport these days. My mother and father will be very upset.' The following afternoon, George started his cross-examination with a few short deliveries.

CARMAN: 'Are you a truthful man?'

BOTHAM: 'Yes, sir. I'd like to think so.'

CARMAN: 'Always?'

BOTHAM: 'As often as you can be. We are not all saints. I once broke a window at school. We all do something wrong.'

He was on the back foot. George moved on to two previous libel actions which Botham had started but not finished. Gray objected. The judge, Mr Justice French, allowed the questioning to proceed. The first action George focused on was against the *Mail on Sunday*.

CARMAN (reading from the newspaper article): . . . 'you "smoked marijuana in public in New Zealand, and had offered to supply marijuana to two girls in a hotel and encouraged them to have sex".'

BOTHAM: 'I think I was meant to have offered them cocaine. And no charges were ever proven.'

CARMAN: 'You held a press conference or spoke to a large group of journalists to say publicly that you had never taken marijuana or cocaine in your life. That was a lie, wasn't it?'

BOTHAM: 'No, because I had to take legal advice and when confronted by journalists you tend to freeze.'

CARMAN: 'It was a lie, wasn't it?'

BOTHAM: 'Yes, sir.'

CARMAN: '. . . Why did you drop the case against the *Mail on Sunday*?'

BOTHAM: 'We came to an agreement because I was not prepared to risk everything I had worked for in my life against a newspaper with a bottomless supply of money.'

George then turned to *News of the World* allegations published in 1986. These claimed that during a tour in the West Indies Botham had had sex with Miss Barbados, Lindy Field, and had taken drugs with her. Again, he had started proceedings only to abandon them.

CARMAN: 'This was a very serious matter. One of the worst allegations made against you?'

BOTHAM: 'Well, there have been many, but that was one of them, yes.'

CARMAN: 'That allegation, that as a married man you had sex with Miss Barbados and took hard drugs with her, clearly ranked as a serious allegation. It must have caused you great distress in your relationship with your wife?'

BOTHAM: 'Yes, sir. Until I spoke to her and told her it wasn't true.'

CARMAN: 'So why, in what ranked as a serious allegation, did you abandon proceedings?'

BOTHAM: 'Because I'd have been taking on a national newspaper. I am a man of limited means. To fight something like that you begin proceedings out of anger and frustration. Then you sit down with your wife and end up laughing at it and you think, why risk it?'

CARMAN: 'Is that really a truthful answer? The overwhelmingly truthful answer is that you did not proceed for the very simple reason that you knew the general substance of what they were saying was true, and would be proved in court?'

BOTHAM: 'No, sir.'

George kept a straight face in lighter moments.

CARMAN: 'Did you joke in a radio broadcast that Pakistan was the kind of place to send your mother-in-law for a month?'

BOTHAM: 'I think I said it was the kind of place to send your mother-in-law for two weeks.'

CARMAN: 'That was a disgracefully offensive observation to the people and cricketers of Pakistan, wasn't it?'

There was more:

CARMAN: 'Why did you not sue Ian Chappell [the former Australian captain] when he referred to you as "an habitual liar who attacked him with a glass"?'

BOTHAM: 'He's an Australian and I didn't take any notice.'

A heated exchange on ball-tampering followed.

CARMAN: 'Were you trying to alter the condition of the ball?'

BOTHAM: 'No way. Altering its shape.'

CARMAN: 'Oh for heaven's sake!'

BOTHAM: 'The shape, not the condition.'

CARMAN: 'Mr Botham, you should have been a casuist.'

MR JUSTICE FRENCH (intervening): 'Now that's a comment, Mr Carman.'

George apologised. The use of the word casuist – a person who solves moral problems with clever but false arguments – was most unlike him. It was not jury friendly. He was making mischief by recalling the language of moral philosophy debates at Balliol. At the end of three days of cross-examination, he produced a letter of apology from Imran. It had been suggested that this might be published in *The Times* in 1994.

CARMAN: 'In the interests of the great name of cricket and in the interests of avoiding some kind of blood battle in these courts and in the interests of good relations between the Pakistan cricketing team and the English team, did you not think that that was a fair and reasonable proposal which you might accept?'

BOTHAM: 'No, sir, I did not.'

CARMAN: 'Did you not think the letter was written in good faith?'
BOTHAM: 'No, sir, I do not. I think it's another smokescreen. I do
not think that is an apology, which is all I asked for.'

Botham later commented in his autobiography on this witness-
box experience: 'Carman's performance was a tour de force.
Snarling, sarcastic and bullying, it was obvious that he was
trying to provoke me into losing my temper. But I refused to
let him. No matter how hostile or cheap his attempts to drag
my name through the dirt became, I was determined not to lose
my cool ... I wouldn't employ Mr Carman. I don't like his
tactics. They are dirty rats'.'

An army of cricketers were called to give evidence on the rules
of cricket, in particular Law 42.5, which governs ball-tampering
and the raising of the seam. Their views were sought on whether
this constituted cheating. The England captain Mike Atherton
took a break from the Lord's Test match against Pakistan to agree
with George that it was 'part and parcel' of the game and that
he was 'pretty relaxed about it'. Derek Pringle, a former England
bowler, said that using a fingernail was 'fair play'. David Lloyd,
England coach, said that he did not accept the practice. David
Gower, a former England captain, said he had never seen Botham
tamper with the ball. John Emburey, the former England spinner,
told George: 'You appear to be more aware of reverse swing
than I am. I've been playing for twenty-three years and still
don't understand it.' The jury were probably left none the wiser.

Geoffrey Boycott, veteran of 108 Test matches, gave the best
copy. He started with his address.

BOYCOTT: '... WJ4 2JQ, Yorkshire ... that's in England.'
CARMAN: 'It hasn't declared a state of independence then?'
BOYCOTT (after a long answer): '... we like to think we're a bit
different.'

He agreed with Imran that the laws on ball-tampering should
be reviewed. George invited him to comment on Brian Close,

his former Yorkshire team mate, who had given evidence earlier that day.

BOYCOTT: 'I think he is a bitter and angry man trying to get his own back which is why he came here to cast aspersions on my honesty and integrity. I have been outspoken and critical of him. I said Yorkshire would be no good until he left the club. He left last year and they are doing well now.'

George asked him if the rules of the game were broken in other ways.

BOYCOTT: 'Yes, with Close as captain in certain games. He would instruct us to . . .'

Charles Gray then objected.

BOYCOTT: 'It's all right for him to criticise me and I can't reply for his untruthfulness.'
GRAY: 'Do be quiet, Mr Boycott.'
CARMAN: 'Do you agree or disagree with Mr Close's comment that it is the game first, team second and the player third?'
BOYCOTT: 'I don't understand his comment.'

Mr Justice French then asked him to leave the witness box. 'Pity,' muttered Boycott, as he returned to the commentary box at Lord's, where England were about to lose another Test. Before this comic interlude, Imran had already given his evidence. After hearing Botham's evidence and then Gower's, George advised him on the ninth day of the case to withdraw the specific allegation of cheating. Imran gave way: 'I respect them both. And if they say they were squeezing the ball, fine, they were squeezing the ball.' To many, this concession meant that he was staring defeat in the face. George played to Imran's low-key style in contrast to Botham's. The focus was shifted towards the idea that his comments to *India Today* may have been misreported. Imran made the following observation on class and race: 'I have never at any stage in my life believed in the class system. I don't look at people and decide what class they belong to. I believe in an egalitarian society. We are Pathans, a tribal group – we have always been egalitarian.'

George told the jury that the action was 'ill considered and ill founded' since breaches of the rules were 'part and parcel' of cricket. As the jury of seven men and five women went out, the smart money had piled up on Botham and Lamb. Four and a half hours later, a majority verdict was returned. Imran had won. 'My God, we've done it,' said Jemima Khan, hugging her husband. His opponents were genuinely 'astonished'. They had been confident of victory. As Botham recounts in his autobiography: 'We were stunned. And the feeling stayed with me for an awfully long time.' Sir Charles Gray is still puzzled by the verdict: 'The result remains a complete mystery to me and to most other people. The jury must have taken the view that sportsmen should not be litigating against one another in court.' An appeal was launched only to be abandoned in May 1999.

It was seen as another victory against the odds for George, and it provided Frances Gibb with the *Times* headline: 'Carman Scores at Cricket After Last Year's Soccer Own Goal'. The following day, even Bernard Levin joined in with a special piece. He called the cricketers 'three grown men behaving like spoilt children'. After confirming that 'Carman is the tops,' he went on to say: 'If parcels of boobies want to throw million of pounds into the nearest dustbin, Mr Carman has the right to use his gigantic talents to point out where the dustbins stand.'

Thrilled to be back on top, George received thanks all round from Imran, Jemima and Sir James Goldsmith. He turned his attention to his health – always low on the priority list. For some time, surgery to remove part of his colon had been required. He had deferred it until after the Botham–Khan case. The operation was judged successful, but pain persisted in his right buttock and eventually a scan was done. This revealed a small tumour on the sacrum bone, which runs across the pelvic region. Cancer was diagnosed. They had found a secondary growth. Debate raged as to the source of the primary, with the most likely candidate being the prostate. One thing was fixed in George's mind – he would continue working until he dropped. That was his life. The thought of retirement terrified him. There was nothing else he enjoyed, as he told one interviewer: 'Retirement actually scares me. I don't play golf. I don't play bridge. I don't garden, so what would be left?'

He approached medicine with the forensic skill of the court-room. Over the next few years, he met with many cancer experts. They were rigorously cross-examined on the salient points. In order to fight his illness as he fought everything else in his life, he wanted to understand his condition first. More and more advice led only to greater confusion. Eventually, he put his illness in a compartment of his mind, having treatment when necessary and forgetting about it when in court. He lived from quarter to quarter when tests would reveal his PSA level, a key indicator in the progress of prostate cancer. Until 1999, he was able to cope without much interference. Some observed that he was finding long cases more of a struggle. 'I began to notice that he had more off days,' says Hugh Tomlinson, who was aware of his condition.

Coping with cancer brought out some of the best in George. He talked about it in a detached manner as if discussing a client's case. It was very impressive to see him deal with the problem in this way. He consciously rejected any idea of chemotherapy, which might have prolonged life expectancy. Everyone would then know. And once they knew, he thought, the work would stop. He wanted what was left of his life to be spent on his feet in court. That was his happiness.

He lived his life as normal outside, telling lots of people about the diagnosis 'in confidence'. Knowledge that he was unwell became fairly widespread in the small world of libel practitioners. It had little impact on his flow of work. The only thought in solici-tors' minds was age. As a man in his late sixties and with plenty of money (they thought) would George retire soon and was the hunger still there? To the last question, the answer was definitely yes. Sometimes he would casually talk about 'packing it all in' and getting a part-time consultancy with a firm of solicitors at '£200,000–£300,000 a year and a car thrown in'. This was idle chatter. Although he did approach one or two City firms, this was never really going to happen. The last few years of practice were destined to provide some of his best performances.

In their first season after promotion, Middlesbrough were due to play Blackburn in a Premier League fixture at Ewood Park on 20 December 1996. They called it off, claiming that they were overwhelmed by injuries or suspensions with no fewer than twenty-four players affected. The club's unilateral decision to cancel the match made the Premier League decide on a three-point deduction and a £50,000 fine. Every point counted in the struggle to avoid relegation. George was called in for an appeal hearing before the Football Association (FA). After meeting with the Middlesbrough manager Bryan Robson, a former captain of Manchester United and England, he promised to do his best.

The sports writers had some fun. In the weeks leading up to the hearing on 26 March 1997, they excelled in their fund of hyperbole. The match of George 'the opponent from hell' against the FA chief executive Graham Kelly 'and his cronies' attracted most attention. 'One withering remark from Carman can turn a man to jelly and among the many unkind things said about Kelly is that he looks like blancmange to begin with,' wrote Jeff Powell. Another comment was that 'To send Kelly in against Carman, an intellectual giant, is cruelty to a simple man.' And finally, 'Kelly is in danger of serious brain damage.' The FA chief may well have read the copy. He did not bow to pressure. George put Middlesbrough's case for nearly six hours at a hearing in a hotel near Heathrow. The three-man commission listened patiently and then confirmed that the original punishment set by the Premier League was 'right and fair'. Two months later, Middlesbrough were relegated.

On any view, the trials of Bruce Grobbelaar assumed

Kafkaesque proportions. Between 1997 and 2001, Liverpool's former goalkeeper of twelve years faced two criminal trials, a libel trial and a lengthy Court of Appeal hearing. The issue was the same in each – match fixing, originally exposed in a *Sun* 'world exclusive' on 9 November 1994 headed 'Grobbelaar Took Bribes to Fix Games'. This claimed that he had taken £40,000 to lose a match against Newcastle on 21 November 1993. Liverpool had lost the game 3–0. Over the next few days, there were three more articles with further allegations. One of these included the suggestion that he had blown his chance of thousands more by accidentally making a sensational save in a game against Manchester United on 4 January 1994. 'I dived the wrong fucking way,' were Grobbelaar's recorded words to describe a goal he saved from Andy Cole. The result was 3–3. *Sun* journalists John Troup and Guy Patrick had worked on the story for months under the control of the paper's Northern editor Peter Sherlock. They were supported by the *Sun*'s new editor Stuart Higgins, who had recently succeeded Kelvin MacKenzie.

It was a classic sting. With the assistance of Grobbelaar's fellow Zimbabwean Chris Vincent – a former army comrade and business associate – the goalkeeper confessed to match fixing. His conversation with Vincent was caught on tape using a video camera hidden in a Southampton hotel room. He clearly admitted to attempting to influence the result in five Premiership games in 1993 and 1994. It emerged on tape that he had done this for money, paid for by a betting syndicate. Vincent talked about a new betting syndicate and a deal by which he would receive £100,000 for successfully throwing a game. Grobbelaar was cautious. Initially, he declined to accept £2,000 in cash which Vincent offered him as a retainer. Five days later, he returned to the same hotel and took the money. *Sun* reporters then caught up with him at the airport. After the articles were published, he sued for libel.

The police soon became interested. In July 1995, Grobbelaar was charged with conspiracy to accept money for fixing matches on behalf of a betting syndicate in the Far East. Wimbledon striker John Fashanu, goalkeeper Hans Segers and a Malaysian businessman, Richard Lim, faced similar charges. There were two trials at Winchester Crown Court, in January and August 1997. The first jury failed to agree. A retrial was ordered, at which all four defendants were acquitted. The libel action against the *Sun* eventually came to court in July 1999, nearly five years after the original article. In another thirteen-day case, held this time in Court 14, George was representing the newspaper. There were other well-known names in court. Richard Hartley QC was acting for Grobbelaar and the judge was the newly appointed Mr Justice Gray.

Hartley explained to the jury that Grobbelaar had been 'stringing Mr Vincent along. It was a high-risk strategy and did not have the result he was hoping for.' In accepting the money and talking about fixing matches, he intended to expose Vincent's corruption. But he was entrapped before he had the chance to report the matter to the police or the Football Association. 'I would never do anything to let my fans down,' Grobbelaar told the jury. The former team mate of Souness in his early years at Liverpool was no less forceful in giving evidence. A strong exchange followed when George got to his feet.

CARMAN: 'Mr Grobbelaar, the position is you are the kind of man who unfortunately will lie and lie and lie if it suits your own convenience – either to save your skin or to obtain money. You are sufficiently immoral that you were prepared in the High Court action to present a false case to the High Court and your opponents, the *Sun* newspaper. Only as a result of the police investigation and police evidence, you were forced to change your story which you did in a later amendment. Do you understand what I am saying?'

GROBBELAAR: 'That is your explanation.'

CARMAN: 'You are a man prepared to change your story to suit your circumstances when revealed against you?'

GROBBELAAR: 'Circumstances can change because you can forget a lot of things. I can't say what I did a year ago.'

The videotaped conversations with Vincent were playing to the jury. On these, Grobbelaar made various sexual observations about a woman in the bar whom he called 'fucking fresh', and he arranged a date in a telephone conversation with another woman called Wendy White whom he had met on a plane. He talked about his marriage: 'I've been in trouble with my wife. My missus has been shit. It's a separation job.' Mrs Debbie Grobbelaar sat in court, listening impassively. In a second tape recording, he talked at length about match fixing and how he wanted the money: 'Greenbacks, greenbacks, just put it in green-backs, and then I'm going to take the fucking full lot and go out of the country.' George put it to him that 'The whole of this tape is showing up the real Bruce Grobbelaar. It is the real Bruce Grobbelaar speaking.' Grobbelaar denied it, saying that he was merely stringing Vincent along and that 'Everything on the tape was a complete lie.'

George moved on to £20,000 in cash found in his sock drawer at home, suggesting that it had been given to him by John Fashanu. Grobbelaar claimed that this came from after-dinner speaking and a charity match in Turkey. He was unable to produce any receipts. He was then forced to admit to lying to *Sun* journalists and to his team mate Steve Nichol about visiting Richard Lim to pick up £1,500. 'You are a goalkeeper who keeps moving the goalposts of truth,' suggested George. 'That's simply not true,' came the response.

Debbie Grobbelaar was a good witness. She told the jury how Bruce was 'naive' and 'under the spell' of Vincent. The British Airways air hostess and mother of two had a pleasant manner and strong jury appeal. George was worried about the sympathy factor. She rubbished Vincent as a 'leech' in their marriage and confirmed the sock-drawer story under cross-examination. George did not press too hard.

CARMAN: 'What's the matter with banks?'
MRS GROBBELAAR: 'Footballers like to have cash.'

The distinguished BBC commentator Bob Wilson and the former England international Alan Ball gave evidence supporting Grobbelaar's claim that he never threw the games suggested by the *Sun*. They confirmed that the videos of the matches which had already been played to the jury showed no signs of cheating. George opened the defence case by introducing the phrase he had borrowed from *The Tempest* to describe Sonia Sutcliffe, 'Grobbelaar and the truth are strange bedfellows,' before referring to him as one 'who seeks to pollute the fountain of justice'. He asked the jury to put aside sympathy and prejudice: 'There are features in this case where you would not be human did you not have some sympathy for Mrs Grobbelaar.' He highlighted signposts to Grobbelaar's lies to the jury. Among these were lying to his wife, to his lawyers, to his team mates and to *Sun* journalists. He added that the footballer's account was 'a lethal cocktail of lies, half-truths and the occasional truth . . . Has this case not revealed a dark side to Bruce Grobbelaar, a degree of intrigue, fondness for deception and interest in money?'

The journalists and the former editor of the *Sun* Stuart Higgins gave evidence. Vincent did not. George believed that the video was compelling proof of Grobbelaar's corruption and suggested to the jury that he was 'not entitled to a penny'. The jury did not agree. They found unanimously in Grobbelaar's favour, awarding him £85,000. Debbie wept openly in court. *Sun* executives said that they were 'surprised at the jury's verdict' and would be appealing. George was shocked. He thought the decision perverse and in the face of the evidence. 'I think George hated being seen to lose high-profile cases and minded adverse jury decisions a lot' is the view of the judge, Sir Charles Gray.

The *Sun* lodged an appeal. The Court of Appeal hearing took place in December 2000 after George had retired. As ever, he was keen to know how it was going. It was still his case. He got me to call Richard Spearman QC from his private hospital room at the London Clinic in Harley Street. Spearman called back from a service station on the M4 and said that it was likely that the *Sun* would win the appeal. George was going to do it again. Judgment was reserved until January. In the event, the three Appeal Court judges, Lord Justice Simon Brown presiding, delivered a unanimous verdict on 18 January 2001 in favour of the *Sun*. They called the jury's decision 'an affront to justice'. It came a little over two weeks after George's death. The post-humous victory 'from beyond the grave' was widely reported. The *Sun* dedicated twelve pages to the result, including a double-page spread and a special cartoon devoted to their favourite barrister. Grobbelaar then took his case a stage further. At the time of writing, the decision of the House of Lords is expected some time in 2002.

Less than a month after acting for News Group in defending the *Sun* against Grobbelaar, George was heavily criticising their sister newspaper the *News of the World* in front of a Rugby Football Union (RFU) disciplinary hearing. He was acting for the former England rugby captain and world-beating number 8 Lawrence Dallaglio. The issue was drugs.

In May 1999, two undercover reporters calling themselves James Tunstall and Louise Wood met with Dallaglio at the London Hilton. They posed as potential sponsors for a four-year £1 million deal. Their meeting followed an approach to his agent by a third reporter, pretending to offer a lucrative sponsor-ship deal from Gillette. It was elaborate and sophisticated entrapment. Over several bottles of champagne, the twenty-seven-year-old Dallaglio told the reporters of his riotous behaviour with two other players at the presidential suite of the Inter-Continental Hotel in Johannesburg.

The honey trap unfolded when the newspaper then broke the story. On Sunday 23 May 1999, the *News of the World* alleged that Dallaglio had dealt in drugs and taken cocaine and ecstasy during a 1997 British Lions tour of South Africa. The day after the article was published, Dallaglio resigned as England captain and pulled out of a tour of Australia. Twenty-four hours later, he told a press conference that he had not dealt in or taken drugs on the 1997 tour. He conceded that he had experimented with drugs as a young man, but said that he had been set up by the newspaper and had lied to the reporters. The RFU appointed a three-man panel to examine the allegations.

There were two issues: drug taking and bringing the game into disrepute. A detailed ten-week probe, conducted under the chairmanship of a High Court judge, Sir John Kay, featured exhaustive enquiries and interviews, some with Dallaglio's playing peers. It resulted in charges against him on both of the issues examined. Lawrence met George in a hotel and later came to see him in Wimbledon. The number of sandwiches consumed by England's number 8 was the source of much amusement. They discussed the forthcoming tribunal, to be chaired by Sir Oliver Popplewell, recently retired from the High Court and very familiar to George as the judge in the Aitken libel case. Two days before the hearing, George pulled off a significant coup for his client. In a behind-the-scenes deal, he managed to persuade the prosecutor, Richard Lissack QC, to drop the more serious charge of drug taking. This was achieved in the face of much opposition.

Left with only the vaguer charge of bringing the game into disrepute, Lawrence and George attended the hearing held on 25 August in seminar room two of the West Stand at Twickenham. Popplewell recalls: 'I had two chaps with me who knew a lot about rugger [John Spencer and Chris Tuffley], which was very helpful. Once they'd dropped the drugs charge against Dallaglio, it was much easier. He pleaded guilty to the other charge and then George started introducing human rights. It might have impressed my colleagues, but it didn't impress me. We really wanted to know about his finances, since we couldn't ban him for bringing the game into disrepute.' Dallaglio ended up with a verbal slap across the wrists and a fine of £15,000. He was also ordered to pay £10,000 in costs. Crucially, this meant he would be in action for the Rugby World Cup that was just about to begin. Lawrence gave George some tickets to say thank you. The following month, I took Charlie and Tristan to watch the international at Twickenham. They loved it. In a great match, full of tries, England beat Italy 67–7. George had passed up on the opportunity to come with us. He preferred to stay at home.

11

The Simple Sword of Truth

That a lie which is all a lie may be met and fought with outright,
But a lie which is part a truth is a harder matter to fight.
                    Alfred, Lord Tennyson, 'The Grandmother'

'We'd better get Carman, before Aitken does,' was Alan Rusbridger's automatic response to the news that the former Cabinet minister was suing the *Guardian* for libel. It was April 1995. After only a few months in the editor's chair, Rusbridger acted decisively. He secured the man he thought would give his newspaper the best fighting chance. And by the time George stepped into the Royal Courts of Justice, two years later, to do battle against Jonathan Aitken's simple sword of truth and trusty shield of fair play, he had had considerable experience, not only in winning prominent libel cases, but also in dealing with Conservative politicians.

Apart from savaging Edwina Currie and indirectly forcing David Mellor's resignation from the Cabinet, he had fought and won separate libel actions for Phillip Oppenheim and Norman Tebbit. Both victories were against David Bookbinder, Labour leader of Derbyshire County Council. In January 1993, he was retained by the *New Statesman* to take on the Prime Minister, John Major, when he sued over an article concerning a former Downing Street chef, Clare Latimer. He pulled out when the *Observer* incorrectly stated on its front page that he had offered 'strategic help and advice, free of charge'. The newspaper printed an apology to George. Major's action was settled shortly afterwards. In April 1994, George successfully represented Margaret Thatcher in a copyright dispute over reproduction of her memoirs without permission by a newspaper, winning very substantial compensation on her behalf.

Until the 1999 disclosure of his Cambridge undergraduate experiences in a *Times* interview, Michael Portillo had retained George to act against any newspaper that made accusations about his past homosexuality. And when his fervently hetero-sexual predecessor as the MP for Kensington and Chelsea, Alan Clark, wanted to sue over stories following his relationships with the Harkness coven – the South African judge's wife and two daughters whom he had seduced – George told him, 'Don't be a bloody fool.'

Other senior Tories, when seeking advice on litigation, left consultations with George reassured by his sanguine conclusion – don't bother. This message was delivered twice to Michael Heseltine, first when he approached him in 1996 on behalf of the entire Conservative Cabinet following the Scott report on the arms-to-Iraq scandal, and later concerning a defamatory remark made by a broadsheet newspaper. Norman Lamont had got a raw deal from the press over Threshergate and in other areas of his personal life. In seeing George on several occasions, the former Chancellor was persuaded each time not to take things further. But the strongest warning was reserved for the unfortunate David Ashby MP, who after sharing a bed with a male friend on holiday in France, 'to save money', wanted to sue the *Sunday Times* over their version of events. Ashby decided to fight his corner, using different counsel. The consequences were disastrous.

Leading the *Guardian* defence against Aitken put all of this very much in the shade. In this case the stakes were so high that, if no settlement was reached, defeat for either side could have the most dramatic consequences, particularly for the Rt Hon. Jonathan Aitken. Born on 30 August 1942, the son of the Conservative MP for Bury St Edmunds, Sir William Travern Aitken, and Penelope, Lady Aitken, daughter of Lord Rugby, the young Jonathan had a privileged upbringing at Eton and Oxford. He read law at Christ Church, failing in three attempts to become president of the Union. At nineteen, he became speechwriter to Macmillan's Chancellor Selwyn Lloyd, who in turn became his mentor.

Jonathan's great-uncle was Max Aitken, better known as Lord Beaverbrook – Canadian multi-millionaire, Fleet Street's most creative and dynamic press baron (immortalised as Lord Copper in Evelyn Waugh's *Scoop*) and wartime Cabinet minister. For many years, he was the second most powerful man in Britain and, in his own view, a potential Prime Minister. Like many old men with money, he played games with his will. From 1960 to 1964, Jonathan was a frequent visitor at his country retreat, Cherkley. They got on well. One day, Beaverbrook praised Jonathan to the detriment of his children and grandchildren, before concluding: 'I'm going to do the greatest thing I can for you – the greatest thing of all. I'm not going to leave you any money.'

After Oxford, Aitken demonstrated strong journalistic ability, prospering as a writer and broadcaster, before becoming Conservative MP for Thanet East (later Thanet South) in 1974. His charm with women was legendary. In 1979, he had a relationship with the Prime Minister's daughter, Carol Thatcher. This backfired, as he became 'the man who made Carol cry' when he chose instead to marry the Yugoslav-born Lolicia Azucki, a wealthy Swiss-based economist.

He failed to achieve ministerial office under Margaret Thatcher, remaining on the backbenches for eighteen years. The compensation was success in business. He made money as managing director of Slater Walker Middle East and became friendly with Prince Mohammed bin Fahd, son of the Saudi king, and with his business manager Said Ayas, who introduced him to Lolicia. He set up his own merchant bank, Aitken Hulme, funded by Arabs, and he negotiated the purchase, for Middle Eastern clients, of the Inglewood Heath Hydro in Berkshire. Again with £2.1 million of Arab money, he bought a majority stake in TV-am in 1981. If his backers had been disclosed at the time, the IBA would have blocked the purchase. When the truth about the source of his finance emerged seven years later, as a result of an *Observer* exposé, he immediately resigned as a director. TV-am presenter Anna Ford proceeded to throw a glass of wine over him at a party when she learned what had happened.

In 1979, Aitken was appointed part-time managing director of Prince Mohammed's company Al-Bilad UK and later became a non-executive director, between 1988 and 1990, of an arms manufacturer called BMARC. At this time, Saudi Arabia was importing billions of pounds' worth of British weapon and arms technology. After the 1992 election, John Major appointed him Minister of State for Defence Procurement, a position which seemed designed to exploit his Middle Eastern knowledge and contacts: 'The best Minister I've ever had,' said Malcolm Rifkind, then Defence Secretary. On 21 July 1994, Aitken was promoted again, to become Chief Secretary to the Treasury, thereby joining the Cabinet.

Three months later, the *Guardian* published an article, on 27 October 1994, concerning Aitken's stay at the Ritz Hotel in Paris between 17 and 19 September the previous year. The events of this weekend would later become the central focus of the libel case. The *Guardian* article raised the issue of Aitken's hotel bill of 8,010.90 French francs, which had been clearly marked: 'Débiteur A/C M. Ayas #626/7.' Why had Said Ayas paid the hotel bill of the Minister of State for Defence Procurement? This question had been at the heart of correspondence between the then editor of the *Guardian*, Peter Preston, and Jonathan Aitken over much of the previous year, with the latter repeatedly denying that he had breached Section 126 of the House of Commons Questions of Procedures for Ministers.

Preston had been alerted to the payment in October 1993 by the owner of the Ritz Hotel, Mohamed Al-Fayed, who furnished him with a copy of the bill. To protect his source, Preston obtained another copy directly from the Ritz on 21 November 1993, by sending a 'cod fax'. This was a request, forged on House of Commons notepaper, but with *Guardian* telephone and fax numbers, purporting to come from Jonathan Aitken's private secretary. Preston continued to exchange letters with Aitken, without disclosing his source to be Al-Fayed.

A very convoluted story emerged. Aitken asserted that his wife Lolicia had paid the bill after he had left the hotel on Sunday afternoon. He sought to support this by using a letter sent to him by Frank Klein, president of the Ritz Hotel. This apparently confirmed the new line that Lolicia had settled the bill in cash since it stated that 'a brunette lady of European aspect speaking French had paid the cash sum of 4,257 francs to the account of M. Ayas'. The 'brunette lady' had in fact been Manon Vidal, a private assistant to Prince Mohammed and Said Ayas.

Critically, before sending a copy of Klein's letter to Preston, Aitken removed the words that appeared after 'paid the cash sum' because it showed a different amount to his own bill. In the meantime, Al-Fayed had independently given Preston a copy of the complete letter. The sharp editing was obvious. To cover his position further, Aitken made up the difference of 3,753.90 francs between his original bill (FF 8,010.90) and the amount paid (FF 4,257) by sending a cheque for the sterling equivalent, £426.88, to Abdul Rahman, Ayas's nephew, together with a letter apologising for the 'mix-up'. Ayas further corroborated the lie by writing a sham letter to Aitken on 23 February 1994 saying that he had seen Lolicia paying the bill.

Preston invited the Cabinet Secretary Sir Robin Butler to have another look into the affair. Butler had already discussed the Ritz bill with Aitken and cleared him of impropriety. The request was refused. On 10 May 1994, the first *Guardian* article on the subject appeared, headed 'The Minister, the Mandarin, the Premier and the Editor'. Aitken dismissed the newspaper's reproduction of the Ritz bill and took no action.

On 19 September, Al-Fayed lost a case in the European Court of Human Rights where he was trying to overturn a report by the Department of Trade and Industry (DTI) into the Harrods takeover. This was the catalyst for Al-Fayed's raging against the

Conservative government, whom he blamed for many of his problems. He decided to make public his allegations concerning four Conservative ministers: Michael Howard, Neil Hamilton, Tim Smith and Jonathan Aitken. Preston was to be his mouthpiece as the *Guardian* started to reveal the story of cash payments in brown envelopes paid to Smith and Hamilton. On 20 October, Smith resigned, to be followed within a week by Hamilton. The *Guardian* article of 27 October published the Klein letter in full alongside the Ritz bill.

In the event, Aitken survived that round. The letter became overshadowed by Preston's use of the cod fax. Conservative MPs smelt blood. The *Guardian* editor resigned from the Press Complaints Commission and, after twenty years in charge, was booted upstairs to become editor-in-chief, leaving the chair to Rusbridger. The *Guardian* got into bed with Granada Television to launch a combined assault on Aitken across a broad front. On 9 April 1995, the newspaper splashed with 'Aitken "Tried to Arrange Girls" for Saudi Friends'. The headline heralded Granada's *World in Action* programme, to be broadcast that evening, called *Jonathan of Arabia*. Between them, the *Guardian* and Granada catalogued corrupt, dishonest and immoral behaviour by Aitken over many years of business dealings with Arabs. This was total war.

Aitken counter-attacked with a well-timed press conference from Conservative Central Office, three hours before the broadcast, in which – reading from the autocue – he adopted the mantle and terminology of the crusading knight (the voice of Britain) from the old Beaverbrook *Express* masthead: 'If it falls to me to start a fight to cut out the cancer of bent and twisted journalism in our country with the simple sword of truth and the trusty shield of traditional British fair play, so be it. I am ready for the fight!'

He remained in the Cabinet for a further three months, before resigning voluntarily on 5 July 1995 to spend more time with his lawyers. For much of the next two years, he involved himself in the detail of his case. Aitken told me about his pre-trial strategy: 'In a big drama like a law case, thorough preparation is a good idea. I went to watch George to get a feel for his style of cross-examination. Most QCs have a sort of handwriting and, if you are familiar with it, you can see a little bit quicker where they're coming from. But when I saw George, there were few surprises. As I expected, he was tremendously thorough. The only thing I learned is that he would go round and round a point like an obsessive yachtsman circling a buoy or a rock, in the hope of catching one more fish.'

Aitken had been watching George's defence of a libel action for Mirror Group. *The Times* reported these courtroom visits under the headline 'Mugging Up'. During this case, George questioned the former Health Secretary Virginia Bottomley. The plaintiff, Dr Percy, won and was awarded £625,000 damages. Percy's counsel was Charles Gray QC, whom Aitken had decided to retain for his libel fight. Virginia's husband, Peter Bottomley MP, also encountered George in cross-examination when suing the *Sunday Express* in 1995. Even though he won, with a damages award of £40,000, he advised Jonathan not to proceed unless he was confident there was no significant flaw in his case. The advice was ignored.

George had defended Aitken's younger sister Maria. The actress's 1988 case had allowed Aitken to get to know him a bit, as he recalls: 'She was in an incredibly unlucky bind. George was needed to cut through a knot which no one else had been able to. Maria and her partner took drugs in a mild sort of way. A series of envelopes, addressed in false names, were sent from Peru to my sister's home address. Each contained a tiny amount of cocaine, very much for personal consumption. Post Office machines detected these envelopes as they came in. She was arrested, prosecuted and heavily fined, pleading guilty.'

Maria's barrister pointed out that it was not certain that all the envelopes had yet arrived. Aitken continues: 'The Customs were very angry that Maria was not imprisoned. Forty-eight hours later, she was rearrested on the grounds that more envelopes had arrived. It was a rather over-zealous or over-vindictive move. In dialogue with her solicitor, Sir David Napley, the Customs would not give way. Maria was on legal aid, but George said he'd love to do it, believing it to be a monstrous injustice. The deal was done before a court hearing as the Customs caved in. George presided eloquently over the withdrawal.' Afterwards, says Aitken, 'we had a very good lunch at 90 Park Lane [at Chez Nico], part of the Grosvenor House Hotel. Very good in the sense that it went on until four o'clock in the afternoon. I hugely enjoyed his company. I thought he was a bit flash, a bit of a peacock, but he had a lot of depth. Prime Ministers sometimes divide ministers into bookies and bishops. He was the bookie type rather than the bishop.'

In the two years that followed Aitken's defiant 'sword and shield' rhetoric, a wealth of solicitors' correspondence made no progress towards settlement. A Wilton's lunch between Rusbridger and Lord Saatchi, acting on Aitken's behalf, came to nothing. Events quickened in the weeks before the case. Like Thorpe just before his trial, Aitken, an Old Etonian politician, fought to keep his parliamentary seat at a General Election. And like Thorpe, he lost. Mirroring the fate of so many of his fellow Tories in 1997, a healthy majority of 11,500 turned into a Labour gain by a margin of 2,878 votes, a swing of 15 per cent. A second, more significant result as far as his case was concerned was the decision by Mr Justice Popplewell, the trial judge, that he would try it without a jury. George had argued strongly against Charles Gray's application. But as Popplewell told me: 'The poor old *Guardian*, they cannot get over it. They still think it was my doing simply to benefit Aitken. And I don't think anything will ever shift them from that view. As the thing went on, the papers become mountainous. One of the grounds not to have a jury trial is if the volume of paper is so great that they're really not going to get hold of it. By the time it got to trial, there were ring binders coming out of our ears. Because there were so many allegations, it grew like topsy.' Aitken's witness statement alone, says Popplewell, was 280 pages. 'There was discretion that, if the volume of paper was too great, it didn't automatically mean that it should be a jury trial. So I took the view that it ought to be tried by judge alone.' Gray says of his application to Popplewell that he was 'surprised we won and just thought it was worth a try. I didn't expect him to agree.'

George took the decision to the Court of Appeal. Presiding was the Lord Chief Justice, Tom Bingham, who, like George, had read law at Balliol, although they were not exact contemporaries.

CARMAN: 'The ordinary layman and the media will say: "This is a bit of a whitewash, it should be left to a jury." There will be criticism which will diminish public confidence in the administration of justice.'
BINGHAM: 'I do not believe public perception will be a reliable guide.'

The Court of Appeal upheld Popplewell's decision. There was horror and dismay at the *Guardian*. They believed that a jury trial would have given them a much better chance of winning. Gray also thought 'it was more likely than not' that Aitken would win. Everything now depended upon Sir Oliver Popplewell, formerly of Charterhouse and Queens' College, Cambridge, who had just retired as president of the MCC, the culmination of a lifelong passion for cricket. An uncontroversial judge and regarded as a safe pair of hands, he had authored reports on the Bradford and Heysel football stadium tragedies. Like Rusbridger, he is a Garrick member. In Aitken's view, he was 'really everything a judge should be: old fashioned, crusty, slightly twinkly, very firm and a very shrewd cookie'. The *Guardian* took a gloomier view, believing that his establishment background and natural conservatism would make him much more inclined to favour Aitken than a jury. George viewed him as very fair and was not as concerned as his clients about the perceived lack of impartiality. The clients' anxiety is further confirmed by the book of the trial, *The Liar*, written by three *Guardian* journalists. This caricatures the judge as an establishment figure 'right down to his striped pyjamas'.

Popplewell dismisses their comments: 'It was marvellous journalism and quite funny. I took it with a great pinch of salt. The complaint was that this judge coming from a public school background would identify with Aitken and would be overwhelmed by him where his honour was at stake. Quite incorrect.' Privately, George was also less bothered than the newspaper about the absence of a jury and was happy to deal with Popplewell alone. Aitken was similarly unmoved by the decision: 'I didn't think it was enormously important, although I know Charles Gray did. I was happy to take my chances with an English jury. The advantage of having the judge alone meant that it would cut down the time massively and reduce the expense. It would have taken another three weeks with a jury because of explanation.' Gray's view echoes that of the *Guardian*: 'Getting rid of the jury was a very key point for two reasons. First, it was generally thought the judge would be more sympathetic to Aitken. I think that's probably true because juries don't like politicians. Secondly, I think George was much more at home cross-examining to a jury than cross-examining in a completely different way as you do with judge alone.'

At the start, George was very excited and more than unusually uptight. Although he never discussed this with his clients, he was concerned about his stamina and health. Some of the cancer treatment made him tired, and this was aggravated by the additional strain of such a demanding case. More than anything, he was worried by the prospect of losing. A well-publicised defeat might have signalled the beginning of the end in terms of work. At sixty-seven, he was very conscious that some were already saying that he was past his best and slower around the court than he used to be. He hated the idea of giving up practice. As he saw it, that was his *raison d'être*.

One indication of his state of mind was how he was at home.

By coincidence, Rachel and I had flown back from Hong Kong, having arranged many weeks before to stay with George. The purpose of our trip was to spend a few days looking for a house to buy in London. Our two young children, Charlie and Tristan, then aged three and a half and eighteen months, flew with us. We met up with Matthew, my eldest son, who lives in Hertfordshire. George's Wimbledon house, where he lived alone, had more than enough room to accommodate a visiting family. We arrived on Friday 6 June, the first day he was on his feet in court. On the Saturday, anxiety about the case soon turned to impatience with the children. He became irritated by their noise, so we tried to keep them in the conservatory. He asked us to leave. We went to stay with friends. Rachel and I watched a couple of days of Aitken's cross-examination the following week. It had been the same story the previous Christmas when arriving with the children from Hong Kong. George had become angry when I arranged for a photographer to visit the house to take portraits of the children. George the lawyer found it difficult to be George the family man. He could not show that he cared in a conventional way. Our children never stayed at his house again.

Aitken's counsel, Charles Gray (Sir Charles Grayman in *Private Eye*-speak) opened the case on Wednesday 4 June 1997. This mild and mellifluous Wykehamist epitomised the gentleman barrister, with the diction and demeanour of Dennis Price in *Kind Hearts and Coronets*. Aitken related to his style: 'They are all racehorses at that level. After discussing it with my solicitor Richard Sykes, I chose Gray in preference to Patrick Milmo, the other silk I had retained, because he seemed slightly younger and slightly more suitable for the course. His quieter style was more appropriate to my case.' George was by now very familiar with his skilled opponent.

Gray stood up in Court 10 to tell the judge that the *Guardian* and Granada Television had 'butchered' Aitken's 'personal, political and professional reputation'. He outlined the six distinct allegations which, between them, they had made about him:

1. He had stayed at the Ritz Hotel in Paris to attend a clandestine business meeting and had lied about his bill;
2. He was in the pocket of the Saudi Royal family and financially dependent on them;
3. He had offered to help Astra Holdings sell arms to Iran and Iraq;
4. He knew that BMARC, of which he had been a director, sold a cannon to Iraq;
5. He did business with Future Management Services, an arms company;
6. He pimped for Arabs by asking Jo Lambert and Robin Kirk, two former employees of Inglewood Health Hydro, to procure girls.

The following day, the former Cabinet minister went into the witness box. He was to remain there for eight full days of questioning. Aitken recalls: 'I had put a lot of effort into preparing. I needed to have crisp answers.' He sells himself short. To those watching, his evidence appeared to be wonderfully controlled, polished, fluent, convincing and confident – all the things you would expect from a highly intelligent, professional politician. He had mastered the detail of his own case to perfection. He started by giving his reaction to the *Guardian* headline of 9 April about arranging girls for Arabs: 'I felt pole-axed by this headline and the ensuing story. It was almost the equivalent of having a heart attack in terms of the shock and pain I felt on reading it . . . it was just such a sordid story and I remember burying my head in my hands and saying really to no one in particular: "The *Guardian* have now said on their front page that I am a pimp."' His son asked: 'What is a pimp, Daddy?'

This last comment caught the following day's headlines, alongside posed photographs of Jonathan, Lolicia and their three children. After reading the *Guardian* article, he made a decision, described to the court in the words of Scott Fitzgerald: 'I said to myself "in the long dark night of the soul", I have got to fight these lies and I will do so.' He also gave his reaction to the *World in Action* programme: 'This was, in my view, character assassination by television, not current affairs television. There was no attempt at balance or fairness or objectivity. It was "get Aitken" time.'

George was very fortunate to have an outstanding junior silk, James Price QC, who was extremely capable in arguing all the points of law. This left him free to concentrate on advocacy. It was a high-risk case to fight and he knew that, despite all the rhetoric, there was not a great deal of ammunition in terms of admissible evidence, apart from the Ritz. This would be the focus of his strategy from the outset. He moved slowly up to the wicket, knowing that this was going to be a long innings. His first question went straight to the heart of the matter.

CARMAN: 'If my Lord has eventually to make the melancholy decision that you have lied to the Cabinet Secretary while a Cabinet minister, that you have lied to the Prime Minister while a Cabinet minister; and that you have lied to this court on all occasions to do with your stay at the Ritz, if that were to be so, you would accept that such a series of lies would prove you totally unfit for public office?'

AITKEN: 'I don't accept any of these melodramatic, hypothetical allegations you are putting to me. But if his Lordship were to make those dramatic judgments it would obviously be a shattering blow for me.'

CARMAN: 'It would butcher your reputation.'

AITKEN: 'My reputation has already been butchered.'

CARMAN: 'It would butcher it again.'

AITKEN: 'It would.'

The following day, Aitken admitted 'subterfuge' over the Ritz in a letter of response to questions from the Cabinet Secretary, Sir Robin Butler, and tried a smokescreen tactic by saying the whole thing may have been a 'set-up'. The real fireworks began on Tuesday 10 June as George challenged Aitken's account of the Ritz weekend of September 1993 and his claim that his wife had paid his hotel bill in cash on the Sunday afternoon after he had left.

CARMAN: 'When you add up that catalogue of improbability, do you not realise how scandalous, incredible and preposterous your story is?'

AITKEN: 'I don't realise any such thing. I flatly reject these flamboyant allegations. There are good, honest explanations for all the points put to me.'

George dealt with his 'web of lies', in which 'improbability was heaped on improbability' (a phrase recycled from the Taylforth case). He highlighted thirteen points where Aitken's evidence was 'tainted with improbability'. These included a letter to Sir Robin Butler, in which he had 'covered his tracks', and his 'conspiratorial agreement' with Said Ayas over the Ritz. George told the court that it was Manon Vidal, private assistant to Prince Mohammed and a French-speaking brunette, who had paid the bill. While crystal clear on his own movements, Aitken became vague about his wife.

AITKEN: 'My wife has been unable to recall the precise details of what did happen – all that Carry on Arabia scene around the Ritz cashier desk on that afternoon.'

CARMAN: 'You say your wife paid it.'

AITKEN: 'I can't even now grip it – exactly who did what where – I wasn't there.'

As he launched into the fourth and fifth days of cross-examination, George thought he was making some headway. He was also buoyed up by the prospect of new enquiries being made by the *Guardian* and by Geraldine Proudler, his instructing solicitor at Olswang. These were promising to yield results, but not yet. It is clear in reading subsequent accounts that his mood remained much more confident during cross-examination at this time than that of many in the defence team, where pessimism prevailed. This was largely a result of the judge's ruling on Monday 9 June in Aitken's favour over the programme's meaning on BMARC – whether he knew or should

3 January 1992: George with Kevin and Ian Maxwell, exercising their right to silence before House of Commons Select Committee hearing over missing millions from the Mirror Group pension fund.

Robert Maxwell – George's first high-profile libel client.

George with Richard Branson – double winners in the libel courts against British Airways, January 1993, and Guy Snowden of lottery operator G-Tech, February 1998.

Defeated by George: Sonia Sutcliffe,
wife of the Yorkshire Ripper, lost
against the *News of the World*
in December 1990.

Jani Allan destroyed by her diary
after suing Channel 4 over alleged
affair with neo-Nazi Eugene Terre
Blanche, August 1992.

Sir Maurice Drake – judge in
the Bauwens, Currie, Elton
John, Sutcliffe and Taylforth
cases.

Gillian Taylforth blown over by the
jury's verdict after a revealing video
was shown in her case against the
Sun, January 1994.

Tessa Sanderson with 'Mr Motivator' husband, Derrick Evans. She won £30,000 from Mirror Group (represented by George), February 1990.

Edwina Currie, won £5,000 against the *Observer* and enjoyed her battle with George, May 1991.

Judith Mellor with Mona Bauwens, September 1992. David Mellor did not put in a court appearance, but had to resign two days after the verdict in Bauwens' case against the *People* when it emerged that she had paid for his holiday.

Richard Hartley QC: George's opponent in the Sanderson, Currie, Bauwens and Grobbelaar cases.

Sporting heroes: George won disciplinary hearings for Michael Schumacher (*left*) and Lawrence Dallaglio (*right*). Bruce Grobbelaar, with wife Debbie (*centre*), won against George acting for the *Sun* in August 1999, only to be overturned by the Court of Appeal in January 2001.

George with Imran and Jemima Khan. Their opponents Ian Botham and Allan Lamb were clean bowled by the jury, July 1996.

Star clients: Elton John wins £350,000 for mistaken identity, November 1993 (*top left*). Tom Cruise wins £100,000 over gay slur, October 1998 (*top right*). Marco Pierre White wins £75,000 over 'sex, drugs, rock 'n' roll' claims, April 2000 (*bottom left*). Marquess of Bristol – a hopeless case. George could not keep him out of prison for drug offences (*bottom right*).

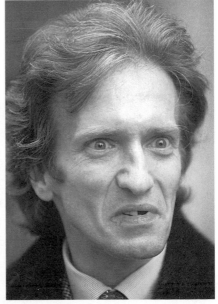

Sir Charles Gray, Aitken's counsel and George's opponent in Jani Allan v. Channel 4 and Botham v. Kahn cases.

Sir Oliver Popplewell, judge in Aitken's libel case against the *Guardian*.

George with his clerk, Bill Conner (*above*), arrives to cross-examine Aitken, June 1997.

Jonathan Aitken studying theology in Oxford, 2001 (*left*). He remembers George 'with respect and affection'.

George with Karen Phillipps,
enjoying his celebrity status (*above*).

George with Mohamed Al-Fayed
celebrating on court steps following
December 1999 libel victory over
Neil and Christine Hamilton (*inset*).

George on retirement in garden of his Wimbledon home, August 2000.

George with grandchildren, Tristan and Charlie.

have known about the illegal arms sales to Iraq. The *Guardian* was forced to remove the defence of justification, and concluded that this ruling gave a strong picture of the judge's state of mind – thought to be pro-Aitken. But just because one plank of the defence had gone did not mean that the war was lost. As Popplewell explains: 'It was a technical victory, but it was only a small part of the trial.' When George and I spoke, he seemed reasonably satisfied as he chiselled away at the edifice, even if he had not produced an obvious breakthrough. Meanwhile, Aitken was employing the full thesaurus of alternatives for the word lying.

Over TV-am he admitted 'lack of candour' in failing to disclose the Arab funding because he had put the confidentiality of investors above the interests of other shareholders and his fellow directors. The following day, he admitted that he had misled the *Newbury Times* by leading them to believe that he owned Inglewood Health Hydro: 'There is no doubt that I dissembled about my role for reasons that seemed valid at the time.' (George developed a great fondness for the word dissemble, recycling it in the Hamilton case more than once.) He also admitted that he had failed to declare his unpaid directorship of Future Management Services, blaming a secretarial error. He claimed that the company made pipes, not arms.

Aitken told the court under questioning from Charles Gray that on the Sunday morning in question he had called the Hôtel Bristol in Villars, Switzerland. His case was that his wife had been staying there, but he called after she had left (to go to Paris) and spoke to his mother-in-law. He said that the two women had shared a bedroom on the Saturday night.

CARMAN: 'You invented the story of the mother-in-law staying that night so she could be the recipient of your telephone call.' [The record of this phone call to the Hôtel Bristol showed on Aitken's Ritz hotel bill.]

AITKEN: 'I didn't invent any such thing.'

George returned to attack the mother-in-law story subsequently, once Aitken's American Express statements became
available under subpoena. These showed that Mrs Aitken had
been charged only for single occupancy on Saturday, when
Aitken had claimed she was there with her mother.

CARMAN: 'I have to suggest to you that the story of your mother-in-
law staying there is untrue again and an untruth told to this court
on oath because you thought there would be no documents which
would ever reveal the nature of your lie.'
AITKEN: 'Your suggestion is wrong and untrue.'

I watched the playing out of the Hôtel Bristol episode in court.
Aitken sounded distinctly uncomfortable. He now dismisses
these exchanges as 'a nasty flurry of punches, but not lethal'.
There was more to come on the *World in Action* rushes –
unbroadcast clips from the *Jonathan of Arabia* programme. On
leaving his house, Aitken had claimed that he had been 'stam-
peded' by a journalist and camera crew and that his daughter
Alexandra had been visibly upset. The uncut version showed
Aitken leaving by himself.

CARMAN: 'Where on earth is your daughter in the film we saw?'
AITKEN: 'We were shouted at, we were, my daughter was upset and
there was a car chase. [Lolicia mouthed at him "Another time"
from the bench in front of the dock] ... A different film.'

Later, close inspection would reveal that the time on a clock
caught in the film showed that it could not have been a different
film. This had been one of Aitken's more difficult moments.
George's epic battle with 'the best-prepared witness' he had
ever encountered was drawing to a close. He was exhausted.
After running into a seventh day, it was the longest single cross-
examination of his career. The final joust centred on the truth.

CARMAN: 'As a man who claims to take up the sword of truth, my
last suggestion to you is this: before this court case, and during

it, you have proved yourself – and I want your comment on this to see if you accept it – a stranger to the truth whenever it suits you.'

AITKEN: 'My comment is that it is unfair and unjust. I believe the issues raised by the *Guardian* and Granada would in the end be vindicated by what I rather rhetorically called the sword of truth and the shield of fair play and I would be seen to be justified in the action I was taking.'

During cross-examination, Aitken had complained about being 'demonised by the *Guardian* and Carmanised in this court'. For many spectators it had not been a decisive encounter. The *Guardian* was 'buggered', according to one press observer. Charles Gray's view of George's performance was that it 'was formidable in terms of stamina, particularly so because he had cancer. But he didn't really get anywhere.' Meanwhile, Aitken believes that he had done well up to this point and had won the judge over to his side: 'I don't think he missed anything. My hunch was that I would have won the case outright, because there were so many allegations on which he would have had to give me the verdict. I think he may well have harboured serious doubts about the Ritz, but without the evidence he would have been unable to say anything more. From his questions, his attitude, his body language, I think he was on our side and was likely to accept that I should be the winner in this case, that I had been very seriously defamed and would award damages in my favour.' This view is further endorsed by Charles Gray: 'I think the judge probably took the view that, on balance of probabilities, Aitken was telling the truth.'

However, the one person who had to decide the case, Sir Oliver Popplewell, is adamant that he had already heard enough to form a clear picture of Jonathan Aitken as early as the third day of his evidence: 'He was a very good witness, very impressive. He'd got a great command of the detail. He'd done a fantastic job selling arms and, whatever one's view about arms deals, it brought the country an enormous amount of money. But by day three it was clear to me that the story about the bills didn't make sense during the examination-in-chief, and in cross-examination I just didn't believe a word he said on the Ritz. George hadn't gone very far before he'd achieved his objective as far as I was concerned: he'd persuaded me that Aitken's account of the Ritz was untrue. It was absolutely fixed in my mind that the story was false.' That was really the centrepiece, Popplewell adds. 'As George indicated at the outset, the whole case really turned on that. The mother-in-law's telephone conversation just put the boot in for me. By then, I had made my mind up that I would not find for Aitken.' No one knew, or indeed would have guessed, the judge's thinking at the time.

George was circumspect and tried not to read Popplewell's mind too much. He was instead becoming increasingly excited by the prospect of further documents materialising. Weeks of detective work in Europe by *Guardian* journalists and Geraldine Proudler's team at solicitors Olswang were beginning to yield results. First had been the Hôtel Bristol record and then the American Express receipt showing single occupancy. The existence of Lolicia's American Express card had only become known at the start of the trial as an indirect result of the Hôtel Bristol enquiry. In discovery before trial (when the parties disclose all relevant documents), only a Barclaycard had been revealed.

Despite urgent requests, full American Express statements had been slow in coming from Aitken. So Amex were subpoenaed on 9 June. The statements revealed a car hire from Budget Rent a Car at Geneva Airport arrival hall on Friday 17 September at 12.02 p.m. The car had been returned two days later in downtown Geneva at the time Lolicia was supposed to be paying the bill in Paris. According to Aitken's evidence, Lolicia had taken the ferry to Calais on Thursday and later caught the TGV train. Further subpoenas had also been sent to Swissair and British Airways. Swissair did not comply because it was outside the jurisdiction. BA came up trumps.

At the end of the day's hearing on Monday 16 June, Proudler got a call to confirm that Lolicia and her daughter Victoria had flown from Heathrow to Geneva at 8.30 a.m. on Friday 17 September on flight BA 724 and Lolicia had flown back from Geneva to London on the Monday at 7.05 p.m. Bingo! Proudler knew they had done it. 'Carman looked like a cat with a gallon of cream,' wrote the *Guardian* journalists later. Before it could be put before the court, the documents were needed. Wendy Harris, a British Airways official, was nominated to provide a detailed, watertight witness statement. George phoned me in Hong Kong with the news. His excitement was almost tangible. 'We've got him! Just wait until it explodes in court.'

Aitken had got so worried about the Hôtel Bristol evidence that he obtained statements from his wife Lolicia and his daughter Victoria in order to substantiate the story further. On 17 June, the seventeen-year-old Victoria Aitken made a formal statement, confirming the fictitious story of her mother's departure for Paris, with the added invention of a phone call to her grandmother at the Hôtel Bristol on the Sunday morning. When he read this, George was shocked, realising that she had lied at her father's instigation. He wanted the evidence in court before she perjured herself further. She was due to give evidence on Thursday 19 June, dubbed Ladies' Day by the press because Lolicia was due to follow her daughter into the witness box.

At 3 p.m. on the afternoon of Wednesday 18 June, Proudler walked into Court 10, where George was questioning Sir Alan Thomas, one of Aitken's witnesses. George had been waiting (impatiently) for her arrival. She handed him a white envelope containing a full statement from Wendy Harris. After finishing with Thomas, George read Harris's statement. He got to his feet again. That day was the forty-fourth anniversary of his call to the Bar. He would later describe it as 'the most dramatic moment in my professional life': 'My Lord, before any further evidence is called by my learned friend, I am now in a position to provide the plaintiff's solicitors, Mr Gray and yourself with a signed witness statement of a lady called Wendy Dawn Harris, who was employed by British Airways. I think, my Lord, if I may respectfully say so, it might be very important for Mr Gray and yourself to read it immediately.' Five minutes later, the Budget Rent a Car documents also arrived to complete the jigsaw.

Aitken recalls the moment: 'Immediately I knew I'd lost. I knew my world was shattered. I think there was also a sense of relief as well as horror because this newspaper drama had gone on so long, at least it was going to end. There was a feeling of "It's over." I saw the possibility of prison within half an hour or so. I asked the question of my team: "Am I in danger of a perjury charge?" Interestingly, they said: "We're not criminal lawyers, but we wouldn't think so."' He had employed an enquiry agent to check whether this information could be extracted from the manifests. He had been told that it could not.

In reflecting on the most unpalatable aspect of his case – Victoria's witness statement in which she committed perjury to save her father – he says: 'I think by that stage I personally – and the family too – had gone slightly mad with the drama. Honestly, we didn't see the dangers in the way we should have done. It was my irresponsibility, but the drama was so obsessional to us all and we all wanted to win so badly, that morality and sanity had gone out of the window. It was obviously an appalling decision from every angle. We were going to fight the fortress to the last gasp. However cuckoo it looks today, that was the spirit of the moment.'

Popplewell was unsurprised: 'I wasn't shocked because this now explained my suspicion over what had happened at the Ritz. This absolutely confirmed it. But I was shocked because it was so untrue and so blatant. When it collapsed, I went up to Lord's and saw John Major and got talking to him about it. He said that he'd got Jonathan Aitken into his room at some stage and looked him straight in the eye and said, "What's the truth about this?" and Aitken had said, "There's absolutely nothing in it," and looked him straight in the eye. And Major said: "Well, I have to believe a Cabinet colleague."'

Gray was astonished: 'It was the biggest surprise I'd had in a courtroom. I was absolutely staggered. He was unbelievably plausible and I never would have conceived that anyone would take the gamble he took. He didn't need to sue.' On Victoria Aitken, whom he was going to call to give evidence, he adds: 'That's the bit of the story that really does stick in the gullet.'

Proceedings were formally abandoned on 20 June when the action was withdrawn. The *Guardian* and Granada were thrilled. They had won hands down through dogged determination and exhaustive research. Their instincts had been right. Even if they had lacked much of the evidence to prove all the specific allegations, they had achieved a superb result on what they managed to get in very difficult circumstances. Delighted for his clients, George took no pleasure in Aitken's discomfort. Schadenfreude was not part of his professional approach. In the coming months, he thought that the *Guardian* took a little of the shine off their victory by indulging in too much sustained self-congratulation. He knew that a perjury charge would undoubtedly result in a prison sentence and felt some sympathy for Aitken's inevitable downfall and disgrace. As he was to tell psychoanalyst Stephen Grosz over dinner in August 1997: 'Jonathan Aitken was not a liar, he told a lie, like many of us do, and had to live with the consequences.'

This charitable approach was sincere. Months after the case, George and Aitken met at a party given by Charles Gray to celebrate his appointment as a High Court judge. As Aitken recalls: 'We had a very good chat for twenty minutes or so. People in the room were stunned. George said: "I'm very sorry for what's happened and particularly glad that Victoria is not in any danger now." There was no ill will or rancour. He'd been fair and honourable. I thanked him for that because, after the case had been withdrawn, the *Guardian* wanted indemnity costs and he got them to agree to 80 per cent of the costs, which was good of him. Of all the people on the other side in the case, he was the only one who had no personal malice towards me. I regarded him with respect and affection.'

On 8 June 1999, Jonathan Aitken pleaded guilty to the charge of perjury at Number One Court at the Old Bailey, the same court where Thorpe had been tried exactly twenty years before. Behind the scenes, Aitken told me that Sir Charles Gray, by then a High Court judge, wrote to his trial judge, Mr Justice Scott Baker, pointing out that under the new rules on damages which prevailed at the time of his libel trial he had not stood to make a lot of money if he won his case and that, as far as Gray was concerned, that had never been his motivation. Aitken was sentenced to eighteen months in prison, serving seven months inside, before being released in January 2000. After completing his book, *Pride and Perjury*, he went to Oxford to study for a theology degree for two years. I visited him there in his student digs when researching this book.

Popplewell wrote to him when he retired, summarising his view of Aitken's evidence as given above, in the expectation that George would include it in his autobiography. Rusbridger expressed disbelief and astonishment when the letter was read to him over the phone. If the *Guardian* editor saw a newspaper article written by Karen Phillipps in the *Mail on Sunday* of 4 February 2001, he may have raised a similarly sceptical eyebrow. In detailing her discussions with George at the time of the trial, she stated: 'It was during one such exchange of thoughts on the Jonathan Aitken case – that I questioned George as to whether it could have been physically possible for Mrs Aitken to have made the crucial journey from Switzerland to pay the bill at the Ritz Hotel in Paris, as had been alleged. This fired George's interest and, with his usual gritty determination, he set about proving whether she had indeed made the trip. He endeavoured to see if the passenger manifests of the airlines could be accessed openly. It was then he made the vital discovery.'

Karen's account may be yet another surprise for the *Guardian*'s superb investigative team and the dedicated lawyers at Olswang headed by Geraldine Proudler. Her claim to have been the invisible hand behind the newspaper's victory certainly bears no relation to the detailed narrative of events given in *The Liar* nor to the lengthy and thoughtful analysis given to me by James Price QC, George's junior counsel.

After Aitken, two more senior Tories knocked on George's door. For the second half of 1999, he advised the Tory Treasurer and Belize-based tycoon Michael Ashcroft, when he sued *The Times*. Peter Stothard, the newspaper's editor, had wanted his own *Guardian*-style coup, and he got Ben Preston, son of Peter, to take a close look at Ashcroft. Allegations about money laundering and drug-related crimes made repeated headlines over the summer and autumn. After months of telephone calls, George and Ashcroft met. In the unlikely surroundings of the Petersham Hotel in Richmond, George told him that his case was outstanding. He had no idea that his client's next stop that afternoon was Rupert Murdoch's flat in St James's. Jeff Randall, then editor of *Sunday Business*, had acted as honest broker in getting the warring parties together. The two billionaires struck a deal and the case was settled.

Another senior Tory to come his way was Lord Archer, with whom George had mixed socially for some years. They enjoyed each other's company and spent hours engaged in conversation at parties and dinners. George knew he was tricky but, like many, was willingly seduced by the charms of a likeable rogue. In October 1999, the former Conservative deputy chairman started libel proceedings against *The Times*. At issue were false allegations that he had had access to information which had helped him defeat Stephen Norris, his rival as Tory candidate in the London mayoral election of 2000. George was retained by his solicitors, Eversheds (the second time he had acted on Archer's behalf). He settled the matter with an apology and modest damages. When new evidence emerged in November 1999 about false statements made at his libel trial of twelve years before, the *Star* saw the opportunity for a re-run and a chance to recover £500,000 damages and nearly £2 million in costs. Archer was finished.

George had given me a tape of a Canada Club dinner held at the Savoy on 13 October 1998 where he was one of three speakers. The other two were Conrad Black and Lord Archer, who joked in his speech that he hoped he would 'never have to face George in a courtroom'. A year later, that prospect might have become reality. Archer's fellow speaker was called on by Lovells, solicitors for Express Newspapers, to act against him in appealing the *Star* libel decision. George agreed to do so, even though he had been advising Archer as a client only eight weeks earlier. He attended a conference at Lovells with David Pannick QC to discuss strategy in civil proceedings. In April 2000, criminal charges were brought against the former Tory deputy chairman, so the civil action had to be postponed. After George retired, Archer wrote to him in October 2000. Concerned about his impending trial for perjury and attempting to pervert the course of justice, he suggested a lunch where they could 'discuss matters'. George did not respond. Instead, he called Jennifer McDermott at Lovells to let her know of the unorthodox request. She recalls that they had a good laugh about it.

Just before his Old Bailey trial in June 2001, I met Archer over lunch at Le Caprice. This was the restaurant at the centre of his false alibi in the *Star* case on the crucial night in September 1986. Ebullient, charming and almost likeable, he talked loudly and at length about George's ability, saying that he wished he were alive to fight his corner now when he really needed it. In professing incredulity that George had been advising the *Star*, he sounded very plausible. The fact that it had been reported in several newspapers must somehow have escaped his attention.

Archer and Aitken have both marked out their place in the history of this era, and in the history of the Tory Party, as chancers who lost. And in playing the libel game they lost so much more than their reputations. For George, dealing with such charismatic yet deeply dishonest politicians was great fun. He liked their risk-taking, reckless approach to life and their desire to battle against the odds and win. In that respect, they were men after his own heart.

12
Tycoons

To be clever enough to get all that money one must be stupid
enough to want it.

G. K. Chesterton

'Hello, George?' boomed the familiar deep voice. With a swift
'Hold on, please,' I handed over the phone. Robert Maxwell
spoke for forty-five minutes or so, testing George's views on a
range of matters. He concluded with a grand gesture: 'I'll send
a plane for you within the hour.' The offer was declined. There
was no problem getting a scheduled flight from Paris. Maxwell
rang off after they had arranged to meet the following afternoon.
It was September 1991. George had come to spend a few days
with me while I was on a business trip. We stayed up until 3
a.m., talking about Captain Bob, who had become a regular
client over the previous eighteen months.

Before 1990, George had done only one major libel case – for
the millionaire businessman Rolf Schild against Express Newspapers. I had witnessed his bitter disappointment at losing this
against Robert Alexander QC in 1982 when the Court of Appeal
upheld a ruling by Mr Justice Mars-Jones. This prevented the
case going any further before a jury. Over lunch at the old Mario
& Franco's restaurant in Chancery Lane, George told Sir John
Junor, then editor of the *Sunday Express*, that he was very
fortunate. The red-faced, beagle-eyed Scot responded only with
a wry grin. Seven years later, George let it be known, among
solicitors who mattered, that he wanted to try his hand again
at the libel game.

One man who took note was Oscar Beuselinck, in-house
lawyer at Mirror Group, then owned by the titanic publisher

Robert Maxwell. For many years, he had run his own firm, Wright Webb, acting for *Private Eye*, Sean Connery and John Osborne among others. Small, Catholic, divorced three times, earthy and fond of the ladies ('If I don't get it three times a day, I feel physically ill'), he developed a natural sympathy with George, who was soon advising on a number of cases. It wasn't long before George was seeing Maxwell personally, tackling a myriad of legal problems. The most important of these was a libel action against the BBC, following a *Panorama* programme entitled *The Max Factor*. For years, the self-educated Czech peasant turned British army officer, Labour MP and ultimately billionaire publisher and media magnate/dealmaker had stifled criticism of himself and his brutal business methods by bullying his opponents and crushing internal dissent. The BBC had thrown down the gauntlet. George saw this as an opportunity to showcase his own talent for destruction.

From the outset, it was George and Robert. They understood each other and got on very well. Both men were outsiders in the world in which they operated with such ruthless determination. Both aroused suspicion and hostility. Maxwell, it must be said, attracted rather more obvious antipathy than his barrister. George liked Robert, or, more to the point, he liked his status and position. Privately, he agreed with the comment that here was a man who 'could charm the birds off the trees and then shoot them'. Nevertheless, he told it to him straight rather than telling him what he wanted to hear. And Maxwell listened. There were endless meetings in the flat/office that occupied much of the chairman's floor at the old red-topped Mirror Building in High Holborn. Robert often interrupted their discussion to take calls, speaking alternately in English, German, French and even Russian (he was fluent in nine languages). When George heard Robert speak with Mikhail Gorbachev, he was impressed. When Robert heard George speak about the law, he was impressed. Increasingly, he seems to have afforded him two commodities rare in the Maxwell vocabulary, respect and trust.

George certainly felt proud to be in his confidence and flattered to have the ear of such an important figure. He enjoyed being close to power, and he tried to exercise some of it on behalf of the charity Shelter, which he supported enthusiastically for a short while. He got Maxwell's promise for a *Mirror* campaign for the homeless. Events took over. It never happened. George parted company with Shelter soon afterwards, tired of giving them money after providing a five-year covenant up front.

As the last weeks of Maxwell's life drew to an unscheduled conclusion, many hours were spent with George and Oscar discussing strategy in the BBC case. They had a final consultation at the end of October. The twenty-stone Colossus arrived at his chambers, wearing a red baseball cap – the first time in living memory that he had gone to see his lawyers in London rather than the other way round. This was a gesture that meant something. Turning to George with a grin, he said of the BBC: 'We'll get the bastards. I know you'll destroy them for me.' A week later, the Bouncing Czech's final contract expired. After a heart attack on the night of 5 November, he fell overboard from his yacht, *Lady Ghislaine*, twenty-eight miles from Gran Canaria. The case died with him.

But the Maxwell legacy lived on. 'Love him or hate him, he touched the lives of many millions of people,' was Kevin Maxwell's response to the news five days later that his father's body had been discovered in the ocean. The publisher's thirty-three-year-old son quickly assumed control of Maxwell Communication Corporation, while his thirty-six-year-old brother Ian took over at Mirror Group. The two principal companies in the complicated Maxwell empire were now in the hands of his two favoured sons. Their problems were legion: massive debts of over £1 billion, volatile share prices and a crisis of confidence among the thirty banks which were keeping it all afloat. Kevin shuttled between London and New York, desperately trying to salvage the situation. It was hopeless. On 4 December, Scotland

Yard's Fraud Squad arrived, wanting to know more about the £426 million that was missing from Mirror Group's two pension funds. These moneys had been used in an elaborate share-support operation. The following day, the administrators came as the brothers gave up the struggle.

Monty Raphael, Kevin's solicitor, immediately retained George. A week later, on Friday 13 December, he made a successful High Court application for the release of his client's passport, which had been surrendered to the police. Kevin needed to fly to New York before Christmas to deal with the fall-out as the business unravelled. The New Year brought fresh problems. The Maxwell brothers were summoned to attend a special televised hearing of the House of Commons Select Committee on 13 January 1992. They were to answer questions about the plundered pension funds. This was the first time such a power had been used since 1982, when Arthur Scargill had been subpoenaed. Kevin and Ian turned up with their lawyers. George acted for Kevin and John Jarvis QC represented Ian. Chaired by the ever conscientious Frank Field, the Committee of MPs intended to probe into the missing millions. A month earlier, George had told the High Court that he had strongly advised his client 'to exercise the rights vested to him by law and to every other citizen not to provide, in advance of any prospective criminal charge, his defence to any such charge'. To reveal his defence, he added, 'would be premature, ill-advised and inappropriate at a time when he is under enormous pressure'.

Before they went in, Kevin and Ian joked with George and Monty Raphael about the torture process that might await them. Once in front of the Committee, expressions were serious as George made it clear that the advice to his client remained the same: 'It is plain and clear and respectful but unambiguous that Kevin Maxwell is not going to answer any questions.' He argued that the brothers had 'a precious constitutional right and an historic one' to stay silent so that they did not incriminate themselves. He went on to explain that 'In my judgment, I say two things on criminal charges: one, that they are likely, and two, they are likely soon. Anyone in peril of criminal charges is entitled from first to last in all circumstances in this country at common law to maintain his right to silence.' Jarvis made the same point on behalf of Ian Maxwell. This historic argument was summarised efficiently by Charles I in 1636: 'Never make a defence or apology before you be accused.' Sitting directly behind George was David Pannick QC, a fellow of All Souls and key member of the advisory team. He noted that 'George was particularly excited that his performance was being televised live.'

As Field and his fellow Committee members went through the charade of attempting to put questions directly to each brother in turn, they received identical responses: 'I will answer through my lawyer.' George reiterated his earlier point repeatedly before concluding: 'It may be that Mr Kevin Maxwell could actively contribute to the deliberations and recommendations of the Committee, but all that is subordinate to the inalienable right of silence.' After nearly two hours, the Committee hearing was over. Broadcast live on the BBC, the highlights were beamed all over the world. The Maxwell scandal was a global news story. It was the first time the general public had seen George in action, on the job. A flood of retainers followed.

Several weeks later, I met George in his chambers. He wanted to go out for the evening. As usual on such occasions, I switched to Perrier after one glass of wine. After some hours, we ended up in a Chelsea wine bar called Draycott's, near where Kevin Maxwell lived. George decided to make an impromptu visit. We arrived on the doorstep at about 10 p.m. His wife Pandora answered. The mother of five children had just finished putting them all to bed. Kevin was in the States. We stayed for an hour or so, listening to her articulate strong views on Robert and what he had done, not just to the Mirror Group and to the pensioners, but also to his family. Her words, eloquently delivered, forcefully demonstrated the awful personal consequences of Maxwell's actions. George nodded silently in agreement.

When asked to defend Kevin, George declined. Over dinner at the Ivy, he 'readily admitted' to the *Guardian*'s legal correspondent Clare Dyer 'that he did not want to be committed to a long legal aid defence'. She told me that 'such admissions are very rare since it is technically in breach of the Bar Council rules'. At their 1995 trial, Kevin and Ian were acquitted on charges of conspiracy to defraud.

Sir Richard Branson is a national institution. His life has been rich, varied, eventful and hugely successful. He is Britain's favourite entrepreneur and one of the best-known faces in public life. Yet many of the tens of thousands of people who have read his best-selling autobiography, *Losing My Virginity*, may have been a little puzzled by the content. For nearly 25 per cent of the book deals with his 1993 libel action against British Airways and the detailed events leading up to his day in court. It is perhaps some measure of the importance of this case to Branson that he chose to make it the centrepiece of his life story in print.

When Virgin Atlantic started operating from Heathrow in July 1991, the airline had already been flying for seven years on transatlantic routes, including New York, Los Angeles, Miami, Orlando and Boston. Lord King, then chairman of British Airways, started to pay closer attention to Branson's upstart airline as Virgin Upper Class in particular started to encroach on BA revenue streams in this fiercely competitive market. Branson became concerned about hostile press stories, which began to circulate during 1990 and 1991. They seemed to be linked to British Airways.

By October 1991, Brian Basham, a public relations consultant, was identified as the source of a number of 'hostile and discreditable' stories about Branson and his airline. It also became apparent that BA was 'switch selling' or poaching, by making contact with Virgin passengers to entice them to change their tickets to

BA. Branson learned that BA employees were shredding incriminating documents, which might be deemed anti-competitive. He wrote to BA on 11 December, setting out his concerns and requesting an investigation. Sir Colin Marshall, BA deputy chairman and chief executive, replied that the allegations were 'wholly without foundation'. On 27 February 1992, a Thames Television *This Week* programme highlighted BA's dirty-tricks campaign. Mervyn Walker, BA's legal director, wrote a letter of complaint to *This Week*, stating that 'I have always regarded Mr Branson's claims as unfounded and in some ways scurrilous . . . the promotion of unjustified, mischievous allegations against us is motivated by a desire to secure publicity for himself and his airline.' These comments were repeated in *BA News*, the British Airways newspaper. The remarks were further confirmed by several letters written by Lord King in response to complaints he had received.

Branson and Virgin Atlantic started libel proceedings on 20 March 1992. BA and Lord King sought to justify their allegations and counterclaimed over Branson's letter of 11 December. At the Hanover Square offices of his solicitors, Harbottle & Lewis, Branson asked Gerrard Tyrrell whom should he most fear being cross-examined by in court. Tyrrell's automatic response was: 'George Carman.' 'Then hire him!' said Branson. George enjoyed Richard's company, discovering that he was every bit as easy to deal with in private as the public impression might suggest. He found him co-operative, eager to listen to advice, tough and used to getting his own way. Richard did not really like lawyers, or men in suits, even though his seventy-four-year-old father, Edward ('Ted') Branson, had been a barrister and for seventeen years a stipendiary magistrate, while his grandfather had been a High Court judge. 'I decide within five seconds if I like someone,' Branson once remarked. George must have made a good first impression. It was probably his unstuffy approach, as much as his ability to understand the issues and present a clear strategy, that won Richard over. He inspired 'total confidence'. In his book, Richard adds: 'With his white hair and impeccable manners, George seemed like everyone's favourite uncle outside the courts. Inside he had the tenacity and killer instincts of a praying mantis. People went to extraordinary lengths to avoid him.'

This was going to be what the press labelled 'the mother of all libel battles'. Harbottles and BA's solicitors Linklaters & Paines, who put nearly forty lawyers on the case, began the discovery process through the courts. Things began to look uncomfortable as documents emerged which added further substance to Virgin's claims, especially the illegal use of Virgin Atlantic computer information. Additional damaging testimony from former BA employees did not help; nor did further disclosure about the activities of Basham and David Burnside, BA's director of publicity.

Meanwhile, George had been having fun. He was looking forward to grilling Messrs King and Marshall. His opening speech to the jury was going to adapt the Saatchi Brothers slogan as follows: 'The "world's favourite airline" has a favourite pastime; it's called shredding documents which are liable to be misconstrued.' Then on 7 December, a Pearl Harbour-like shock: BA capitulated, paying £485,000 into court on the advice of Linklaters. King and Marshall wanted to avoid the consequences of what Bernard Levin was to describe in *The Times* as 'Gorgeous George ripping them to pieces'. That could have created corporate meltdown. George began exhaustive negotiations with Christopher Clarke QC, representing BA. For two weeks, they hammered it out, back and forth. George was able to twist the knife a bit. Clarke's client was on the floor, with little room for manoeuvre. By Christmas, he had secured £500,000 for Richard Branson and £110,000 for the airline. The deal was done. This remains the largest single uncontested award for libel damages to a company.

The case was not due in Mr Justice Drake's court until 11 January 1993, but the story of a settlement broke as the *Sunday*

Times splashed with BA's climbdown on 27 December. 'Virgin Screws BA' ran the *Sun*'s low-key headline, four days before the hearing, on 7 January. News of the £610,000 total damages award had leaked out. It was another scoop for David Yelland, the paper's City editor. Five years later, Rupert Murdoch made him editor of the paper. When George read out an agreed statement to a packed Court 13 at the Royal Courts of Justice, the press benches were desperately looking for some added copy. They got it. BA's grovelling apology made all the front pages. The good publicity was worth much more than the libel award. Branson was happy to share the spoils by giving £166 to each employee as a thank-you. There was good publicity for George too. 'Having George Carman was at least 30 per cent of the reason why we won,' volunteered Branson afterwards.

Over a light lunch in the conservatory of his house at Holland Park, Richard was entertaining Guy Snowden, founder of G-Tech, the world's largest lottery operator. It was Friday 24 September 1993, nine months after the libel victory against BA. The Virgin King's attention now focused on a new prize: the opportunity to win a seven-year franchise to operate the UK national lottery, which had been proposed by John Major's government. This was set to be the world's biggest lottery, with estimated annual revenues approaching £5 billion. Branson was just about to launch a non-profit bid, after lobbying government ministers with the idea for five years. Snowden had been pleased to accept the invitation to lunch. He was concerned by the threat of a Branson bid. The G-Tech-led commercial consortium Camelot was at that stage front runner (and ultimately winner) in the race to operate the lottery. Lunch conversation at Holland Park inevitably centred on one topic. The two men were joined for baked salmon, salad and chilled chardonnay by John Jackson, the co-ordinator of Branson's lottery bid and, at the time, chief executive of the Body Shop. What happened next, or rather who said what, became the subject of Branson's next foray into the libel arena.

Almost exactly five years after his victory over BA, Branson squared up to Guy Snowden against the background of the familiar wood panelling of Court 13 at the Royal Courts of Justice. It had taken that long to reach court because the issue of libel did not arise until Branson gave an account of the lunch on a *Panorama* programme more than two years later, in December 1995. Following the programme, both sides made comments to the press, which resulted in Branson issuing a writ for libel on 4 January 1996 against Guy Snowden and G-Tech. And, as in the BA case, Snowden countersued nine days later. This time, there was no prospect of settlement.

Harbottles retained George. His opponent was an established star of the criminal courts. Richard ('Dick') Ferguson QC, a pugnacious sixty-two-year-old Ulsterman with lilting tones, listed his recreations in *Who's Who* as 'drinking pints of Guinness and watching Arsenal play football'. Snowden and G-Tech's solicitors had gone outside the libel Bar to find a tough cross-examiner who might break Branson. The central issues in the case were simple: bribery and lying. Branson claimed that Snowden had tried to bribe him over lunch to drop his lottery bid. Snowden claimed that he had not. One of them was lying. A jury would have to decide who was telling the truth about the lunch, Snowden or Branson, supported by the independent testimony of John Jackson. It was to last three weeks in court.

The judge, Mr Justice Morland, famed for trying the James Bulger murder case, had known George for nearly fifty years. There was a lot of common ground. As exact contemporaries at Oxford and later on the Northern Circuit, they had appeared against each other from time to time during the 1960s and 1970s. Although he was scrupulously fair throughout the trial, familiarity with George did no harm. Morland had been at Stowe, the most beautiful public school in England, where Richard Branson was also educated, although they were some twenty years apart. He joked in interview about whether this should have been disclosed to the court.

George opened the case to the jury on Tuesday 13 January 1998: 'It is as plain as a pikestaff that what Guy Snowden was about that day was floating a bribe in front of Richard Branson in order to get him out of the bidding and pave the way for G-Tech and Camelot to go on without his dangerous rival. There is no shilly-shallying about this, no room for doubt, misunderstanding or misinterpretation.' He summarised the lunch conversation as follows: Snowden was asked by Branson to assist with his bid. In turn, Snowden asked Branson to join the Camelot consortium. Branson declined. Then Snowden said: 'I don't know how to phrase this, Richard. There's always a bottom line. I'll get to the point. In what way can we help you?' He paused before continuing: 'I mean, what can I do for you personally, Richard?' Branson, George said, was 'absolutely astonished'. After 'an ugly moment of silence', he asked: 'What on earth do you mean?' Snowden replied: 'Everybody needs something.' Branson told him: 'Thank you very much, but I'm quite successful. I only need one breakfast, one lunch and one dinner a day. The only way you could have helped us is by joining the consortium.' Branson then went to his bathroom and wrote a note of the conversation. This became known as the 'loo note'.

The weather had played a part in guaranteeing Branson's appearance in court to hear these words. For many weeks beforehand, he had been more concerned about going round the world in a balloon than listening to George argue his case. He had repeatedly asked if he had to attend all of the hearing and whether a long absence would jeopardise his chances with the jury. George was astounded. Branson gave him regular updates on the weather conditions around Morocco, from where he wanted to launch the first non-stop balloon flight around the world. This would predetermine his time in court. He planned to give evidence, dash off to Morocco and jump into his balloon, leaving George to continue the fight while he circumnavigated the globe. In the event, the weather was against him and he stayed for the duration.

Ferguson went in hard, calling Branson a 'bitter man' and a 'crass amateur' at running lotteries. He drew contrasts with his client Guy Snowden. In court, he said, everybody was equal – 'public schoolboy, self-made man, barrister's son, son of a bulldozer driver, the English billionaire and the American millionaire, the loser and the winner'. Unfortunately, the fifty-two-year-old Snowden was as wide as he was tall. He looked every inch the caricature of a 1920s Chicago gangster, needing only a cigar and a fedora to complete the picture. The physical contrast with the slim, tanned Virgin King was not one which Ferguson needed to bring to the jury's attention. They could see it for themselves.

Into the witness box stepped a nervous-looking Richard Branson. He was uncertain and hesitant, lacking confidence in the courtroom, a situation where he was not in control of events and with a great deal at stake. His anxiety had been evident on the morning of Sunday 11 January, two days before the case, when he spent several hours on the phone to George. I had just arrived at Wimbledon armed with a video camera from a New York business trip. Intrigued by Richard's nerves, George asked me to film him as, using a telephone speakerphone, he conducted yet another complete dress-rehearsal of his examination-in-chief. We watched it later. The two-hour tape of two separate telephone calls shows George acting out an obviously well-worn pattern of question and answers about the lunch, the conversation, the bribe and the note-taking. Richard can be clearly heard playing his part. It highlights the intimacy and good relationship between barrister and client – much of it a question of hand-holding and reassurance.

Under cross-examination, Ferguson accused Branson of embellishing his story by adding the words: 'What can I do for you personally, Richard?' Branson replied: 'There's nothing that needs strengthening in this case. I do not embellish things. I gave him three opportunities to say this was all a big mistake and at the end there was deathly silence.' He lost his temper with

Ferguson, accusing him of 'trying to distract the jury' over the wording of the alleged bribe attempt. He agreed that Snowden could be destroyed by the allegation, but added: 'If you think that bribery is wrong then, yes, his reputation should be destroyed.' Ferguson questioned the authenticity of the 'loo note'. There was an angry response.

BRANSON: 'With respect, you are not saying I'm lying but you seem to be questioning my integrity at the moment.'

FERGUSON: 'You're very sensitive, Mr Branson. When I get to your integrity you'll know about it.'

Earlier, George had examined Richard, asking why he had brought the case. He responded: 'If there's ever any question mark over your integrity it's very important one defends that. I had been accused of being a liar in the strongest possible terms. I felt it was important that the truth came out. In life all you have is your reputation, both personally and in the business. Millions of people put their trust in me every year. They put their lives with me on my aeroplanes and go on my trains. We have people who invest their money with us and people have got to trust you.' In giving a more detailed account of the lunch that George had outlined, Branson described Snowden as 'odious' and 'sweaty' when he was making his bribe attempt. This was then confirmed by John Jackson, their fellow lunch guest and recently appointed chairman of Sketchley plc. He said that he 'nearly fell off the chair' and was 'flabbergasted' when he heard Snowden's 'crass bribe attempt'.

A rather different picture of the lunch conversation emerged from the larger-than-life figure of Guy Snowden. He said: 'I had the world at my feet. I had a great company. The moment I first heard this [the allegation of attempted bribery] I found it to be incomprehensible.' He told Ferguson that he had gone to 'explore with Mr Branson why he wanted to be in the lottery. I wanted him to share with me what I suspected was some commercial tie-in with the lottery. Richard Branson had become annoyed during the lunch when I asked him what commercial gain he wanted to get out of running for the lottery. I think I upset him.' But he continued: 'I said what else can we do? He said he was a very successful man, and only needed to eat three times a day. I was there to have a business discussion. In no way did I say personally.'

George had been relishing the prospect of cross-examining Snowden, thinking that he would expose his true colours. He did not have to wait long. His junior, Hugh Tomlinson, recalls: 'Contrary to popular myth, George was not a great preparer. Before he cross-examined Snowden, we had discussed it, but he hadn't really thought it out. He hadn't expected that he would have to start when he did. He ad-libbed for an hour and a half. It was absolutely brilliant, wonderful to watch.' George began:

CARMAN: 'You would accept, wouldn't you, that £400 million or £500 million [the profit Camelot expected to make over their seven-year franchise] might provide a lot of advantages to good causes?'
SNOWDEN: 'We are already raising £1.5 billion for good causes.'

George pointed out that all the net proceeds of a Branson-run lottery would go to charity.

SNOWDEN: 'He can do with it whatever he wants. I've got my share-holders to pay. If Mr Branson wants to give it to charity or burn it, it doesn't matter to me.'

He entrapped Snowden by getting him to admit that his words to Branson, 'Is there some other business we could do?', could not have been misunderstood. Snowden also agreed that payments to G-Tech and Camelot lobbyists appeared 'awkward'.

Peter Davis, the lottery regulator, gave evidence. Previously he had said that Branson's 1994 account of how he had warned him about Snowden and the bribery attempt was untrue. In the witness box, he changed his mind. 'I am afraid you have put doubts in my mind,' he told George. Disaster for Snowden. In his closing speech, George attacked with force, enlisting Pope's help again: 'The defendant's case was one of complete intellectual disarray. [Ferguson] seemed to lurch around from opening to closing walking on a tightrope, willing to wound, but afraid to strike . . . They do not have the courage to say that Richard Branson has lied.'

On 2 February 1998, after three hours of deliberation, the jury returned to award Branson £100,000 in damages; he also obtained costs estimated at £2 million. He had been vindicated. Punching the air in victory on the courtroom steps, he was surrounded, as he had been every day of the trial, by his wife, father and sisters. George and Richard were a winning team again. Snowden resigned from both Camelot and G-Tech, receiving $13 million in compensation for his efforts.

The case went to the Court of Appeal, listed for March 1999. Snowden's leading counsel this time was the intellectual heavyweight Gordon Pollock QC. The motorcycling head of Essex Court chambers, the top commercial set, was recognised as a star performer across many practice areas. He was something of a bruiser too. Andrew Caldecott QC, Snowden's junior both at the trial and in the Court of Appeal, believes that George had put 'a critical document which was not properly admissible' in front of Snowden, relating to his supposed earlier knowledge of Branson's bribe claim. 'It happens to us all,' says Caldecott, wishing to make light of George's slip-up. In his written notice of appeal, produced some weeks before the hearing, Pollock was far less charitable. He referred to inadmissible documents and made a strong personal attack on George's conduct of the case. I first learned of this the day George himself found out, when he called me in a bad state at 1 a.m., extremely agitated by the personal nature of the attack. Worse was to follow.

On the morning of the appeal, the phone rang as I walked into my office just after 7.30. It was George. He wanted me to come and see him urgently. As often before a big case, he was staying at the Howard Hotel, a five-minute walk from the Royal

Courts of Justice. I knew too well from the voice that he was in trouble and jumped in a taxi straight away. When I arrived, he was being sick after a heavy night. Such scenes had been a very familiar part of life since early childhood. But to watch a man in his seventieth year still abusing his body in this way was painful.

He simply could not bear the thought of any personal attack on his professional ethics, which suggested lack of integrity and improper conduct. It was rough stuff – and part, he understood, of Pollock's stock-in-trade. But personal criticism was something he hated, so he had gone on an almighty bender. He had done the same thing before an important Court of Appeal hearing for the *Guardian* in a case brought by PC Reynold Bennett and others. When he arrived in court after a late-night session, his junior thought she was 'going to have to prop him up'. The issue was identical – personal criticism of his conduct by opposing counsel.

The Branson appeal was due to start at ten o'clock. I helped to get him dressed, fixing his studs and stiff collar and washing his face with a flannel. I poured tea. He smoked endless Marlboro Lights. I tried to sober him up, hoping that he would make it. A slow shuffle towards the Strand indicated that he wouldn't. When we reached the Law Courts, George went to the robing room. Without knowing who I was, Nick Higham, the BBC arts correspondent covering the case, stood in the corridor and told me that he was 'expecting Carman to get a pasting'. Meanwhile George, now in his wig and gown, was in trouble again in the gents' lavatory, and I had to hold him up.

Sitting next to him on a bench outside, I nodded to his junior Hugh Tomlinson, who took one look and immediately realised what had happened. He made the necessary excuses to the three Appeal Court judges. As I walked him across the marble floor of the Law Courts' main hall, a number of barristers and solicitors stared at George in amazement. We returned to the hotel, where his doctor Annie Coxon arrived to put him on a drip and stabilise him. She was very used to dealing with George's crises at all hours of the day and night, frequently taking his calls at 2, 3 or 4 a.m. His clerk Bill arrived to check that he was okay.

Old habits die hard. Two or three weeks would rarely pass without a boozing session. His age and condition meant that he was more easily affected by alcohol, often becoming knocked out for a couple of days as a consequence. Less common was bingeing heavily the night before he was on his feet. In his later years, George was generally much more careful in working out when he could drink without direct effect on his work.

When the appeal was eventually heard on 20 May 1999, the three judges listened to Pollock's arguments that George had broken the rules of cross-examination and prejudiced the jury, thereby making a fair trial impossible. Pollock said that his behaviour 'in a word is dirty pool and it is not supposed to happen in front of a jury'. Higham got his copy for the BBC. But although 'they were very uneasy', according to Caldecott, the judges kicked the arguments into touch. Appeal dismissed. Branson and Carman had won again.

Together with his lesser-known brothers, Ali and Shah, Mohamed Al-Fayed bought Harrods for £615 million on 11 March 1985. A decade later, George was giving regular advice to the most controversial businessman in Britain in the chairman's suite of offices on the top floor of the top people's store. As in his dealings with Maxwell, George spent many hours with Al-Fayed over a period of five years, discussing the day-to-day intricacies of litigation, without once appearing in front of a jury on his behalf. The range of libel advice was considerable, including the long-running battle against the American magazine *Vanity Fair*, eventually settled in the autumn of 1997; the action against Tom Bower, author of an 'explosive' unauthorised biography in 1998; and the case which got closest to reaching a fight in court, against the former deputy chairman of Harrods Christoph Betterman, in February 1996. All of these actions were eventually dropped or settled.

On 31 August 1997, Princess Diana and Dodi Fayed, Mohamed's son, were killed in a car crash in the Place de l'Alma tunnel, Paris. George had previously advised Diana on one or two legal matters, but nothing that was ever likely to reach a courtroom. In the weeks leading up to their deaths, however, intrusion by the press during the couple's Mediterranean holidays had reached an extraordinary level. In mid-August, Mohamed approached George, who was in Singapore savaging Prime Minister Goh in the political libel case already mentioned, to advise the couple on taking legal action. He was due to have informal discussions with them in early September.

Throughout the mid-1990s, Al-Fayed worked closely with the *Guardian*, helping to bring down several government ministers while providing some of the crucial information about the 1993 Paris Ritz weekend which helped to destroy Jonathan Aitken four years later. Of all those whom he helped to remove from office, the one Conservative who was determined to wreak revenge at all costs was the MP for Tatton, Neil Hamilton. He had been Corporate Affairs Minister at the DTI, from April 1992 until 27 October 1994, when he was told by Michael Heseltine to resign. The instruction was given a week after the *Guardian* published revelations about cash payments made to him by Al-Fayed under the headline, 'Tory MPs Were Paid to Plant Questions Says Harrods Chief'. Hamilton sued together with Ian Greer, the parliamentary lobbyist.

In July 1995, George represented the *Guardian* and got the case stopped on a complicated point of law relating to Article 9 of the Bill of Rights 1689. Hamilton, supported by Baroness Thatcher among others, got the law changed in his favour with an amendment to Section 13 of the new Defamation Act 1996. Greer and Hamilton then fell out. Greer had failed to disclose payments. Hamilton was proved to have been economical with the truth in revealing the nature of his financial relationship with Greer to Michael Heseltine when questioned about it in October 1994. As the former Deputy Prime Minister recounts in his

autobiography *Life in the Jungle*: 'His understanding had dif-
fered from mine. There can be no way of reconciling such a
difference of interpretation.'

The case was eventually dropped on terms humiliating for
Hamilton. The *Guardian* ran with 'A Liar and a Cheat'. On 16
January 1997, Channel 4 broadcast a programme, *A Question of
Sleaze*, in which Al-Fayed repeated the allegations of corruption.
Hamilton issued a libel writ against him. On 1 May 1997, he
lost his seat at the General Election. In an unprecedented show
of unanimity, the Labour and Liberal Democrat parties had
agreed not to put up candidates against him in Tatton, leaving
the way clear for the independent anti-sleaze candidate Martin
Bell to romp home with a majority of 11,077 votes. Two and a
half years later, Hamilton risked everything on a courtroom libel
battle with Al-Fayed, again in Court 13 of the Royal Courts of
Justice. At last, George was going into battle for Al-Fayed in a
case of high drama and much media attention.

The inevitable question is what did George think of his client,
Mohamed Al-Fayed, the flamboyant Egyptian billionaire? The
answer is complicated, matching the complexity of the man.
Certainly, he was not oblivious to Al-Fayed's many faults nor
to his capacity (as his publicist Max Clifford put it to me) 'to
shoot himself in the foot'. George would also have endorsed
Clifford's comment that 'He's his own worst enemy, but that
to me is part of the attraction. The problem with Mohamed is
that he does say what he thinks and what he feels without
considering the consequences.'

George spent much of his time trying to explain those consequences to Al-Fayed, who took little interest in the law, only in
results. Subtleties were lost on him as he became easily bored
by lengthy processes. He wanted to cut the Gordian knot of
every problem with an instant solution. For a lawyer, he was a
nightmare client, concerned only to launch a diatribe against his
opponents. An army of Harrods in-house lawyers did not help.
When the chips were down, as in the Hamilton case, the prospect

of giving evidence concentrated his mind a little better. He listened to a point, promising to do what George told him. But ultimately it was a charade.

George would describe meetings with Al-Fayed as 'impossible' or just laugh at the absurdity of it all, imitating his thick Egyptian accent and the cascade of expletives. For the most part, he went with the flow, laughed at the jokes and knew when he could take no more. Behind his client's feigned lack of interest was a strong gut instinct for self-preservation. Once the boredom threshold was reached, he would disappear, leaving George in mid-sentence, and return with a teddy bear or a cigar. Presents were part of his culture. Alert to the possible dangers of accepting even a modest gift, these would be gratefully declined. The only exceptions were Harrods Christmas hampers, delivered without fail for six years, and the transfer between homes of the Bosendorfer baby grand in 1999. A call was made to Al-Fayed to ask if he could arrange for Harrods specialist movers to deal with the piano. He was delighted to oblige.

The best indication of proximity in the relationship with Al-Fayed was that for four years after his cancer was first diagnosed in 1996 George shared his personal doctor, Annie Coxon. Based in Harley Street, she had had a strict Catholic upbringing before her conversion to Islam. An intelligent, compassionate and dedicated woman, she had the patience and presence of mind to handle George, who had worked his way through many different doctors in his life, falling out with most of them. For Al-Fayed, health was paramount, and the continuous concern for his favourite barrister was entirely genuine. There were many offers to send him for treatment to Johns Hopkins and the Mayo Clinic in the States. In the event, they were not accepted, but inevitably they affected his assessment. With many criticisms of Al-Fayed, George would agree: difficult, yes; impossible, yes; outrageous, yes; awkward, yes. But kind and considerate too. And that mattered.

Immediately after the case opened on 15 November 1999,

there were three days of legal argument about the admissibility of evidence relating to a consultancy payment of £10,000 made by Mobil Oil to Hamilton in 1989. George got a favourable ruling from the droll Mr Justice Morland, the same judge as in the Branson–G-Tech case. This was a crucial break for Al-Fayed, allowing the case to be fought on two fronts. A trial within a trial emerged on the Mobil issue, completely independent from Al-Fayed's evidence. Again, there was an element of the 'rabbit out of the hat' for George, since the crucial evidence did not arrive at the offices of D. J. Freeman until midnight on Friday 12 November.

The jury knew none of this, and the trial proper began on Thursday 18 November. George opened with a bang. Hamilton, he said, 'was a greedy and unscrupulous politician, who was on the make and on the take and who over the years has shown his character to be deeply flawed by a degree of dishonesty, by half-truths and lies, disguising his financial activities'. He catalogued Al-Fayed's gifts to Hamilton: the many cash gifts (totalling up to £30,000) paid in bundles of £50 notes put into brown envelopes, the presents of Harrods gift vouchers totalling £8,000, and Neil and Christine Hamilton's stay at the Paris Ritz Hotel in 1987, when they spent £2,000 on meals and vintage wine (paid for by Al-Fayed). He talked of the couple's 'uncontrolled greed and unbridled extravagance'. He explained that the cash was paid because Hamilton was retained by Greer to ask questions on Al-Fayed's behalf in the House of Commons. Al-Fayed would give it to Hamilton when the two men were alone together, or it would be left for collection. George also highlighted the Mobil payment as the '£10,000 demand that shocked an oil firm'.

In contrast to George, who was labelled 'Scary Silk' by the press, Desmond Browne QC, Hamilton's counsel, the grandson of the 9th Earl of Bessborough and an Old Etonian, was dubbed 'Posh Silk'. Prim and precise, Browne did not pull any punches either, saying that Al-Fayed 'had no respect for the truth', that he was 'the Phoney Pharaoh of Harrods' and 'the Ali Baba of Deceit' who was 'a deeply vindictive man, ready to take his revenge on those who he sees as responsible for the lies he tells'. He said that Al-Fayed 'had forfeited all sympathy' by spreading false stories about the death of his son Dodi and Princess Diana. Even the *Financial Times* headlined day one as a 'slanging match'. This was only a warm-up.

Al-Fayed's stay in the witness box, at five and a half days, lasted nearly as long as that endured by Belmarsh Prison's best-known former inmate Jonathan Aitken. George did not keep his Egyptian client long, just long enough to tell the court of the cash and gifts paid to Hamilton: 'He had discovered the golden goose . . . for me he is nothing, he is not a human, he is a someone who would sell his mother for money – no dignity, no honour, nothing.' He explained how Greer had told him how 'You can rent an MP like you rent a taxi,' and he declared that 'The voter has to know, the ordinary people have to know what kind of people they have put in power.'

Browne started a marathon cross-examination by scrutinising Al-Fayed's age. There was a long debate about his year of birth – 1929 or 1933? As with Ken Dodd, four years seemed to have gone missing in the mists of time. Browne moved on to his name, accusing him of using the prefix 'Al' to make himself sound grander in the Arab world. Al-Fayed replied: 'You can call me Al Capone if you like.' He had originally cracked this joke in conversation with George a couple of weeks earlier. George told him to drop it into his evidence. He did so seamlessly. Over the next week, things were not always so jolly.

The next day saw a catalogue of allegations from Al-Fayed: that the Duke of Edinburgh had 'masterminded the murder' of Diana and Dodi, that Michael Howard, the former Home Secretary, had 'taken a bribe of £1.5 million' and that Hamilton had 'hired rent boys'. Browne took him through a videotaped lunch with Tiny Rowland in which Al-Fayed had said of Hamilton: 'He took maybe £30,000 in cash . . . he's a prostitute, a homosexual.' When questioned on this, Al-Fayed told the court: 'It was casual discussion about rumours.' He went on to talk about Mrs Thatcher, who 'just threw me to the dogs' because she 'just wanted to cover up her son's arms deals'. Browne challenged him about seven staff members at Harrods whom he had 'bugged' and 'vindictively harassed', including Betterman, the former deputy chairman. Al-Fayed dismissed these as of no consequence.

On Al-Fayed's fifth day in the witness box, Browne turned to money and his weekly cash withdrawals.

BROWNE: 'You have four children – £120,000 a week is a fairly handsome family budget.'

AL-FAYED: 'It is none of your bloody business, it is my business . . . get on with your cross-examination and don't waste the time of everybody.'

Browne was now getting to the heart of his case. He listed inconsistencies in Al-Fayed's evidence, saying that it was not supported by 'a single document'. The insults continued.

BROWNE: 'If it is true that cash had, on your instruction, been prepared for collection by Mr Hamilton, you would have said that yourself long before September 1996.'

AL-FAYED: 'I cannot comment . . . because you are talking a load of crap.'

To add to the heat of this cross-examination, Browne became very agitated at George's highly audible stage whispers while he was on his feet. His patience finally gave way. 'The noises really are becoming intolerable,' he said to Morland. The judge, obviously amused by George's gamesmanship, responded: 'You'll just have to do the best you can, Mr Browne.'

George re-examined Al-Fayed, asking him about his failure to obtain citizenship.

CARMAN: 'Can you tell the jury how you feel about that?'

AL-FAYED: 'It's very sad and unconvincing. For somebody like me who has given thirty-five years of his life . . . [at this point his voice became emotional and he wiped away a tear]'

CARMAN: 'I think you've answered the question.'

AL-FAYED (tearfully): 'And he is insulted, humiliated, his son can be murdered, he can face in front of crooked people raised to power. They know they are guilty . . . [pointing to Hamilton] he knows, he take cash, and then I have to continue such trauma for the rest of my life. [Turning to Morland] I'm sorry, your Lordship.'

Finally on the question of the payments, Al-Fayed agreed with George that he was not good on detail.

CARMAN: 'Do you remember the important things?'

AL-FAYED: 'Sometimes.'

CARMAN: 'Do you have a clear memory or not of paying Neil Hamilton?'

AL-FAYED: 'Definite.'

Alison Bozek entered the witness box. After being Al-Fayed's secretary from 1981 to 1994, she had qualified as a solicitor. She talked about payments to Hamilton: 'One particular occasion sticks very clearly in my mind. I went into Mr Al-Fayed's office and he had his briefcase on the desk open in front of him. He took out a wodge of cash and put it into an envelope, a white envelope into which he put the money, and he scrawled on the envelope Neil Hamilton's name. I can remember to this day Neil Hamilton's name scrawled on the envelope.' She denied lying when Browne suggested her account was false: 'That's absolutely untrue, Mr Browne. I wouldn't risk all the hard work I have done qualifying to be a lawyer. It has taken nine years and I wouldn't risk that for anybody, I can assure you.' Iris Bond, who had worked at Al-Fayed's Park Lane offices for twenty-one years, supported Bozek's evidence. She confirmed that she had witnessed three occasions when cash had been organised for Mr Hamilton. Finally, a security officer, Philip Bromfield, confirmed that he had handed over envelopes to Hamilton at Park Lane.

The trial within a trial began as the Mobil payment now entered the scene. Peter Whiteman QC, a tax consultant to Mobil, testified that he had been 'very surprised and embarrassed' when Hamilton asked about a fee with the words 'What do Mobil pay?' The former MP had been used to help the company's opposition to the Finance Bill of 1989: 'It was a very short amendment [to the bill]. I did not anticipate for one moment that he would seek payment,' said Whiteman. A retired tax director of Mobil, Lionel Blumenthal, confirmed that he had been 'shocked and horrified' by Hamilton's request for £10,000 and that, although a consultancy agreement had been drawn up, he had 'no doubt that the reality was that we were buying off Mr Hamilton'.

On day fourteen of the case, Neil Hamilton began his evidence. 'Pack of lies' became his catchphrase. He used it repeatedly when asked about Al-Fayed's evidence. Anger, outrage and distress were also on offer as he dismissed as 'absurd' some of the allegations, saying that he 'went to the Ritz as a friend'. *The Times* caught one quotation in a sub-headline: 'But for the devastating impact of Mr Fayed's lies, I think I could have expected to take a front-rank position in the Conservative party in this parliament.' A bold claim. He added that his reputation had been damaged, he had lost his seat and 'It has been virtually impossible for me to find any work.' The following day, Thursday 9 December, Browne continued questioning Hamilton until 3.30 p.m. George welcomed the mid-afternoon break for a couple of quick cigarettes, before storming into action. He had been staying as usual at the Howard Hotel. Evenings had been spent trying to combat a heavy cold by downing hot toddies with his junior, James Price QC. The medicine had worked. Twenty-two minutes after starting his cross-examination, a dramatic exchange took place.

CARMAN: 'Are you really saying you would have had a realistic chance of sitting on the front bench now?'

HAMILTON: 'Mr Mandelson is back in the Cabinet.'

CARMAN: 'And when was Mr Mandelson criticised by a select committee and threatened with suspension [from the House of
Commons]?'

HAMILTON: 'Well, he was subject to a very great deal of criticism.'

CARMAN: 'This is about your claim for damages and loss of your
career prospects. Are you seriously saying to the jury, "Award me
damages for the loss of my career prospects, which include the
possibility that I would be serving as a front-bench spokesman"?'

HAMILTON: 'I am very happy to exclude from any damages the
possibility that I would have been a front-bench spokesman.'

CARMAN: 'Are you abandoning that?'

HAMILTON: 'I am quite happy to abandon that specific point.'

Hamilton was humiliated, forced to drop a claim that he had
made only the day before. On the next morning, George moved
relentlessly on. His theme was greed. He accused Hamilton of
lying to Michael Heseltine, lining his own pockets, fiddling his
tax return and 'throwing dust in the eyes' of those investigating
his financial affairs. The Paris Ritz once again became the centre
of attention and in particular the Hamiltons' six-night stay in
September 1987. 'There were no Big Macs or chicken sandwiches' had been part of his opening speech. George now concentrated on the couple's lavish consumption.

CARMAN: 'When you look at the fact that dinner with champagne
every single night never cost less than £200 in 1987, to call it " a
bit over the top" is a violent understatement, isn't it?'

HAMILTON: 'I know you can have your fun with this and I don't
blame you. It is of course an embarrassment. Looking back on it
now, we wish we hadn't done it. But what is done is done.'

CARMAN: 'Have you any shame over it?'

HAMILTON: 'Well, of course we do.'

George then went through the Ritz interlude meal by meal,
bottle by bottle, slowly accumulating the images of greed in the

jurors' minds. There were many tense and compelling exchanges in George's duel with Hamilton. The former minister was edgy, in contrast to the quiet, sarcastic deliberation of his tormentor. He tried to fight back with snappy quips of his own. When George mentioned the name of a former Harrods employee, Hamilton said he was in prison.

CARMAN: 'Why did you say that, Mr Hamilton? Was it to smear Mr Fayed?'

HAMILTON: 'It's the same technique that you are using against me. Two can play at that game.'

This was followed by:

CARMAN: 'You must rest assured that when I say I will come back to something I will.'

HAMILTON: 'I am resting very assured, Mr Carman.'

And then:

HAMILTON: 'I believe that is prejudicial.'

CARMAN: 'Many of my questions are intended to be prejudicial, Mr Hamilton, otherwise I would not ask them.'

HAMILTON: 'You have never hidden your light under a bushel, Mr Carman.'

And finally:

CARMAN: 'Do you pay close attention to anything you find particularly disagreeable?'

HAMILTON: 'I'm paying close attention to you.'

Towards the end of the cross-examination, Hamilton explained what winning the case would mean to him: 'If I win this action, I think I will be completely vindicated and I will be able to pursue a career in many walks of life.' He concluded: 'I don't have to be in this court to vindicate my character and I'm prepared to be cross-examined by the most fearsome advocate in the land on matters which are, in many respects, a grave

embarrassment to me.' Hamilton, who had qualified and practised briefly as a tax barrister, was fluent, articulate and well
rehearsed, but one exchange above all others highlighted his
semantic problem with the truth.

CARMAN: 'If when you answer someone's question you show a lack
of candour, do you still say you are telling the whole truth?'
HAMILTON: '. . . it is impossible to answer a question couched in
terms of such generality.'
CARMAN: 'Do you understand the words "tell the truth"?'
HAMILTON: 'Yes.'
CARMAN: 'If you answer a question with a lack of candour, do you
think you have given the whole truth?'
HAMILTON: 'I find it difficult to give an answer to that question . . .'

One of Hamilton's better answers had been: 'I am not going
to answer for my wife, Mr Carman. As you know, she is more
than able to answer for herself.' Christine Hamilton, author of
Le Bumper Book of British Battleaxes, had stood as a permanent
fixture at her husband's side during several years of scrutiny and
ridicule. They were inseparable. With blonde, swept-back hair
and mostly red check suits, she had spent four weeks glaring
fiercely at George with her piercing blue eyes. Now it was her
moment.

Through tears, she told Browne that Neil had lost one and a
half stone in weight and that he was a 'generous, not a greedy
man'. At one point she broke down. She said that she had gone
through Neil's pockets every night and there was no cash from
Al-Fayed. She said there was 'no money, no courier, no collection, no vouchers, nothing'. She called George's accusations
'absolutely grotesque'. As for the Ritz, she denied his suggestion
of greed in their consumption of vintage champagne, adding
that she wished she had 'never stepped across the threshold of
that beastly hotel'. George was deliberately economical with
Christine, keeping her evidence to a minimum, much to the
chagrin of reporters. Too much pressure might backfire with

the jury, he thought. The last witness was Brian Dodd, the former head of security at Harrods, who guaranteed himself headlines with a parting shot: 'Al-Fayed is the biggest bloody crook in town.'

In his closing speech, Browne said that Hamilton had had 'a long hard battle to clear his name' against the 'habitual liar' Mohamed Al-Fayed. He said that the Egyptian 'had robbed Hamilton of his reputation – personal, political and professional – and had stolen from him years of his useful life'. George concluded that Hamilton had 'disqualified' himself from damages 'because the case against him is made out on the evidence'. He said that Hamilton had 'made a naked appeal for sympathy' by referring to his limited means. He said that the way Al-Fayed had been cross-examined was 'designed to create and build up against him an irresistible climate of prejudice' which occasionally 'had a racist element'.

Mr Justice Morland's summing up was balanced and well considered. He warned the jury that it was 'dangerous' to accept Al-Fayed's 'inconsistent and unreliable' evidence without corroboration. He said of the Egyptian: 'He has a warped appreciation of what is fact and what is fiction and what is truth and what is fiction.' He warned against finding for the Harrods owner 'unless you are convinced that evidence independent of Mr Al-Fayed's, which you find highly convincing, confirms Mr Al-Fayed's evidence in a material way'. Of Alison Bozek, he said: 'She is a very important witness. Are you satisfied that she has told the truth?' The same point was made of Bond and Bromfield. On the Ritz, he said it was important that what the Hamiltons had done was proved to be 'corrupt' and not merely 'greedy' behaviour. In damages, he suggested an upper ceiling of £150,000. Finally, on Mobil, he said: 'If that transaction had been dishonestly concealed, that was corrupt.'

The jury of six women and five men (one had stood down through illness) took eight hours to reach their unanimous verdict in favour of Al-Fayed at 2.30 p.m. on 21 December. The shortest day of the year was the longest day in the lives of Neil and Christine Hamilton. They walked out of the courtroom, exhibiting dignity in defeat, to stand arm in arm outside the Royal Courts of Justice with brave words for the waiting throng of cameras and journalists. But their faces told the true story of devastation, disaster and humiliation: the three words which dominated the following day's headlines. George waited more than forty minutes for Al-Fayed's arrival in the court building. He wanted to share publicly in the moment of glory – it meant so much. Al-Fayed emerged on the pavement, holding both arms aloft in victory. George and Mohamed then stood together on the court steps, smiling and hugging in celebration for the cameras, flanked by Susan Aslan and the team at D. J. Freeman. It was the end of the year, the end of the Millennium, the end (for the moment) of the Hamiltons and the end, the Tory Party hoped, of sleaze in British politics.

For George, it was nearly the end of his glittering career. This was his last great public triumph. His retirement eight months later came before the Hamiltons' appeal, which took place in December 2000. When that decision came through, George was thrilled that the Court of Appeal had upheld the jury's verdict, confirming and underlining his achievement. This last judgment proved that he was a winner right to the close of proceedings.

13

The Three Graces

We think caged birds sing, when indeed they cry.

John Webster

This chapter is given over to George's three wives: Ursula, Celia and Frances. After lengthy interviews with each of them, these accounts accurately and fairly reflect their experiences of marriage. For Ursula and Celia, the words which follow are entirely their own. After reading the transcript of her interview, Frances found it traumatic to see her own words in print, describing the events of her marriage. She asked instead if I would produce a brief summary of our conversation.

George once said that 'Barristers don't make good husbands,' and, in another interview, 'The best barristers are not good husbands because they always put the job first.' In a 1997 interview with the BBC journalist Martyn Lewis, he expanded further. Lewis said: 'You have been married three times. Do you regard your personal life as a failure?' George replied: 'I don't regard it as a failure. I think that is an over-simplification. I am sure the failure of those marriages ultimately is something for which I bear responsibility, but nevertheless one shouldn't regret that fact. I look back on the positive features. I look back on what I learned from them. I look back on the fact that much happiness was mixed with the unhappiness that eventually emerged. So life is not all good or bad. It is a glorious mix and I am not prepared to confess to failure in my personal life, although it could have been very much better if I had been able to work at it harder.'

Ursula

When introduced to George in the autumn of 1954, Ursula Groves was twenty-two and he was twenty-four. They married in July 1955 and remained together for three years, before separating in 1958 and divorcing in 1960. She remarried in 1971 and had a daughter, Alice.

We met in the Clifton Hotel, owned by his brother-in-law's family. George was noticeably small, but was clearly a very smart cookie. Like me, he had just lost his mother, who had died from cancer shortly beforehand. This made me feel sympathetic towards him. She had been a huge influence in his life and he obviously missed her a great deal. He kept phoning me up when I was keeping house for my father. So we went out together, but not very much.

Like a lot of people, I was taken by his dry wit and intellect, but I was very surprised when he asked me to marry him, since we didn't really know each other very well. I had been out with several boyfriends and was quite popular. Maybe I was a bit of a snob then, because a barrister seemed to be better than anything else that was on offer and I was flattered. I thought he needed a strong woman behind him, but I was also aware that this was to some degree a marriage of convenience, with mutual benefit. For George, I was probably a good catch because of my family connections.

When we got engaged, he gave me his mother's diamond engagement ring. I said yes and then told him he should go and see my father, Peter Groves, to ask him for my hand in marriage. My father ran the local brewery in Salford, which had been in the Peer-Groves family since the 1820s. He had been to Charterhouse, before getting a first at Cambridge. George got on well with him and they talked for hours. He thought George could do some of the things he hadn't and helped him by sending him to Conservative selection committees, since he was very active in politics. My uncle, Grimble Groves, had been a Tory MP. George was too effete for a working-class Manchester constituency and was never the sort to have pints in a bar. He was much better on the piano at Yates's Wine Lodge, playing lots of popular songs for the old ladies, who loved it.

He was always very concerned about his image and putting on a front. He chose St Anne's Church in Manchester, because it had status and was near the Café Royal, where we had a reception for 200 guests. For our honeymoon, we went to Venice. There was a thunderstorm and George was terrified, hiding under the sheets, like a rabbit in a hutch. This was the first indication I had of his paranoia. Beforehand, he had been so controlled, polite and charming to everyone we met. I discovered in time that he had lots of different psychosomatic problems. You needed to handle him with kid gloves at all times and be very careful what you said.

I soon realised that he was a strange person, but did not mind since my own family was quite eccentric. He seemed to be deeply ashamed of his family background and did his best to hide the detail. I felt very sorry for his father, Alf. He was such a nice man, proud of his son, but also frightened of him, because he was so clever, and at the same time so hurtful. George would not come down to his father's level, as he saw it. Once, when we had driven to court in Preston, he took a detour on the way back home, parking outside a very small terraced house, two up, two down. He said to me: 'My grandfather lives here, but you can't come in because he wouldn't know who you are.' He went in for ten minutes while I waited in the car outside. He was embarrassed and didn't want me to meet him, because he lived in very humble circumstances. George mentioned to me the following year that he had died. He did not go to the funeral.

He argued a lot with his sister Joyce. They were both very highly strung, like their mother. I had met Evelyn briefly before I knew George, when I studied at Blackpool Catering College for three years in the early 1950s. Alf had helped financially when Joyce got married. George was jealous, even though our fathers had each given us £1,500 when we got married, which was quite a lot of money then. My cousin also lent him a new car that he smashed up, which was a great shame.

Money was a problem with George, who lived way beyond his means, spending too much in the clubs, always happy to buy drinks for other people. He would also buy me grand dresses and suits which he chose to impress others, but never stopped to get the small things that mattered, like a box of chocolates or a bunch of flowers. After we had been married for eighteen months, his overspending got to such a degree that the house in Sale that we had bought had to be sold and we lived in a rented flat in Wilmslow.

His mother had left him some of her valuable antique jewellery and my grandmother had also given me several lovely pieces from Asprey's. They were all pawned. Whenever we went to lavish functions such as the Jewish wedding receptions of the barristers he knew, and especially when we went to see his sister, we had to get them out of hock. Later, most of the jewellery and furniture had to be sold to pay the substantial debts he had built up by the time we divorced.

George was very disappointed that my family, who had money, did not put more of it my way. His father gave him a few handouts, but he was never out of trouble. I earned more than he did, which he hated, resenting the fact that I had to work at all. He said that my job, as a canteen manageress at Great Universal Stores, was lowly and menial. He said this was not the sort of thing for a barrister's wife to do. I was working hard for him to succeed since he was not earning much at the time and needed support. He seemed to enjoy having power over me, shouting and putting me down in every way he could, because he was more intelligent than I was. It was part of the way he controlled me.

He asked me to watch him in court if I wasn't working. He was very sharp and quick on his feet, charming the judges by quoting judgments and using lots of Latin phrases. Fred, his clerk, used to say to him: 'Mr Carman, what do you do with your money?' I think he knew the answer. As well as getting him to chase his outstanding fees, George was very ambitious to do more important cases and to get on.

Before marriage, I had been looking forward to a bit of romping on the bed, but there was nothing. The marriage was never consummated. Like a lot of women starved of sex, I became very emotional and we had lots of arguments about it. I tried all sorts of things to make myself attractive to him. I went to a Lucie Clayton modelling school and I lost weight. At home, he wanted me to dress up and parade for him in the same way as the showgirls did in the clubs that he liked to go to. So I did. But he still couldn't have sex. Underneath, I was probably aware when we got married that he was hiding part of his sexuality. I would not have been surprised if he had told me he was bisexual, but he didn't. I knew the pattern from one of my uncles who lived with us as a child and was openly gay. I never discussed it with George, even when he used to get postcards from Manchester with strange cryptic messages in coded language. They were obviously from another man, not a woman.

The time he spent in the nightclubs and mixing with underworld life put him only a hair's breadth away from the people whom he had to represent in court. I think he drank so much because he was highly strung and, like a lot of people, to escape. It helped him relax. I went with him sometimes and quite enjoyed it. We went to all sorts of strange places – they were not exactly Annabel's. One was run by a couple of wrestlers and, in another, we used to have a laugh with the comedian Tommy Cooper. But George was a snob and he did not really want his wife to be part of that scene. He liked to go off by himself, disappearing all night and coming back without any explanation. He knew a wide range of people and drank with many different types. Yet he was essentially a loner without any really close mates, although he could really turn on the charm when he wanted.

Part of the problem was that he got into arguments and could fall out with people quite easily. Manchester people did not like it when he became too smart with them at their expense. They were also wary of him.

Most nights of the week, he would get drunk and come home late. He always had to 'see people' and 'discuss his work'. Then, after a few months of marriage, for no apparent reason, the beatings began. They usually followed his drinking bouts, which could put him in a foul temper. I would get bruises, black eyes and cut lips. Often, I would curl into a ball on the floor as he punched and kicked me. I did not retaliate, letting my body go floppy until, eventually, he stopped. At the time, I thought it was because he was worried about lack of money and not having enough work. On reflection, I think it was partly a form of sexual gratification, since a lot of his anger was linked to his frustration, and partly a form of manipulation. I wish I had been as tough then as I am now. I was walked over and I never told anyone at the time. He never said sorry or explained why he did it and I never asked him about it or complained. This probably sounds strange, but I looked up to him and, because he was so clever, I forgave him, despite the humiliation I felt.

When I committed adultery and told him what I had been up to, he went ballistic. He was really surprised because he didn't think I was sexy and could not really understand it. His attitude seemed to be, well, I can't have her, so no one else is going to either. We did, however, have one night of passion after we separated. At about that time, he met Celia, who was singing in a nightclub. He was obviously very taken with her, talking about the paintings of flowers that she would do backstage. When we discussed divorce, George was afraid that I would come out with details of violence, so he got a private detective to give evidence that he had committed adultery. We got on better after the separation. He used to come round every week to give me £5 maintenance, using it as an excuse to keep control and see what I was up to. I now see that as part of his manipulation. When he stopped coming, the money stopped as well.

I came out of the marriage damaged and with very low self-esteem. Yet, in a strange way, after we split up I missed his intellect and his tremendous, quick ability with words. I was always very taken by that. I went to America for three years, visiting George's friend Professor George Steiner. Afterwards, I had an unconventional life for many years to escape what had happened, travelling the world as a hippy, before I remarried and had a daughter, Alice, in 1972.

A friend pointed out to me a newspaper interview with George in 1991, which said that he had only been married twice. I went dashing down to the library to look in *Who's Who*. He had deliberately not listed me in it. I thought, I'm not going to have that, so I approached a newspaper, because I was furious and wanted to put the record straight. I had worked hard to support him and he had conveniently forgotten about me. Maybe it was because the marriage in his mind was never a proper marriage. I don't know. He did terrible things, but maybe I'm old now and more detached. On reflection, I suppose that I feel sorry for him and will always think of him as poor George.

Celia

When she met the twenty-eight-year-old George in 1958, Celia was a twenty-year-old singer, performing on stage in the Piccadilly Club in Manchester. They married in July 1960, separated in 1972 and divorced in 1976.

After my first night singing in Manchester, I got some flowers with a note signed 'from George', who then came to introduce himself as George Cavendish. Some days later, he told me that his real surname was Carman and that Cavendish was a pseudonym he used. He was sweet: polite, softly spoken and extremely attentive. He was older than my friends and I was flattered by the attention. He seemed quaintly old-fashioned. But I did not dislike that. My booking was only for a week and I returned to London, where I lived with my parents. He arranged for another club owner, whom he knew, to book me for a further week. This ended up with George playing the piano each night while I sang.

He discussed his life with me in great detail, telling me that he was separated and in the process of getting a divorce. I found out that I had a similar sort of strict Catholic upbringing to his, having been educated in a convent, and thought that it must be very difficult for him to contemplate divorce. He told me that, since he hadn't been married in a Catholic church, it had not been a proper marriage. Before George, I had not had many boyfriends because I was keen to develop my acting career after RADA. My mother had been a businesswoman and was very ambitious for me. My father had been gassed in the trenches and was very reserved.

George drove to London to see me at weekends, taking me out for dinner in lots of different restaurants. He was a great letter writer and would send flowers regularly. One weekend, when we were sitting together on a bench outside Kenwood House, he asked me to go back and live with him in Manchester, that same evening. He was very insistent and I agreed. When I telephoned my mother to tell her, she was very upset. After staying together for a few months, I moved back home because he was violent towards me on several occasions. I did not tell anyone. Endless phone calls and flowers followed, and he would park outside my parents' house for hours, waiting for me to come out. I relented and he proposed marriage to me shortly afterwards by saying: 'I want you to be the mother of my son.' Eventually I agreed and we had a Catholic wedding in north London. My family were not at all happy. My elder brother Donald, who is twelve years my senior, thought George was arrogant and not the right man for me. I did not meet his family at all until after we were married. We had no honeymoon because George was working. We drove home to Manchester. When we arrived, there were make-up stains on the bed, which was not a great start. I remember George said: 'What do you expect? You haven't been here living with me.'

While he could spend hours chatting to people he knew over the bar, it did not take long to discover that he also had a great capacity for abuse when he had had a few drinks. Often this would be directed at people he did not even know. He could be incredibly rude and insulting, saying to someone, 'And what kind of job do you do?', before tearing them to shreds for no reason at all. It was totally unnecessary and unprovoked. He once came home after being punched in the face, which did not really surprise me by that time.

I would have preferred to wait before starting a family, but George wanted to start immediately. So I became pregnant within a few months. His attitude changed completely and the physical side of our relationship ended. For the next twelve years, there was no intimacy or affection at all. I blamed myself, although I could not see a reason for it. When I found out about the women whom he was seen with, I could not understand it. Some of them were rough and unattractive, yet he seemed to flaunt them as if they were desirable. It did not make sense to me.

When I was pregnant, he made no attempt to help. He never took me shopping for food or even made a cup of tea. In fact, trivial as it may sound, he never made me a cup of tea. He suffered from lots of vaso-vagal attacks when I was pregnant, because of nerves. It became apparent that he was something of a hypochondriac. Most nights of the week, he stayed out drinking and I would go and meet him in bars, until I became too heavily pregnant. He also returned to violence and once hit me in the stomach outside our house. But I never discussed this with him or anyone else. I was too ashamed and afraid.

On the night Dominic was born, George told me that he was drinking champagne in a club to celebrate. A drinking friend of his from John Gorna's office, called Donald Short, came to see me in hospital the following morning with a fuchsia plant. George arrived later, but did not send any flowers. He was very proud of having a son, but never played with Dominic or read stories to him, becoming quite irate if he banged his cup with a spoon or cried loudly.

George would typically phone up in the evening at 7 or 7.30 and say: 'I'm just having a quick drink. I'll be home for dinner in half an hour.' I would take this to mean that he would not come back until 12 or 1 in the morning, sometimes later. And I was usually right. He would drive back every night, no matter how drunk he was, until he had a bad car accident, which scared him. After that, he developed a phobia about driving and got taxis everywhere.

When my mother and sister came to stay at the house, he would keep away and not come back until late. By then George could not put on an act even for a few days and made no pretence to be polite or to spend time with them. He did not see his own father very often, since they did not see eye to eye, although he asked for his financial help several times when he had been gambling. Eventually, this was refused because Alf knew why George needed the money.

Once his day in court had finished, the casino became the number-one thing in his life, after he had warmed up at the bar for a few hours. He started by taking me, on the pretext of going out to dinner or the theatre, but instead I had to watch him play cards. I hated it. When we could not afford to go on holiday or have furniture in the house or sometimes have money even for the basics in life, to see him put down £100 or £200 on the table would really hurt. I would think, we could have done this or we could have afforded that, if he had not lost the money. But he was horribly addicted and nothing would prevent him. I soon stopped going. He would then regularly not come back until 3 or 4 a.m. Sometimes, he did not come home at all and I did not know where he was. This became the normal routine of life.

I left him once in 1966. Taking the overnight train to London, Dominic and I went to my mother's house. After we arrived, a policeman came to the door. George had reported me to the police for illegally withdrawing Dominic from the family home. It frightened me and my mother, so we turned round and got the first train back to Manchester. In the middle of shouting at me, he also took Dominic off on several occasions, leaving him with his London friends in Holland Park and elsewhere. He never told me where he was at the time.

George's fellow barristers seemed to hold him in high regard, though some of them were a little wary. I think they could see beyond the charm. Many, like his head of chambers Godfrey Heilpern, were quite family-orientated, which was at odds with George's style. But, although we did not mix with them very much socially, George liked most of his chambers colleagues and enjoyed talking about work with them. He would also talk to me about his cases for hours on end. Sometimes this was very interesting. At other times, I found it boring and told him so, which really annoyed him.

I knew I wasn't marrying a rich man, but it seemed that there was never enough money to do anything. The house had to be sold to pay off the bank overdraft, which had gone way out of control through gambling. George said we needed to rent a place for a short while. He was lucky to find somewhere cheap. Over the next few years, he never had the money, or desire, to buy another house. Every day George lived life exactly as he chose, never explaining or apologising for his behaviour. If you asked him why, there would be real trouble. By asking a question or trying to begin a discussion, you were criticising him and he would become very aggressive. Even though a small man, like an angry Jack Russell he made people scared to confront him. They tried to keep their distance, but he was very good at involving people to get them on his side.

George was often violent. He would punch me and bang my head against the wall. He broke things in the house frequently.

After one Sunday-lunchtime drinking session, he came into the kitchen, threw out the cutlery drawer and pulled out two large carving knives, saying: 'Which one do you want in you first?' I have tried to block the memories of violence like this out of my mind and don't like to remember it, but I think it should be known that violence continued throughout our marriage. To talk about it now is a healing process and I see now after a number of years that I was damaged by the experience. I wish I had talked about it before, but I didn't to protect him.

He often brought Dominic down out of bed and then abused me in front of him. This was terrible. To avoid being treated as a resident punchbag, I developed the habit of keeping out of his way when he came back drunk and late. I knew by the look in his eyes when I opened the door if he was about to hit me. Sometimes, I hid in the garden for safety. The worst aspect was that George was so intelligent and articulate and yet so brutal and barbaric. It was very difficult to contend with mentally because of the fear and humiliation it caused. I had no idea that he had been violent towards Ursula. I thought it was just me that brought this out in him and that it must be my fault.

When people talk about violence in a marriage, they usually mean physical violence. But much worse for me was the mental violence. This was the really sinister part of George. The tongue-lashing and constant erosion of self-esteem was punishing. He was expert in the business of slow and sustained humiliation over a long period. One small example sticks in my mind. He once brought home a girl whom he had picked up, called Barbara. He got Dominic, who was then eight years old, and told him to 'kiss the pretty lady' in front of me. It made me feel sick. I said nothing because in those days I was so conditioned that I dared not speak. People may ask why on earth a woman would stay in a relationship like that, but I just did. I was mesmerised in the situation and could not get out of it. George was the ultimate control-freak.

He bought himself a pair of velvet trousers with a coloured

embroidered butterfly on the front. For a man who dressed conservatively, it was a bizarre choice. Something flipped and I ripped it off. I cannot explain why but somehow it was symbolic of his whole attitude – the delicacy of the butterfly somehow made me snap. Maybe it reflected the refined cruelty of which he was capable. He made an art form of it. I decided to consult my solicitor, Michael Sachs, who was later appointed a High Court judge. George was scared by this and persuaded me that things would be different, that he would change and that we could have another child. When he became a QC in 1971, he was very pleased. He told me: 'Celia, I'm going right to the top and I'm going to take you with me.' He was offered a place in excellent chambers in London and played with the idea, but would not take the risk of moving. This always struck me as odd for someone who gambled so much.

George introduced me to George Best, who phoned me up. We had an affair that lasted for a few months. George did not know what was going on. He took the view that it was okay for him to go off and do what he wanted, but it was not acceptable for me to do the same. When he did find out, he went berserk, discussing it in great detail with lots of people. He wanted me out of the city straight away, so I went to live on my own in London. After a couple of months, I returned to Manchester and he begged me to come back for good, but I just couldn't. He asked me if he could get the divorce on the grounds of my adultery. He said it might affect his career and any chance that he might have of becoming a judge. I did not want any more hassle and was quite happy to agree. I spent many months sitting in a London flat on my own, asking myself why it had all happened. I just couldn't face anybody.

George had tremendous ability and more than his share of luck, but there was an extraordinary destructive urge within him and an anger that never made sense. If only he could have somehow got himself together as a person, we could have had a wonderful family life. I have tried to forgive him for what he did to me, but I cannot yet forgive what he did to the rest of his family.

Frances

When she met George in December 1973, Frances was working as a chef at Dalhousie Castle in Scotland. He was forty-four and she was twenty-three. Living together soon afterwards, they married in March 1976 and separated in 1983. They divorced. She remarried in 1984.

George took Frances to a number of good restaurants. Impressed by his sophistication and focused commitment to work, she was persuaded to live with him in Manchester. He sent her to the Pamela Holt model agency, where she learned to model, present herself and make conversation. He would inspect her nails and hands and prided himself on choosing most of her clothes, never allowing her to wear trousers, because they weren't feminine. Overall, he thought he had done a good job. She was told not to work because he expected her to look after him. It had never occurred to her that she would not be allowed to work any more. He ordered her to watch him in court in all the big cases. Even though she was passionate about creating wonderful food, he regarded catering as menial. Frustrated, she became conditioned to thinking of herself as worthless and second rate as he constantly put her down, destroying her self-confidence. He made her feel that she should do what he wanted, by organising and controlling her life.

They married after two years of living together. Her father was devastated. George did not want to know her parents, which distressed her because she came from a close family. She wanted to have a child and needed to have an operation to straighten out one of her fallopian tubes. She devised all sorts of ways to chat George up, but he wasn't interested and stopped showing any affection towards her. They never had a proper physical relationship, before or after marriage. She now believes he thought that sex was dirty. His violence angered her. She was a fighter who fought back when he attacked her during their terrible rows. She decided then that he wasn't balanced. During one argument, he threw her down the stairs and cracked her hip. Even then, she stayed, believing she could put things right.

He spent a lot of time drinking in nightclubs. She often went to get him out of trouble. In a desperate attempt to stop his gambling, she threw chips all over the table at the Playboy Club. The manager asked her to leave. On earlier occasions, she had telephoned the club, begging them not to cash his cheques. George was furious. After one of his worst binges, she saw him lose £60,000 when there were many overdue bills to pay and the bailiffs were due in. The house was sold to cover everything. She felt very ashamed.

An epileptic, Frances was annoyed that George used her condition as an excuse when he changed his mind about being a judge in Hong Kong. Most of her fits were caused by George shouting and interrupting her sleep. But since the day she left him in 1983, she has been entirely free of them. She learned how to control her condition and can now drive.

She thought of ways to escape without huge upheaval, trying to match him up with a wealthy Singapore businesswoman, who wasn't interested. When she finally had the courage to leave him, he started to phone up her parents, saying that she was having affairs, which was untrue. He wanted her to stay because he was losing a possession. Desperate to get out of the marriage, she would have paid George to get a divorce. She accepted his request to admit adultery, though she had always been faithful. To get away, she would have agreed to anything. After divorce, George would often phone up to discuss his many relationship problems, but they met again only twice. Although very hurt when he refused her request for some legal advice at a time of great personal difficulty in 1991, she was not entirely surprised.

Conclusion

There is a natural tendency to shut out unpleasant episodes in life. You try to forget but you can't. And George's behaviour towards my mother is something I would like erased from my mind. His tactics varied. Subtle bullying and intimidation were routine. Physical violence was quite regular. Ritual humiliation was a speciality. The verbal and physical attacks that I witnessed are my most vivid childhood memories. George needed an audience. From the age of four or five, I was made to watch each punishing performance as he degraded her in front of me with violent, caustic language and with blows from his fists. As it progressed, he explained in detail why she deserved this treatment. She did not fight back.

When he struck her, I remember standing between them, trying to stop him. Sometimes this helped to cool things down. The effects would still be visible on her face and arms for days afterwards. Drunk and in an aggressive state, he would often arrive home looking for a fight. He never used a key when he had been drinking, letting the bell ring incessantly until you answered. If I wasn't already awake, the noise of shouting would wake me. Like a man possessed, he aimed to destroy with a tirade of insults and threats, delivered with an incredible force, sometimes for hours at a stretch. His energy was inexhaustible. He would break china and glass against the wall. Complaining that the house was untidy, he would throw everything out of all the drawers. I recall standing in our kitchen aged nine as he smashed two windowpanes in the kitchen door with his bare fists after my mother had locked him out. Anaesthetised by drink, he did not notice the blood dripping from his hand. Such events were commonplace.

Although he was small, George became powerful with that peculiar strength which derives from anger. I noticed this as a teenager when intervening more successfully in his fights with Frances. His physical mistreatment of her was less frequent than it had been with Celia, but it was every bit as unpleasant. The effects were awful. She suffered many epileptic attacks caused by his late-night arrivals and sustained verbal abuse. Yet he never apologised, regarding it as just part of life. In our house, that is what it was.

The worst part of living with all this was the silence. Nothing was said when it was happening or in the years afterwards. Everything was kept quiet to protect George's reputation. I told no one what he was like or what he did, partly through shame and partly through fear. I never discussed with Frances his violence towards Celia or vice versa. After their divorces, neither Celia nor Frances talked about what had happened. In some ways, I wish I had asked George why he did it. This may have helped him accept the consequences of his actions and might have stopped him doing it. In meeting Ursula properly for the first time in April 2001, I recognised the expression in her eyes as she spoke. I understood her traumas and her memories. More than forty years after leaving, she could not forget George.

Lengthy taped interviews with Ursula, Celia and Frances tell a familiar story. Three different women, all with the same message, the same experience: a tale of damaged lives and secret suffering. Whatever demons tormented him, this is something for which George bore responsibility, but for which he never once showed regret.

14
Members of the Jury

[On looking at an hourglass]: To our eyes, it appears that the
sand runs out only at the end and, until it does, it's not worth
thinking about.

> From the film *Death in Venice*, based on the story
> by Thomas Mann

The last year of George's life proved to be just as eventful as
the first seventy. In January 2000, he announced the 'amicable'
dissolution of New Court Chambers. This had been on the
cards for some months. The twenty-six barristers would go their
separate ways from April. A quick move elsewhere inevitably
caused some disaffection as George joined a large and successful
set, 4–5 Grays Inn Square, headed up by Elizabeth Appleby QC.
They were delighted to have a big star name to make up for
imminent departures. He took the room vacated by Cherie Booth
QC, who was leaving to join a new human rights set called
Matrix Chambers. Former joint chambers head Michael Beloff
QC announced that he was going shortly afterwards. 'I don't
think they know quite what to make of me,' George said. He
took a back seat in chambers matters, expressing views only on
a planned merger and on expenses allocation – an endless source
of debate among barristers.

In April, Charles Kennedy, the Liberal Democrat leader,
approached him at a party. They had met before. 'Are you
going to go on for ever like Ted Heath?' Kennedy asked. The
conversation changed direction. 'Would you like to sit as a Lib-
Dem peer?' Not knowing if the offer was serious, George laughed
it off. Kennedy persisted. He asked George to speak further with
the Liberal peer Lord Razzall. The prospect of becoming Lord

Carman meant establishment recognition at last. George was thrilled. In the event, his name did not appear on the Liberal Democrat shortlist submitted to Tony Blair before the summer parliamentary recess. No reason was given.

He continued working in case after case. There were endless consultations. Anna Ford came to see him with her husband John Scott, a former US astronaut. 'I've never shaken the hand of a man who's been on the moon before,' ventured George. In court, the April 2000 victory for Marco Pierre White was followed by a libel involving a poison-pen letter and the key personnel at Derby County Football Club. Branson retained him in a new libel action against Tom Bower after the latter's biography was published. There was another retainer for a casino licence application in Southend. 'Very well paid,' commented George. Back at the Royal Courts of Justice, he was doing an interlocutory for a second Marco Pierre White libel case, this time against fellow chef Tony Allan. The faces in Court 13 were familiar. His junior was Victoria Sharp. His opponent was Desmond Browne QC. The judge was Dame Janet Smith. It was mid-July. This would be his last court appearance.

Over several weeks, he had become very excited about an interview by Ginny Dougary, 1999 interviewer of the year. A major *Times* profile was promised. 'She spent over four hours with me. God knows what she'll write,' George told me. Their meeting had been in early May. Impatient to see the article, he phoned her up several times to find out when it would be published. Eventually, on 13 July 2000, five pages of purplish prose headlined 'The Risk-Taker' appeared in a Section 2 profile, illustrated with copious photographs. George and Karen were positioned together on the newspaper's front-page masthead. It made a statement. 'Pretty good,' he said. He especially liked Dougary's description of his 'sexy little paunch'. The interviewer's more subtle observations showed why she had won the award. For most interviews, he remained cautious, watchful and concerned. There were so many things he did not want to talk about and yet he craved the publicity. The same dilemma arose with each request.

Dougary had got him to open up – a bit. It was quite an achievement. Among many observations was his comment on the actor who played him in the television reconstruction of the Hamilton–Al-Fayed case: 'The wretched man delivering my lines wasn't very impressive . . . I think my friend John Thaw might have done it rather better.' Although George had met Thaw a couple of times, it did not make him a friend. Some clients would be described in the same way. The elevation of well-known clients, celebrities, selected judges and distinguished barristers to the status of friend was an impression developed as part of vicarious living. Occasionally they were friends. More often they were not. Their acquaintance added substance to an empty life.

George passed out at a summer chambers party held at Lord's cricket ground and was attended to by St John's Ambulance. On the last Sunday in July, he called me to complain that walking by himself to Wimbledon village – less than a mile – had caused him discomfort. Two days later, he took Karen to the Cipriani in Venice: his final visit to the city of masks. We went on a family holiday to America. In mid-August, I called him a couple of times, expecting him to be at home. I left messages. I called again on 26 August, four days before our return to London. This time he was there, in a very anxious state, annoyed that he had not been able to make contact. Having our hotel name without the telephone number was not good enough. Unknown to me, he had returned from Venice ten days earlier. Cancer had taken a grip. Facing the prospect of going into court on walking sticks or in a wheelchair, he had decided to pack up. It had been a very traumatic decision.

We returned to newspaper headlines of his retirement on Wednesday 30 August. The press had gathered for a photocall in the garden at Wimbledon. George was captured smiling in open-neck shirt on a sun-lounger as Karen strolled by in stilettos.

With Macmillanesque understatement, he said that 'a little local difficulty' had forced him to quit after forty-seven years as a barrister. The Bar, he added, 'has been a way of life, a challenge and a vocation. I feel that part of me has gone, never to return.' He was furious that such a good stock of cases on the books – involving Albert Reynolds, Branson, Grobbelaar and Marco Pierre White, to name but a few – would have to be sent back for good.

The next few days were spent thinking about a television appearance. He decided that disclosure of his prostate cancer would 'prevent speculation' and might enable him to become an advocate for one of the cancer charities. It would also allow him to announce plans for his forthcoming memoirs. On Sunday 3 September, he chose to go on *Breakfast with Frost* in preference to an invitation from Sir Trevor McDonald on ITV. In a measured and efficient performance, he revealed how cancer treatment had been combined with his work schedule: radiotherapy treatment at 8.30 a.m. sometimes preceding his day in court. It was further proof, if needed, of his courage and determination to fight.

The *Sunday Telegraph* that morning spoiled his early start at the BBC. Under the headline 'Carman Comforted by Caring Karen', a report referred to Karen as 'an independent spirit who has a wide circle of friends including another wealthy septuagenarian, the boxing promoter Jarvis Astaire'. The news that they were still seeing each other infuriated George. Following David Green's abrupt departure from her life in 1993, Astaire, who was six years older than George, had assumed an important role as a good friend. Following their 1995 Concorde trip together to New York – 'We are together,' Astaire told the press – she became a regular visitor at his Sackville Street offices. Further articles were published following the *Sunday Telegraph* piece as she was seen regularly knocking up with Astaire at Queen's Club and out at dinner with him the night after George announced his retirement.

I gave Karen a wide berth and stayed at Wimbledon a couple of nights each week when she was 'at a party' or 'charity dinner'. This was agreed between us. George was annoyed and embarrassed at being made to look a fool by the various stories. He discussed it as usual with those who would listen, including his housekeeper, doctor, accountant, cancer nurse, Frances and Phyllis among others. He even spoke to Al-Fayed about one erroneous story concerning himself and Karen in his magazine *Punch*, before in mid-October instructing solicitors who negotiated a half-page apology and £12,000 in libel damages – paid to Cancer Research.

Craving Karen's attention, he turned a blind eye to the obvious in his desire for her to be his nurse – not an easy role to fulfil without formal training. Meanwhile, George kept the other eye open. He became very agitated at Karen's absence, even if this was just for a few hours. In the considerable time she spent with him, particularly in the last few weeks, events took some toll on her composure. But she retained a calm, quiet and unemotional dignity throughout.

Lending his name to a cancer charity had appeal. Courted by several, he settled on the Cancer Research Campaign after their director general Professor Gordon McVie visited him at home. Endorsing such a worthy cause was a good way of keeping busy. He did a couple of television interviews on the duty of government to do more about research into prostate cancer. His own treatment then took priority. Any practical involvement in charity work effectively ended. Planning an autobiography emerged as George's new passion. He quizzed London's leading book agents on how the process worked and then spent weeks carrying out the negotiations himself so as to save himself tens of thousands of pounds in commission. It was an absorbing process. The day-to-day machinations fascinated him. He treated it as a huge game. Updating me with each twist and turn, he finally secured a £500,000 combined deal with publishers HarperCollins and serialisation in the *Sunday Times*. Given his great anxiety about having enough money to meet growing medical bills, expected to run into hundreds of thousands a year for private treatment, this came as a relief. Potential shortage of funds was another looming problem. Arrangements were made with his bank to draw down on the equity in the house, just in case.

Conversation settled on the contents of his book. Every aspect of personal life was to be excluded – 'far too difficult to talk about'. Apart from brief recollections of childhood and Oxford days, the rest would focus entirely on his cases. This was to be a very one-dimensional effort. I bought him a good tape machine. He never used it nor did he write one word. In reviewing the familiar territory of his career, the process of writing scared him. He did not know where to start. It became obvious that he was playing for time. He chastised his solicitors Harbottle & Lewis for dragging their feet with amendments to the various contracts – another topic that consumed many hours of discussion. They did nothing wrong. George was looking for an excuse not to begin. By entering a state of denial about his illness, the autobiography was an important distraction, but no more. In the event, no contract was ever signed and the deal was never formalised.

Another diversion was the telephone. For years it had been his crutch – an instrument of intimacy that enabled him to speak freely and more personally than in a face-to-face encounter. In chambers or at home, weekday or weekend, day or night, George had enjoyed talking to a coterie of female friends, called in a rota. He chatted and gossiped over many afternoons and evenings. Men were a second-best option. Although he got on with many of his colleagues, male friends were not close in the conventional sense of pals and buddies. Many admired his skill. Very few got to know much of the man underneath. Telephoned best wishes from old friends like Pat Russell and Tom Crone or newer acquaintances like Lord Hanson or Max Clifford were welcome, but less visceral. George's chambers colleague Hugh

Tomlinson says: 'He was not a man who made friends easily.' This is supported by Charles Howard QC: 'It's strange to work alongside someone for twenty-five years and not identify their mates. There didn't seem to be anyone from Oxford or the North. Instead there were many acquaintances and people who were friendly because they did cases with him.'

Among those on his contact list, Adrienne Page and Victoria Sharp made themselves available whenever he called their chambers or home. Adrienne Page recalls: 'For years, he would ring me up at weekends. He wanted to talk and to gossip. He talked to me for hours about everything. I felt I knew him like a very close girlfriend.' It was a similar picture for Victoria Sharp, who explains: 'I'm afraid George brought out my mothering instinct.' She adds: 'I've got four children. He would ring me up at home at about one o'clock on Sunday and say: "I'm not calling at an inconvenient moment, am I?" In the end, I spent more time talking to him than to my husband.' This continued when he was ill. Both went out of their way to listen to George's news and to detail the latest Bar chat. They kept a line open for him to the professional life that had ended.

Phyllis was another regular: 'In his last few months, he called me often when on his own apart from the nurse.' The house-keeper Jacki worked for seven years at his Wimbledon homes. Her days were habitually spent listening to George chat over mugs of tea and endless cigarettes. When he was ill, she did a good job in keeping his spirits up. His nephew Nicholas, an actor, came to see him, taking a break from filming commitments. As a first-time visitor to the new house, he was surprised that his uncle felt comfortable in such anonymity – a contrast to the grandeur of the Garrick where they had once dined.

The deep affection for him at the libel Bar showed when they gave George a retirement dinner at the Ritz on 19 September 2000, attended by most of his courtroom colleagues. They presented him with two magnificent books on the art and architecture of Venice, later displayed proudly in Wimbledon.

Many feared for him in retirement. They sensed his loneliness, now magnified by age and illness, and highlighted by his emotional speech to the assembled group of twenty-four lawyers and judges. At home he avoided discussing his developing cancer. It did not begin to hit me until meeting with him in Harley Street on 7 November. Delayed at the CBI conference by train go-slows, I arrived halfway through a consultation in Dr Coxon's room with Mr James, a consultant who had come down from Birmingham. As we walked out into Harley Street, George told me: 'He confirmed twelve to eighteen months. That's all I've got, at best.' There was not much to say to that. I made some remark like: 'Well, you've got to make the most of it.' Whether or not the consultant's words had surprised him, the pace of deterioration accelerated from that point on.

After four years of treatment and acting as a close confidante – frequently taking his troubled calls in the night – Dr Coxon was reluctantly forced to give up George as her patient. The reason was professional conflict with another doctor. Speaking at length about it in interview, she remains both annoyed and upset. For a few weeks, George opted for different treatment at the Royal Marsden before reverting to the London Clinic. Conflicting medical advice offered confusing alternatives. As with many terminal patients, George may not always have been in the best position to make the right choices. Coxon maintained contact through his cancer nurse Trish, an experienced specialist in her field, who had become another trusted intimate. Over several years, she spent many Sunday mornings with him alone, giving injections and listening to him talk. He would often ask her to stay until lunchtime or afterwards.

Coxon's departure coincided with the doctors not speaking to me directly. Communication became at times contradictory and opaque. In mid-November, George went into the London Clinic for several weeks. I saw him there every day. On 30 November, we watched the entire fiftieth Miss World contest as he hoped to catch a glimpse of Karen, who was attending the event with Julia Morley. When he returned home in December, I felt marginalised and excluded. His judgment was failing with his declining health and increased morphine dosage. We continued to talk about the book. It gave him hope. He even mentioned making a comeback by doing the Branson case, almost saying as much to Clare Dyer at the *Guardian*. He spoke with Branson on the phone several times, particularly about his lottery bid.

Retirement and age often bring with them invisibility. For public figures, this can be an unexpected shock to the system. Family and other interests usually compensate. This was not for George. Desperate to remain in the limelight rather than fade away, he was delighted when Hat Trick Productions asked him to appear on *Have I Got News For You*. Previous invitations had been declined. A slot was fixed for December. Within weeks, he changed his mind. He also accepted invitations to go on *Newsnight* and to be a *Question Time* panellist on 11 January.

Jeremy Paxman visited Wimbledon in mid-December and George asked me to come over for the day. A reduced drug dosage ensured that he would be more lucid when questioned. The accompanying television crew looked shocked at his physical state. He could still walk with assistance but the various tumours in his skull, liver and throughout the pelvic region were now in control. Peering over several rounds of M & S sandwiches supplied by Jacki, the two grand inquisitors weighed each other up with idle kitchen chatter. A tour of the modern Venice paintings passed without comment. George's performance on camera was powerful as much for a brave attitude to illness as for his concentration on past glories. 'I've started praying to St Jude, the patron saint of lost causes,' came the reply when Paxman asked if he would beat the illness. The fifteen-minute interview, broadcast a week before Christmas, was his last public performance – relaxed and straightforward.

Only George knows if he died at peace. I last saw him when I stayed for the weekend of 30–31 December. Apart from the nurses, who changed twice a day, we were entirely alone. As I left on Sunday afternoon, when Karen returned, he was sleeping peacefully after I had read to him for some hours. The morphine dose was by then quite high. His death at lunchtime on Tuesday 2 January 2001 came sooner than anyone had expected. The prospect certainly concentrated his mind. Regular visits by a nun from a local hospice had led to discussions with Father Michael Seed. They had first been introduced by Michael Day, managing director of the Ritz, at the Howard Hotel in November 1999. Months later, Seed, who had accepted Ann Widdecombe and John Gummer as Catholic converts and claimed controversially to have converted Alan Clark on his deathbed, made several visits to Wimbledon. He talked alone with George, who welcomed the attention. Their conversations – about twelve hours in total – moved from room to room. Progressing from theological discussion to personal recollection, the questioning tone and probing manner changed over time to calm reflection. Rarely pure and never simple, personal beliefs are impossible to quantify. Maybe George maintained a delightfully wavering attitude. But I think it likely, despite renewed intellectual curiosity in his boyhood faith and the presence of three priests at his Westminster Cathedral funeral, that he remained an intelligent, thoughtful agnostic. From everything he said and did, the only thing he ever believed in with total conviction was himself.

The funeral service included a beautiful rendition of Ave Maria. My cousin Nicholas and I did the readings. George had asked me to read from I Corinthians 13: 1–18, the original King James version, with the line 'through a glass darkly'. Although announced as family only, a number of people decided to come to the service: Jacki, his housekeeper, Trish, his nurse, Bill and Paul, his former clerks, Hugh Tomlinson, Charles Howard (with his wife Rosie Boycott) and Gail Carrodus from his chambers, Pippa Jessel, his friend, and Caroline Williams, the mother of George's godson Sam. I was pleased that they made the effort. One unfamiliar face gave me her best wishes afterwards. It was only on meeting her three months later that I realised that it had been Ursula, his first wife.

Discussions with Karen were kept to a minimum after the funeral. Jeremy Thorpe, Ken Dodd and Richard Branson were among those who caught press attention at the memorial service, held at St Clement Danes in the Strand. This had been carefully planned by George with Karen some weeks before his death. I chose not to discuss it with her. Jarvis Astaire's attendance astonished me given what had been reported in the newspapers about his friendship with Karen. Frederick Forsyth composed a special tribute. Lord Alexander then set the establishment seal on George's contribution to public life. In a memorable address of crafted eloquence, his conclusion was thoughtful and dignified. A notable feature of glowing obituaries had been the prominence of the headlines. These continued to set George apart from his peers. Cherie Blair, who also attended the memorial, wrote to me the day following his death, remarking that 'He would have loved the publicity.' Sadly, she was right.

There is no final verdict to be delivered. Judgments made in writing this book do not entitle me to sit as judge and jury in conclusion. When assessing the facts presented, interpretation is everything. It is for each reader to decide. George was fond of saying that people are not black or white, but infinite shades of greys and his life covered the full spectrum. Certainly he left his mark on the legal profession. His courtroom success came in spades and, as an advocate, he held all the aces. Skill and luck played their part. He took risks and they paid off. These talents were born with George, not made by him. On his feet in court, he had presence. People took note. They expected a good performance, and they got it. In wig and gown, he grew in height and stature. The years fell away. He had charm. He had charisma. He was in control. In isolating the important point that mattered, he ignored the many that did not. His speeches and phrases were both memorable and accessible. An instinctive grasp of the language was married to an actor's timing. Speaking slowly, listening carefully, talking to the jury, not at them – these were his methods. Not least, he knew the value of silence – the power of the pregnant pause. 'He knew what the media wanted, and tried to make sure that there was always something reportable, even on the dullest day in court,' concludes Marcel Berlins, doyen of legal journalists.

When the law became complex or difficult, he kept it simple. Carefully observing how ordinary people think, feel, breathe and move, he studied the human condition with singular thoroughness and used that knowledge to good effect. His extraordinary ability was dedicated to one persistent aim – winning in court. Few other barristers or prominent public figures pursue the lifestyle that George pursued, or do so for as long as he did. And yet it somehow enhanced his courtroom persona.

Armed with skill and determination, George was a street fighter who battled hard for every achievement. Even though he dined at their table and drank at their parties, he never formed part of the establishment. By remaining on the outside looking in, he remained detached from every club, every group, every clique. Independence and the courage to stand alone developed his strength on the long road from South Shore, Blackpool to becoming the star of the Bar. Driven by ambition every step of the way, his will to succeed was exceptional and his combination of talents unique. Not only for young barristers, but for anyone with ability who aims for the top in their chosen field, George's achievements as an advocate show what can be done. But success built on skill and passionate dedication is only part of the story. He would also have liked to be remembered by those who follow him for making it to the top against the odds. That more than anything fired his relentless desire to keep winning.

An extraordinary hollowness added to the hunger. Success did not do much to fill the void. It only served to increase his isolation further. Loneliness on that scale is rare. Its origin was fear: fear of losing, fear of failure, fear of being alone, fear of being found out, fear of dying – all played their part. The real

George Carman could not stand up to be counted. To paraphrase T. S. Eliot, he prepared endless faces to meet the faces that he met, but was never himself, whoever that person was behind the façade. Because George's life formed itself in masquerade, the true identity of the man underneath remains unknown.

Many elements of life can be duplicated or replaced – but you have only one father and George was unlike any other. His contradictions and unpredictable personality made him challenging. His powerful intellect and ferocious talent gave me much to contemplate. Yet you cannot choose your parents nor can you change them. A father with extraordinary gifts brought much opportunity and privileged awareness. He taught me how to think, how to communicate and how to argue. He gave me an appreciation of language, an understanding of the law and an insight in to moving minds. He left me with the memory of powerful speeches, wonderful cross-examination and immense pride that will never disappear. Somewhere in the game, George fell short. For ordinary pleasures, he gave little time or attention. For ordinary living, he showed only passing concern or involvement. For ordinary family life, he lacked enthusiasm and interest. Ordinary people belonged to a world he observed closely but was unable to enter. From all this, one certainty emerges: George was no ordinary man.

Index

'DC' indicates Dominic Carman and 'GC' George Alfred Carman, QC.

Index

Photographic Sources

Author's Collection: 1, 2, 3, 4, 5 top, 6 bottom, 14 top left and right/bottom left, 16 bottom. Jane Bown: 7 bottom. News International: 8 bottom. PA Photos: 7 top right, 8 top, 9 top/bottom left, 10 top right, 11 top/bottom left and right, 12 top left, 13 top right/bottom left. Popperfoto/Reuters: 15 centre. Rex Features: 10 bottom right, 12 bottom, 15 top. Mirror Syndication International: 5 bottom, 7 top left, 13 top left/bottom right, 14 bottom right, 15 bottom. Topham Picturepoint: 6 top, 9 bottom right, 10 top left, 11 centre right, 12 top centre, 16 top. Universal Pictorial Press: 10 bottom left, 12 top right.